RUSSIAN RESEARCH CENTER STUDIES

★ 52 ★

MANAGERIAL POWER
AND SOVIET POLITICS

MANAGERIAL POWER
AND SOVIET POLITICS

Jeremy R. Azrael

★ ★ ★ ★ ★ ★

HARVARD UNIVERSITY PRESS

Cambridge, Massachusetts

1966

TO MY PARENTS

ACKNOWLEDGMENTS

Although the ultimate responsibility is mine alone, this study would not have been possible without a great deal of outside support. To begin with, my research has been greatly facilitated by grants and fellowships from the Ford Foundation, the Inter-University Committee on Travel Grants, the Social Science Research Council, the American Council of Learned Societies, the Russian Research Center of Harvard University, and the Social Science Research Committee of The University of Chicago. Thanks to this support, I have been able to conduct research in the field, to take time off from the normal press of academic duties, and to enjoy skilled research assistance in the persons of Mrs. Jean Hellie, Miss Julie Gordon, Henry Bienen, Martin Miller, and Stephen Sternheimer. For all of these privileges I am deeply grateful, and I gladly acknowledge my debt to all concerned.

Like so many students of Soviet politics I am obliged beyond all calculation to Professor Merle Fainsod of Harvard University, a stimulating and devoted teacher, to whom I have always been able to turn for judicious counsel, expert advice, constructive criticism, and warm encouragement. In addition, and in much the same way, I am obliged to Barrington Moore, Jr., who not only helped supervise the dissertation of which this study is a much transformed outgrowth but who also was the first to direct my attention to many of the broader problems that were implicit in my subject and had to be explored before my research could pretend to any general significance. While I fear to be measured by the standards of these two men, I am proud to recognize them as mentors and to cite their works as models that I have tried to emulate.

If I have been fortunate in my teachers, I have also been fortunate in my colleagues. Two of these, indeed, Professors Leon Bramson and Leonard Binder, I would almost prefer to rank as teachers in the sense that they have had a decisive influence on my understanding of society and politics. In addition, Professor Binder has made invaluable comments on particular aspects of the present study, and the same is true of my respected colleague, Professor Jerry Hough. Without their help this study would have been far less adequate, and it is likely that

ACKNOWLEDGMENTS

many of the imperfections which remain can be ascribed to my failure to abide by their advice.

Finally, I am indebted to my family. To my wife Gabriella, who has been patient beyond measure and unstinting in her assistance and support. To my daughter Deborah, who has been kind enough to resent my weekends "at the office" and understanding enough to forgive them. To my daughter Ruth, whose consideration was expressed in delaying her arrival until I had completed my manuscript. And finally, but by no means least, to my parents who have been sage counselors, selfless advocates, and dear friends. It is to the two of them, with love, esteem, and gratitude, that I dedicate this book.

J. R. A.
Chicago, Illinois
March 1966

Contents

MANAGERIAL POWER
AND SOVIET POLITICS

★ 1 ★

INTRODUCTION

Karl Marx's proposition, "the country that is more developed industrially only shows . . . the less developed [country] the image of its own future," was a commonplace at the time it was written and has remained so to the present day. The majority of its proponents have also agreed that economic development numbers "political modernization" among its natural concomitants. Within these boundaries, however, there has been persistent disagreement about the meaning of political modernity and its implications for civil liberty and human freedom. In particular, there has been an on-going debate between two distinct schools, which can be called the liberal-democratic and the administrative-technocratic. These designations, it should be stressed, do not necessarily refer to the value preferences of particular theorists, but rather to the principles of authority that the latter associate with political modernity.

According to the adherents of the liberal-democratic school, the extension of individual liberty and popular self-government is an almost inevitable concomitant of economic development. To be sure, many contemporary political sociologists qualify their confidence in the democratizing "logic" of economic development by recognizing that rapid industrialization in an economically backward society is likely to entail a sharp curtailment of individual liberty and popular self-government. However, they remain convinced that the *ultimate* outcome of economic development is certain to be democracy. This is true, for example, of Gabriel Almond, who uses the "Anglo-American" political system

1

as a paradigm of political modernity and treats "modern," "Western," and "Western democratic" virtually as synonyms.[1] It is equally true of Daniel Lerner, who defines political modernization as "the transition to a participant society" whose "crowning achievement is constitutional democracy." Finally, the same point holds in the case of a distinguished study group from the Massachusetts Institute of Technology which treats nondemocratic tendencies as "distortions" in or "diversions" from the modernization process.[2]

Although the view that industrialization entails democratization is probably preponderant in the literature on economic development and political change, it has never gone unchallenged. In particular, it has always had to contend with the argument of the administrative-technocratic school, which holds that industrial growth inevitably gives rise to a system of bureaucratic or scientistic domination that is incompatible with political liberty as it is understood in the West. This argument can be traced back at least as far as Saint-Simon, who predicted that the spread of industrial technology would lead to the progressive replacement of politics by administrative planning and the emergence of a society in which all effective power was concentrated in the hands of an industrial-scientific elite.[3] It then found support and confirmation in the writings of Weber and Michels. Neither of these men was a thoroughgoing determinist, but Weber nonetheless viewed the typical modern society as an "iron cage" of bureaucratic control, and Michels saw the "iron law of oligarchy" as inherent in complex organization.[4] Moreover, their followers have become more rather than less deterministic, and the contemporary literature on political development abounds in such statements as "industrial society is run by technocrats, inevitably."[5]

In view of the dramatic character and rapid tempo of political and economic change in the Soviet Union, it is not surprising that the USSR has provided one of the main focal points for contemporary discussions of the relationship between industrialization and political modernization. And, in view of the degree to which these discussions have been dominated by the two schools that I have been describing, it is not surprising to encounter numerous analyses that envision the inevitable emergence within the USSR of either a democratic or an administrative state. This perspective has been particularly prevalent among Marxist and neo-Marxist analysis such as Otto Bauer, Isaac Deutscher, and Herbert Marcuse, but it has found many other protagonists as well, including W. W. Rostow, Zbigniew Brzezinski, and Adam Ulam, to name only a few of the most prominent.[6] Statements such as Brzezinski's "development and maturity render dictatorship of any sort . . . historically obsolescent" or Ulam's "the 'natural' process in the USSR must be one of erosion of totalitarianism" could be duplicated almost *ad infinitum*.[7]

Those who view a fundamental transformation of the Soviet political system as inevitable are generally agreed that the most critical variables affecting the rate and direction of political change are increased education, increased economic welfare, and increased occupational specialization. These variables, which are viewed as functional requisites of industrial development, receive greater or lesser emphasis at the hands of different authors, but they are characteristically treated as part of an indivisible syndrome and assigned priority over all other variables as determinants of political modernization. Moreover, in those few cases where discussion proceeds beyond the question of general causality to the operational dynamics of political change, there is widespread agreement that the principal "representatives" of the logic of industrial development within the political arena, the most effective agents of political modernization in the actual policy-making process, are the members of the technical intelligentsia and, above all, the managerial elite. Characterized as they are (or are assumed to be) by comparatively high socioeconomic status, a comparatively high degree of professional-

3

ization, and comparatively direct access to the political process, the managers emerge as natural candidates for the role of "the power in the shadows," the "gravediggers" of Communist dictatorship.[8] Whether they are to play this role strictly on their own behalf and hence create a full-fledged technocracy; whether they are merely the vanguard of an entire "new class" of bureaucrats who will establish a highly authoritarian but somewhat less science-oriented administrative state; or whether they are but the precursors of an upsurgent populace that will establish a system of free and open politics — answers to these questions vary from scenario to scenario. Whatever the denouement, however, primary attention is almost always focused on the managers.

Such a focus is apparent in the works of most of the analysts mentioned above. It is even sharper in the work of men such as Joseph Berliner, George Lichtheim, and John Kautsky. Berliner, for example, argues that industrial maturation in the USSR is currently giving rise to a victory of the "optimizers," represented by the managers and economists, over the "dialecticians," represented by the party ideologues and apparatchiki. Similarly, Lichtheim contends that "behind the official facade of 'Communism' in the Soviet orbit there emerges with ever greater clarity the outline of a new society in which the planners hold control." And Kautsky observes that

the vast bureaucracies of the single party and its many organizations of the government, of the armed services and police, and, above all, of the managers and technicians in industry in fact assume more and more decision-making authority. For a while [the established political leadership] . . . may succeed in dominating them by playing one bureaucracy against another . . . but after a generation or so the new elites of . . . bureaucrats and managers are likely to be able to assert their power.

In sum, all of the authors noted, and many others besides, wholeheartedly subscribe to Raymond Aron's judgment that, in the Soviet Union, "technological complexity will strengthen the managerial class at the expense of the ideologists and militants." [9]

In view of the near unanimity regarding the critical significance of the managerial elite, it is somewhat surprising to find
that the managers' political role is among the least thoroughly
analyzed phenomena of Soviet life. There have been two major
studies of the economic role of the managerial elite, but the few
available investigations of managerial behavior within the political arena are sharply restricted in their chronological coverage
or very narrowly focused in their range of inquiry.[10] Yet politically relevant source materials are at least as readily accessible
in the case of the managers as in the case of other Soviet elite
groups, such as the military and the governmental, which have
been the subject of effective, full-length studies. Although the
available data are often fragmentary, they are by no means
insubstantial in either quantity or quality. To subject these
data to thorough analysis is the purpose of this book. Until this
task has been completed, it is manifestly impossible to evaluate
the pervasive belief that the managerial elite holds the key to
the political destiny of the Soviet Union, let alone to evaluate
the probability of change proceeding in one or another direction
and at one or another tempo.

Is it true that the managers have acquired an increasingly
powerful voice in the policy-making process? What truth is there
in the view that the managers have served as representatives of
the broader ranks of the technical intelligentsia or "new class"
within the political arena? Have the managers utilized their
political influence to move the system in the direction anticipated
by the liberal-democratic or the administrative-technocratic
school? These are among the questions I shall try to answer
through empirical investigation. They are questions that can be
answered on this basis, albeit only tentatively. And it is the more
important that the answers be registered because, as we shall
see, they raise serious doubts about the validity of many of the
propositions noted in the preceding pages.

To raise doubts is not to disprove. In the first place, some of the propositions in question clearly embody important insights. They may need reformulation, but they cannot be dismissed. In the second place, many of the relevant propositions embody ancillary hypotheses that cannot be tested solely on the basis of a study of the political role of the managerial elite, however central the latter may appear. Moreover, even those propositions that are narrowly focused and explicitly designate the managers as the principal bearers of the logic of industrial development cannot ordinarily be put to anything resembling a conclusive test. It is virtually impossible, for example, to ascertain the precise limits of managerial influence, and there is hence no way to guard against the possibility that other variables might have played a more decisive role in determining any given political outcome. In addition, and for present purposes more importantly, one cannot disprove propositions that contain a built-in escape clause in the form of an undefined and infinitely elastic conditional variable. Such a variable, in turn, is present in almost all of the propositions here at issue, including those that might at first appear to stand or fall on the specific question of the political behavior of the managers. This variable is usually called "industrial maturity."

Almost all of the projections regarding the liberalizing or technocratizing role of the Soviet managerial elite include industrial maturity as a *sine qua non*. Further, they often contain a warning to the effect that one should not necessarily expect to find the outlines of the future reflected in the realities of the present. At the same time, however, they almost never include a precise definition of industrial maturity, which can thus assume the character of a visual horizon, always receding as one thinks one is approaching it. Yet, whatever the exact meaning of the term, it is difficult to think of the Soviet Union as so little advanced along the path of industrial maturation that observable managerial behavior does not prefigure the state of affairs that will prevail once the ultimate destination is reached. It is well to remember in this connection that, for all of Russia's relative economic backwardness, industrialization had put down firm roots well before the revolution. It is also in order to recall that the Soviet Union has been among the world's leading industrial powers for over thirty years. But, even if one grants that industrial maturity is still to be achieved, an analysis of what is and what has been would seem to have direct bearing on the range of propositions at issue here. In a technical sense such an analysis can prove almost nothing. It can, however, reveal a great deal that has immediate relevance for the continuing discussion of the political consequences of economic maturation in general and for the political role of the Soviet managerial elite in particular.

For the purposes of this study, the Soviet managerial elite will be defined as those executives who have borne primary responsibility for the administration of Soviet heavy industry. Since it is the high-level officials of the central industrial bureaucracy and the directors of major enterprises who appear to have enjoyed the most direct access to the political process, they are the men who will receive the most attention. However, my analysis will also encompass middle-management personnel insofar as such coverage is possible on the basis of the available data. And, from time to time, managers in fields other than heavy industry as well as industrial planners will enter prominently into the discussion. On the one hand, it is clear that some fairly precise delimitation of subject matter is essential both for the sake of manageability and in order to avoid the common practice of treating all officials whose work is in any way related to the conduct of economic affairs as "managers." Under the best of circumstances, such a practice is apt to transform the "managerial revolution" from a problem into a tautological, self-fulfilling prophecy, and under conditions in the Soviet Union, where almost all political roles involve a measure of economic decision making, such a resolution is inevitable. On the other hand, too rigorous a demarcation of the subject also seems inappropriate.

This is so not only because I am seeking to explore a relatively new field, but also because one of my primary objectives is to investigate the interrelationship among various strata and functional groupings within the Soviet industrial establishment.

That the members of the managerial elite have played a significant role in Soviet political development can scarcely be doubted. Moreover, the available data confirm that the managers have played this role in a manner that justifies their treatment as a political group rather than as an aggregate of discrete political actors. In the first place, it is evident that managerial status has had an important influence on the political behavior of the men concerned. This behavior has at times been decisively conditioned by such nonoccupational variables as social status, class origin, and party affiliation, but values, attitudes, and perceptions derived from and rooted in the dynamics of occupational involvement have never been far below the surface and have frequently been dominant. In addition, most industrial executives have consciously recognized that they have important interests in common. The industrial establishment has been the scene of considerable internal dissension and internecine conflict, but its leading cadres have nonetheless been characterized by strong esprit de corps. Finally, there is a good reason to believe that the managers have sometimes collectively engaged in more or less disciplined and coordinated political action. So far as one can judge on the basis of the available evidence, they have never emerged as a formally organized "faction," but they do seem occasionally to have developed a common political strategy for the purpose of influencing public policy in a predetermined direction.

In the vocabulary of the group approach to politics, the Soviet managerial elite has been more than a categoric group comprised of men who share some objective trait in common. Similarly, it has been more than a potential or latent interest group comprised of men who share certain special interests but who do not necessarily recognize that these interests are shared or engaged in collective action. Although the managers have not been a formally organized secondary-interest association, they have functioned as a manifest interest group within the political arena. And, on occasion, they have even functioned as a fairly cohesive political-action group animated by a widely shared and deeply felt commitment to something approaching a distinctive policy platform.[11]

To speak of the Soviet managerial elite in the vocabulary of the group approach to politics is obviously to introduce a comparative dimension into the discussion. It is to suggest that at least some facets of Soviet politics can be usefully analyzed within a conceptual scheme that is applicable to the analysis of other modern political systems. At the same time, however, it is definitely not to deny that in many critical respects the Soviet system is radically distinctive. It is not to subscribe to Alfred Meyer's argument:

In the USSR . . . [the power] elite is composed of industrial executives; military and security officers; leading scientists; opinion makers . . . and, finally, professional politicians who constitute the party *aktiv*. Although relations between the various elements have fluctuated in the past and can be expected to do so in the future, one might generalize that in governing the society the professional politicians must carefully steer a middle course by balancing various groups of experts against each other as well as against the hard-shell ideological dogmatists. Their problem is somewhat similar to that of professional politicians in constitutional governments who steer between various pressure groups and the watch-dogs of democratic and constitutional purity.[12]

Far from supporting such a view of the Soviet political process, my analysis will stress the dissimilarities between the Soviet and other systems. Thus, I shall argue that for purposes of political analysis it is of decisive significance that the group activities of the Soviet managerial elite have never been accorded political legitimacy, that members of the group have occupied bureaucratic positions within a centralized state system, that recruitment into the managerial elite has been governed in large part by political criteria, and that collective action on the part of the managers has been a high-risk enterprise likely to evoke a terroristic response from the political leadership. Most of these variables, in turn, refer to practices that are more or less distinctive to Soviet politics and have played a critical role in Soviet political development.

Whether these and other similar variables operate to produce a system that should be treated as belonging to a unique political type — the totalitarian system — is an important question, and one to which I shall return. For present purposes it is enough to note that this study will raise serious doubts about the utility of presently available *models* of totalitarianism for the analysis of Soviet politics. In particular, by evidencing the existence of widespread esprit de corps and politically oriented group cohesiveness among the managers, it will automatically point up some major discrepancies between the actual functioning of the Soviet political system and those models of the system that depict it as an organizational monolith dominated by a narrow band of rulers who exercise virtually total control over an atomized and anomic society. These models (which are, of course, intentionally exaggerated ideal-types) will not thereby be invalidated, but it should become apparent that they can profitably be revised so as to take better account of empirical realities.

The pages that follow are organized according to a simple historical design, with a primary breakdown into chapters dealing with discrete "political generations." First I examine the management doctrines of prerevolutionary Bolshevism to determine the expectations of the new Soviet leaders regarding the relationship between managerial authority and political power. Then I go on to examine the political attitudes and behavior of the "bourgeois specialists," the managers and engineers inherited by the Bolsheviks from the *ancien régime;* of the "red directors," the Communists who were assigned to management posts in the first years after the revolution and who continued to dominate the industrial establishment for the next two or three decades; and of the managerial elite after the Great Purge. And, finally, I examine the evidence that is available on the men who are now entering the ranks of the managerial elite and are likely to dominate the Soviet industrial establishment in the foreseeable future. Although each of these chapters makes use of essentially paralled categories of analysis, they are not completely symmetrical. Since the amount of available information on any given question varies greatly from period to period, certain categories of analysis are more completely "filled" in one chapter than in another. In such cases, the data have, so to speak, been given their head: problems for which data are readily available have received extensive treatment, while problems that are equally urgent but less amenable to reasonably "hard" empirical analysis are treated only briefly, if at all.

Although I have not been afraid to indulge in informed speculation or conjecture, I have tried not only explicitly to note such instances but also to hold them to a minimum. In this way, it has proved possible to make fuller use of the rich stores of reliable information that have so often been ignored or inadequately utilized in the interest of broad-gauge speculation and dramatic generalization. Nonetheless, despite their asymmetries and limitations, it is hoped that the following pages do reflect a consistent pattern of analysis, and that the results represent not only a detailed and factual case study but also a contribution to the broader study of Soviet politics and of comparative politics in general.

★ 2 ★

BOLSHEVIK MANAGEMENT DOCTRINE
BEFORE THE REVOLUTION

Socialism has no . . . need to concern itself with the organization of industry, since
capitalism does that.   Georges Sorel

Anyone who approaches prerevolutionary Marxist-Leninist theory in search of a comprehensive and systematic doctrine of industrial organization and management is foredoomed to disappointment. The patristic writings provide no warrant for present-day Soviet claims to the effect that "Marx, Engels, and Lenin left quite unambiguous and quite precise instructions regarding the chief principles of socialist economic management." [1] Indeed, such claims run directly counter to the testimony of the founders of the Bolshevik regime. Thus, in the immediate aftermath of the revolution, Lenin himself acknowledged that there was no "concrete plan for the organization of economic life," while Trotsky frankly conceded that, in the sphere of the organization of labor, the victorious Bolsheviks confronted "new questions and new difficulties . . . [for which] socialist theory had no answers." [2] This point once established, however, it must not be pressed too far.

If the classical theorists' concern with such problems was sporadic and discursive, it was nonetheless real and it would be wrong to underestimate either its scope or its intensity. In fact, Marx, Engels, and Lenin did address themselves to "the chief principles of socialist economic management." And, when the

12

pertinent passages are considered in the aggregate, the outlines of a reasonably coherent management doctrine do emerge. Moreover, the doctrine thus revealed is of more than theoretical significance: it provides considerable insight into the actual evolution of Soviet industrial policy following the revolution. Not only were a substantial number of the problems which conditioned that evolution anticipated in prerevolutionary theory, but also a substantial number of the theoretically indicated solutions were put into practice. Often, to be sure, the results were disastrous, and new solutions had quickly to be devised. But the new solutions were themselves born amidst doctrinal controversy, and in many instances official policy continued to conform rather closely to the tenets of prerevolutionary management doctrine. Certainly the divergence between theory and practice was far less extensive than is commonly alleged, especially by those who interpret the theory in question as an exercise in pure utopianism.[3]

Probably the first thing to be noted about the "utopianism" of the prerevolutionary discussion of industrial organization and management is that the very reticence with which this discussion was conducted testifies to the presence of a distinctly antiutopian orientation. To be precise, I would argue Georges Sorel was being a good Marxist when he insisted that socialism need not concern itself with the organization of industry, and would suggest that the patristic authors' unconcern with problems of industrial organization stemmed in large part from an assumption that the postrevolutionary world would leave the management system of its predecessor more or less intact.[4] Nor is this assumption particularly surprising when one understands that the Marxist theorists believed that management was essentially a function of technology. Since this was combined with the further belief that the introduction of socialism would not entail radical technological change, it automatically led its adherents to discount the possibility of radical changes in the organization

13

of industrial authority.[5] Indeed, in Marx's eyes, it was only the "vulgus," with its congenital inability to conceive of old forms in new contexts, which could fail to recognize that the socialist economy would be organized according to "forms developed on the lap of capitalist production." [6]

Whereas the introduction of socialism would undoubtedly entail greater centralization and more comprehensive planning, according to the patristic authors, the attendant organizational changes would be quantitative rather than qualitative. At most, they would involve nothing more than an extension and more consistent implementation of established procedures. And, in those cases where capitalist development had proceeded to the stage of "state capitalism," they would be very slight indeed.[7] In such cases, as Lenin subsequently made clear in both of the two major articles he devoted to the subject, virtually all of the organizational requisites of socialist management would be ready to hand, and the socialists would merely have to adapt the existing management system to their own distinctive purposes.[8]

In arguing in this manner, Lenin was not deviating from Marxist orthodoxy. Although his argument might seem to run counter to Marx's well-known injunction against any effort by the socialists to expropriate rather than to smash the bourgeois state machine, the injunction was never intended to be all-inclusive; indeed, Marx specifically criticized those who interpreted it in a comprehensive fashion. What had to be smashed, he stressed, were "the merely repressive organs of the old government power" — as for the rest, they could and should be preserved to perform their "legitimate functions." [9] Nor is there any doubt that economic agencies fit the latter category as Marx conceived it.

Writing before the era of "state capitalism" and, more particularly, before World War I, Marx did not conceive of economic-managerial agencies as important components of the bourgeois state machine. It was precisely such agencies, however, that he intended to exempt from his injunction, and Lenin was undoubtedly on safe doctrinal grounds when he introduced a distinction between the coercive and the productive machinery of the bourgeois state, contending that productive machinery "must not and should not be broken up" but simply "wrested from the control of the capitalists . . . [and] subordinated to the proletarian soviets." [10] That Lenin saw this productive machinery as so highly developed that the socialists would have little to do in the way of industrial "organization-building" differentiates him from Marx, but the difference is one of chronology, not ideology. In both cases, the prognosis regarding forms of management is a good deal less than visionary, if it is not downright conservative. Moreover, no startlingly new content was to be injected into the old management forms. In particular, these forms were not to be drained of authority and filled with freedom: they were to remain essentially what they were — not "merely repressive," but by no means completely nonrepressive. In short, the patristic writings did not posit the disappearance of management as a distinctive *command* function.

In Western commentaries, the Marxist-Leninist vision of socialism is often summarized by citing the well-known formula, "the governance of men will be replaced by the administration of things." [11] This formula, in turn, is cited as evidence that the patristic texts envision a society in which authority no longer has a place in human relations, industrial or otherwise. But where industrial relations are concerned, such an interpretation is altogether untenable. Those who advance it fail to recognize that the classical writings follow Saint-Simon's practice of using the term "governance" to apply to exploitative and oppressive domination, and the term "administration" to apply to rational and scientific leadership directed toward the ultimate best interests of the ruled. Saint-Simon's image of such leadership was authoritarian in the extreme and by no means excluded coercion, and Marx and his followers took over Saint-Simon's meaning as

15

well as his terminology.[12] Indeed, they went out of their way to underscore this meaning by referring not only to the "administration of things" but also to the "leadership of production" when they anticipated the social factions that would persist once the state had withered away.[13] And it is clear that what they meant by leadership was imperative coordination, entailing the exercise of comprehensive authority within the realm of production.[14]

In *Capital*, Marx specifically affirms that "the labor of supervision and management is naturally required whenever the direct process of production assumes the form of a combined social process and not of the isolated labor of independent producers." Then, lest the point be missed, he proceeds to make his meaning even more explicit by remarking that, quite independently of capital, "all labor in which many individuals cooperate necessarily requires a *commanding will* to coordinate and unify the process." [15] Nor is there any doubt that Marx expected socialist society to be subject to this requirement, for a curtailment of mass production had no place among the changes he associated with the arrival of socialism. On the contrary, according to the Marxist scheme, mass production was destined to burgeon after the revolution, and it was therefore completely consistent to argue that the scope of managerial authority would actually increase once capitalism was overthrown. Although Marx himself did not so argue, Engels did, and there is no reason to doubt that he was expressing his mentor's views.[16] Certainly there was no doubt on this score on the part of many early critics of Marxism, who saw the latter as nothing less than an ideology of emergent technocracy.

To Marx's great rival Bakunin, for example, Marxism foreshadowed a system in which the workers would be "under the direct command of government engineers who will constitute a new privileged scientific political class." [17] Similarly, Herbert Spencer believed that the introduction of Communism would probably lead to "a grinding tyranny . . . under which the mass of the people . . . labored for the support of the organization which regulated them." [18] Again, the Russian-Polish anarchist Machajski, who exercised a profound influence on the Russian revolutionary intelligentsia for a brief period at the turn of the century, wrote in 1898 that "socialism, for all its 'proletarian' protestations, is the ideology of the rising new middle class of intellectuals, professionals, technicians, and white collar workers." He predicted that the result of a socialist revolution would be the establishment of "a hierarchical system under which all industries are owned by the government . . . [whose] officeholders, managers, and engineers [will receive] . . . salaries . . . much higher than the wages paid for manual labor and . . . henceforth constitute the new and only ruling class." [19]

Indicative though these comments are, it is going too far to read Marx or even Engels and Lenin as advocates of full-fledged technocracy. To do so is to ignore the fact that increased managerial authority was to be confined exclusively to the realm of production. More important, the socialist authors envisioned a system whereby managers would ultimately be elected by the public and instantly recallable on popular demand.[20] In this regard they differed markedly from Saint-Simon, who appears to have believed that the ability to "administer" effectively was confined to a narrow circle of natural aristocrats of the intellect whose fate could not be left to the vagaries of the public will.[21] Nevertheless, critics such as Bakunin, Spencer, and Machajski come substantially closer to the truth than those who do not recognize that classical Marxism insists that extensive managerial authority is endemic to modern production and will survive not only the overthrow of capitalism but also the establishment of socialism.

If Marx and his followers foresaw relatively few changes in the basic forms of management or in the fundamental character of the management function under socialism, they were less restrained when they spoke about the men who would occupy

17

managerial posts. Here the case for the realism of prerevolutionary management doctrine undoubtedly tends to break down. In particular one must somehow come to grips with the famous patristic vision of the complete demise of individual specialization and the rise of a situation in which occupational roles would be interchangeable at will, so that "all will take a turn in management and will soon become accustomed to the idea of no [professional] managers at all." [22] Even here, though, it is important to stress that the demise of functional specialization was envisioned as an exceedingly protracted process, which would culminate only after a massive rise in education. In the interim, the most that could be hoped for was a gradual reduction in the gap between mental and physical labor and the immediate transfer into the hands of ordinary rank-and-file citizens of those functions which bourgeois society had surrounded with an artificial aura of complexity.[23]

The founders of Marxism assumed that such functions were numerous, and it is apparent that they seriously underestimated the amount of expertise required for the effective performance of even the simplest administrative and parapolitical tasks. Yet it is equally apparent that they did *not* include management in their catalogue of readily popularized functions. Although all of the patristic authors, and Lenin in particular, indulged in a certain amount of purposeful obfuscation on this score, it is evident that they saw the management function as pertaining to the realm of "mental labor," and clearly understood that it could not be performed without substantial intellectual qualifications and considerable specialized training. All of them, including Lenin, fully subscribed to Engels' injunction that "in order to command productive forces and set them in motion we need . . . trained people, many such people." [24]

The basic consideration behind Lenin's effort to obscure his recognition of the inherent complexity of industrial management was a desire to capitalize on anarchist sentiments prevalent in a sizable segment of the Russian population.[25] The principal tactic he adopted was to shift the focus of his discussion rapidly back and forth from the question of accounting and control *over* production to the question of the management *of* production, thereby creating the illusion that his remarks on the former function applied also to the latter. These remarks, in turn, stressed precisely that "accounting and control . . . have been *simplified* by capitalism . . . and reduced to . . . extraordinarily simple operations . . . that any literate person can perform." [26] Yet, at the same time, Lenin was anxious not to mislead his own followers or to discredit Bolshevism in the eyes of the more "responsible" elements of society.[27] He was usually careful to indicate that he did not intended his remarks on accounting and control to apply to management.

In speaking of "accounting and control," Lenin regularly defined his terms to include only the most routine and prosaic clerical operations.[28] Also, when he turned his attention to management proper, his statements on the need for high qualifications were almost always quite explicit, although often set in contexts designed to discourage reflection on their meaning. Thus there was nothing in the least ambiguous about his assertion that under socialism the leadership of economic ministries would be in the hands of "commissions of specialists." [29] The same is true of his assertions to the effect that one of the first acts of the proletariat upon coming to power would be "to set economists, engineers, agronomists to work out a 'plan'"; that the proletariat would at once "hire their own technicians [and] managers"; and, finally, that the victorious Bolsheviks would give all those who had experience in organizing banks and enterprises "their suitable and usual work." [30]

As this last assertion indicates, Lenin fully expected the initial staff of the socialist managerial apparatus to be recruited from among the managerial cadres of bourgeois society.[31] And there is no question that Marx and Engels entertained a similar expectation.[32] Although the socialist regime would hasten to train selected members of the proletariat in managerial skills and thus be able to place class-conscious workers in key management posts well before the arrival of full-fledged socialism, the managers of socialist industry would for a considerable period undoubtedly be holdovers from the capitalist system. Indeed, it could scarcely be otherwise, for capitalist society did not ordinarily provide the proletariat with access to the requisite knowledge and training. However, the patristic authors did more than acquiesce in the inevitable; they accepted it with relative equanimity. For, with one important qualification that we shall examine later, they expected the holdovers from capitalism to be reliable and perhaps even dedicated servants of the socialist cause. As Lenin put the optimum variant of the case, "these gentlemen work today subordinated to the capitalists; they will work still better tomorrow subordinated to be armed proletariat." [33] Nor is it in anyway a disqualification of my argument that Lenin here refers not to managers as such, but rather to "the scientifically educated staff of engineers, agronomists and so on," for the same cooperative behavior was also expected from executive personnel.[34] The only exceptions would be those managers who were themselves capitalist entrepreneurs, and, as the Marxist theorists were well aware, the replacement of the entrepreneur-manager by the professional management specialist was an integral part of the process of capitalist development.[35]

The expectation that the managerial and technical cadres of bourgeois society would prove reliable and perhaps even dedicated servants of the socialist cause derived in the first instance from the Marxist theory of classes. According to this theory, these cadres were unquestionably members of the proletariat, though their labor was mental rather than physical. As Marx himself pointed out, they were both "wage laborers" and producers of "surplus value," and, as such, the full satisfaction of their class interests could only be achieved under socialism.[36]

20

While they were likely — indeed certain — to be inordinately slow in achieving true class-consciousness, by the time capitalism reached its highest stage of development they would be fully aware of their identity as members of the proletariat and prepared to welcome and even actively to facilitate the advent of socialism. Thus, Engels expressed confidence that with the decline of capitalism "enough young technicians" would be attracted to the socialist banner to enable a revolutionary regime to "organize the management of factories . . . under the direction of party comrades." Similarly, Lenin considered it quite natural that engineers would respond to the prospect of an imminent revolution by forming "a union of socialist engineers" dedicated to "defense of the interests of the workers . . . in complete harmony with the workers' organizations." [37] And, even if a revolution occurred before developments had reached this point, the socialists would still have no cause to despair.

If the members of the technical and managerial intelligentsia had not yet achieved true class-consciousness, they would nonetheless be predisposed to cooperate in socialist construction. In all probability they would be on the verge of achieving full class-consciousness, and the revolution itself would serve as a catalyst in bringing this process to completion.[38] Furthermore, if there were some delay, the situation would still not be critical. The men in question would at least be full-fledged professionals, and in the interim their commitment to professionalism would serve as an adequate pledge of their general reliability.

Karl Kautsky undoubtedly deviated from strict Marxist orthodoxy when he advanced the proposition that the intelligentsia did not have any class interest, but "only professional interests." [39] Still, if Marxism insisted that all men did have class interests, it made ample allowance for faulty perceptions of these interests, and it explicitly recognized that in the short run "false consciousness" could have a decisive bearing on behavior. Further, the patristic authors also realized that members of the intelligentsia were peculiarly apt to conceive of themselves in class-transcendant images and to feel great pride in their self-ascribed status as unbiased devotés of "objective" science.[40] Hence, Kautsky was not deviating from orthodoxy when he argued that the members of the intelligentsia were likely to prove "most readily accessible through their professional, scientific point of view."[41] Certainly there can be no doubt that Lenin considered this argument completely orthodox, since he paraphrased it time and time again. And, like Kautsky, he saw an inherent logic in professionalism that pointed to acceptance of and support for socialism.[42]

At the very least, according to Lenin, professionalism embodied an ethic of apoliticism that predisposed its adherents to serve conscientiously any regime calling upon their talents. This predisposition, in turn, was apt to be particularly strong where a socialist regime was concerned. By the time capitalist development began to approach its zenith (and nadir), it would be apparent to all concerned that only socialism could eliminate the anarchy of capitalist production and clear the way for unimpeded scientific and technological progress, and it was safe to assume that technical and managerial professionals would respond accordingly. To be sure, until professionalism gave way to true class-consciousness, the holdover engineers and managers might cavil at some socialist measures (such as equal pay for all workers). They might also waver in their adherence to certain socialist goals. But their doubts would soon be overcome and their full assimilation in socialist society would be both rapid and devoid of serious complications. Although certain temporary concessions might be necessary to reinforce professional loyalty (a grant of higher-than-average wages, for example), these would be few in number, and any pressure for further compromises would be easily contained by counter-pressures emanating from the broader political environment.[43]

Whereas the managers of socialist industry were to enjoy substantial discretionary authority, they were not to have anything like full autonomy. Not only would their day-to-day activities be subject to more or less continuous surveillance in the form of "accounting and control by the armed populace, by the entire people in arms," but also, and more significantly, they would not be allowed to decide questions of basic economic policy. At least, they were not to be so empowered unless (or until) they qualified as "acknowledged representatives" of the proletariat. For the right to determine overall patterns of resource allocation and commodity distribution was to be granted exclusively to such representatives, acting within the framework of a centralized, hierarchically organized system of governmental councils or (in Russian) soviets.[44]

These councils were to be executive as well as legislative organs, for the theoreticians were acutely sensitive to the danger of administrative deviation from legislative intent. They believed that this danger was endemic to "bourgeois parliamentarism" and held that the only way it could be eliminated was to place legislative and executive responsibility in the same hands.[45] In short, until politics withered away, special pains were to be taken to ensure the supremacy of the political leadership over all facets of state administration, industrial management prominent among them. The goal was to create a situation in which managerial authority would be strictly delegated and carefully circumscribed within a network of operational safeguards. These checks were to be so designed that they would not be unduly restrictive where the direction of the production process per se was concerned, but they would nevertheless be sufficiently stringent to ensure that the directors would function in an essentially instrumental capacity. In Lenin's words, the directors were to be given no choice but that of "simply carrying out . . . instructions as responsible . . . moderately paid 'managers.'"[46]

23

Although the prerevolutionary discussion of the political context of socialist management was too general to provide answers to many important questions, its basic approach was far from utopian. Given managers and engineers who were at least predisposed to accept established political authority, if not actively committed to the cause of socialism, it was by no means visionary to believe that a socialist political system would be able to secure responsible industrial administration and management. Nor was the assumption behind this belief in any way farfetched.

The question of class membership aside, phenomena such as the rise of Saint-Simonism in France and the rapid spread of Marxism among the technical intelligentsia of prerevolutionary Russia provided reasonable grounds for the notion that socialism was likely to have a strong appeal to engineers and industrial managers.[47] Even more important, the concurrent proposition that many managerial and technical cadres would respond to the advent of socialism in terms of their self-conceptions as politically neutral professionals was empirically well-grounded, though as yet historically untested. The spread of professionalism in conjunction with economic development and its wide diffusion among the technical intelligentsia of advanced societies were significant facts, and — as subsequent history was to confirm — there was good reason to suppose that professionalism would be a major asset to a newly empowered regime bent on establishing its effective domination over a modern industrial society.[48] And it was, of course, precisely such a society that Marx and his followers had in view when they addressed themselves to problems of industrial organization and management.

While all of the patristic authors, and Lenin in particular, were revolutionary enthusiasts, with a strong voluntarist streak, their central theory was rigorously deterministic. In all of their more detailed writings on the nature of socialist society, socialism was conceived as the end product of a long process of capitalist development. This presupposition applied with particular force where the subject under discussion was socialist economic management and the recruitment of managerial cadres for socialist industry. Far from assuming that professionalism, let alone socialism, was the prototypical ideology of the managerial and technical intelligentsia, the Marxist theorists believed that detachment and alienation from capitalist society would develop only very gradually in response to the growing tendency of capitalism to place obstacles in the way of technological innovation and the spread of unemployment and impoverishment within the ranks of the technical intelligentsia itself. Until these processes had gone quite far, it was by no means impossible that the managerial and technical intelligentsia would be even more capitalistic than the capitalists themselves. In any event, they would certainly be deeply committed to the capitalist order and profoundly hostile to all attempts at revolution.[49]

The type of response that was anticipated from the managers and engineers in the event of an attempt to overthrow capitalism before it had run something approaching its full course of development was graphically described by Engels in a letter to August Bebel. Writing in 1891, Engels warned Bebel: "If, as the result of a war, we come to power before we are prepared for it, the technicians will be our chief enemies; they will deceive and betray us to the best of their ability." [50] And Engels was aware that the ability in question was bound to be considerable. To be sure, it might be possible to terrorize the technicians into formal submission, but the very conditions of backwardness that made terror necessary would make mere submission more or less irrelevant. Given such conditions, it would be more than ever imperative for a socialist regime to launch a program of rapid economic development, and such a program could only succeed if the technicians actively cooperated.[51] Such cooperation, however, was scarcely likely in the case of men whose initial hostility was compounded by the regime's recourse to terror.

25

Indeed, the problem of growth aside, it was far from certain that the use of terror would suffice to prevent rapid economic collapse. If terror was an effective weapon against overt sabotage, it was likely to be much less effective against covert "wrecking," the more so because the "armed workers" and their "acknowledged representatives" would probably lack sufficient education to comprehend even the gross outlines of management procedures.[52] In short, if for no other reason than the hostility of the managerial and technical cadres with whom it would have to deal, a premature revolution was likely to end in unmitigated disaster, with the attempt to establish socialism giving way either to a restoration of capitalism or to the consolidation of a bureaucratic superstate in which the managers and technicians would themselves play a prominent part. Such, Engels indicated, had been the fate of the French revolutions of 1848 and 1871, and it was the virtually certain fate of all other revolutions occurring before History had paved the way for their success.[53]

There is no doubt that Lenin was familiar with Engels' warning. Moreover, in those of his comments on industrial organization and management referring specifically to Russia, he revealed a distinct awareness that Engels had intended his warning to apply precisely to countries such as Russia.[54] Nevertheless, he was unwilling to concede that he was planning a premature revolution. And he insisted that, in the event of a Bolshevik seizure of power, the majority of the Russian managerial elite and technical intelligentsia would cooperate with the new regime, thereby enabling the Bolsheviks to organize Russian industry in accord with the precepts laid down in Marxist management doctrine.[55] Upon coming to power, the Bolsheviks would undoubtedly encounter more problems in dealing with the managerial holdovers of the *ancien régime* than would most of their Western European counterparts, but these problems would not be insurmountable and their solution would not require any unwarranted political compromises.

In short, while Lenin acknowledged that Russia was relatively backward, he insisted that it had crossed the critical historical divide which made socialism possible, if not absolutely necessary. Yet this very insistence revealed hidden uncertainty, and at times, as we have seen, Lenin's confidence obviously faltered in the face of Russia's massive economic and cultural underdevelopment. The Mensheviks who charged him with adventurism, and prophesied that if the Bolsheviks seized power they would be unable to win the cooperation of the technicians or establish their mastery over the industrial establishment, had a highly persuasive case in Marxist terms, and Lenin was too good a Marxist to be wholly unpersuaded. Furthermore, theoretical considerations apart, Lenin was well aware that Bolshevik efforts to recruit managerial and technical personnel into the party had been signally unsuccessful. Although many members of the technical intelligentsia were Marxists and some had been associated with Bolshevik-led circles during their student days, in 1917 only a handful of Russia's 15,000 or so engineers and industrial specialists had any formal ties with the party.[56] Whatever his doubts regarding the reliability of Russia's managers and engineers, however, Lenin never doubted that the only proper course for the Bolsheviks was to seize power at the earliest opportunity. Accordingly, when it became clear, in October 1917, that the Provisional Government had disintegrated enough to be an easy target for such a steeled instrument of political warfare as the Bolshevik Party, the *coup de grâce* was promptly delivered.[57] With its delivery, Lenin's professed faith in the applicability of the patristic management doctrine to Russian conditions was put squarely to the test.

★ 3 ★

THE BOURGEOIS SPECIALISTS

> Engineer Zabelin: I don't know if there's
> much I can do.
> Stalin: That, of course, we don't know.
> Zabelin: I'll never make a Bolshevik.
> Stalin: That's possible.
> Zabelin: You're planning to build socialism
> in Russia and I don't believe in socialism.
> Lenin (with a sudden flash, cheerfully):
> But I do. Who's right?
> Zabelin: I realize what I say is like child's
> prattle to you.
> Stalin: But you're not an expert on social-
> ism.
> Zabelin: No, of course not. I can't say I
> know much about it.
> Stalin: Then why pass judgment on some-
> thing that's not in your field?
> Nikolai Pogodin,
> *The Chimes of the Kremlin*

The revolution quickly dispelled whatever illusions might have
existed regarding the technical intelligentsia's pro-Bolshevik
sympathies. Far from supporting the Bolsheviks, the vast majority of engineers and industrial specialists was squarely behind
the Provisional Government and strongly opposed to the October
coup. While only a small percentage of the technical intelligentsia appears to have gone so far as to enlist in the White
camp or to join the emigration, a large percentage appears to
have participated in an organized campaign of boycotting Bolshevik-controlled offices and refusing to comply with Bolshevik-

inspired orders. This campaign enjoyed the sponsorship of many of the country's leading technical societies and engineering associations, and it quickly assumed massive proportions, especially in the leading industrial and administrative centers.[1]

It was their participation in this campaign that earned the members of the technical intelligentsia the derisive — and sociologically misleading — sobriquet of "bourgeois specialists."[2] More important, it was their participation in this campaign — which the Bolsheviks quickly labeled a campaign of wrecking and sabotage — that was largely responsible for the ruthless "military measures" that the regime applied within their ranks.[3] While the use of these measures gave rise to frequent excesses, it would be a mistake to appraise the coercion exercised against the technical intelligentsia after the revolution as nothing more than a particular manifestation of a general Bolshevik penchant for the use of terror. Except for the compulsion exercised by the Cheka and the so-called Committee for the Struggle Against Labor Deserters, absenteeism and insubordination might have gone on for an extended period instead of diminishing rapidly toward the end of 1917 and disappearing almost entirely in early 1918.[4] Had this been the case, it is quite possible that the Bolshevik regime would not have survived its birthpangs. At the same time, however, once the need for compulsion and its importance have been recognized, major qualifications are in order.

It is doubtful that the application of military measures even suffices to explain the brevity of overt resistance by the technical intelligentsia. Certainly it does not explain, but rather renders all the more remarkable, the radical change that occurred in the behavior of the "bourgeois specialists" once resistance was suppressed. For, in a large and rapidly increasing number of cases, resistance appears to have given way not to passive compliance with orders but to conscientious collaboration and active cooperation. In short, developments proceeded in a manner that Engels would have considered inconceivable in the circumstances, and in a manner far surpassing even the most sanguine of Lenin's prerevolutionary forecasts.[5]

THE TURN TO COLLABORATION

Lenin heralded a "huge reversal" in the outlook and behavior of the members of the technical intelligentsia as early as April 1919, and the regime's success in maintaining a level of production adequate to meet the exigencies of the Civil War period is testimony to the accuracy of his appraisal.[6] Moreover, despite the subsequent allegations of a number of Soviet authors, there is nothing in the record to indicate that the trend toward cooperation was disproportionately strong among the lower-level cadres in whom Lenin had placed particular faith in his prerevolutionary writings. Certainly, at a minimum, it was not restricted to such cadres. Thus, to cite but one of many possible examples, it was precisely upper-level cadres, including P. I. Palchinsky, *de facto* head of the Central War Industries Committee under the tsar and deputy minister of trade and industry in Kerensky's government, who were the dominant figures in the group of specialists that Lenin called together in early 1920 to prepare a comprehensive plan for the electrification of the Russian countryside.[7] This example is particularly noteworthy, in turn, because Lenin always depicted the enterprise displayed by the members of this group (which eventually formed the nucleus of the State Planning Commission or Gosplan) as both symptomatic and symbolic of the trend within the technical intelligentsia at large.[8] Indeed, Lenin was so favorably impressed with the aid that the so-called Goelro specialists gave in concretizing what was in many respects his grandest and most cherished economic vision that he fell for a moment into what can only be described as a state of chiliastic euphoria.

This mood was already evident when Lenin identified the Goelro Plan as a "second party program," the economic counterpart, as it were, of the political platform drawn up at approximately the same time by Bukharin, Preobrazhensky, and others; but Lenin went even further and suggested that this second party program would quickly assume priority over the first. And, as if this were not enough, he further suggested that the change in the status of the two programs would be accompanied by a change in the status of the two groups concerned: the party elite on the one hand and the bourgeois specialists on the other. This was the essence of his declaration to the Eighth Congress of Soviets (December 1920) that the adoption of the Goelro Plan marked "the beginning of the happy era when politicians will grow ever fewer in number, when people will speak of politics more rarely and at less length, and when engineers and agronomists will do most of the talking." [9] Lenin might not have made the point explicitly, but it was apparent that for some time to come the only available engineers and agronomists would be bourgeois specialists.

As an index of Lenin's practical political plans, this declaration, with its dramatic echoes of *State and Revolution,* was highly misleading. As an index of the behavior of the bourgeois specialists, however, it was quite revealing, for Lenin was not given to unfounded enthusiasm.[10] Further, as I have indicated, it is virtually certain that the trend to which Lenin was responding became progressively more dominant. By 1922, for example, at a time when education was just being resumed on a fairly substantial scale after an almost complete hiatus during the period of revolution and civil war, things had progressed to the point where Lenin could suggest that the training of Soviet replacements for the bourgeois specialists might be proceeding *too rapidly.* Nor was this an idle suggestion, for in fact little effort was made during the next several years to accelerate the training of "red" or "proletarian" specialists.[11] Instead, the prevailing spirit was one of great satisfaction with the capacity and level of performance demonstrated by the old technical cadres.

To cite the views of a Soviet leader intimately involved in

economic affairs, none other than Felix Dzerzhinsky, chief of the dread Cheka and chairman of the Supreme Council of the National Economy (VSNKh), stressed in a 1925 speech that, "if we have achieved a level [of industrial recovery and development] . . . that we did not anticipate, it is only because our party has been able . . . to draw the nonparty technical personnel into our creative economic work." [12] Similarly, the veteran Communist engineer Gleb Krzhizhanovsky, chairman of Gosplan and former head of the Goelro Commission, reported in the same year:

every time we have raised questions regarding the pressing tasks and urgent needs of our industry, we have encountered from the side of our technical personnel not merely formal answers to our enquiries but a most active response. It is unquestionably true that we are here in the presence of that inspired working zeal without which there can be no victory on the . . . difficult labor front.[13]

These statements clearly convey the dominant attitude, and the prevalence of this attitude, in turn, is graphic evidence of the degree to which the technical intelligentsia had adopted a cooperative, supportive approach to the regime.

In seeking to understand the genesis and development of so close a rapprochement after such unpropitious early contacts, one must take into account a number of factors relating both to the character of Bolshevik policy and to the beliefs and predilections of the members of the technical intelligentsia. Three such factors, in particular, stand out.

First, some specialists undoubtedly began to cooperate actively as a result of the regime's increasing willingness to compromise its egalitarian principles and to pay qualified personnel high wages in return for their assistance.[14] Certainly, at a minimum, there is no reason to assume that all or even a majority of the members of the technical intelligentsia were free from venality or immune to appeals to personal self-interest. At the same time, there is unquestionably a tendency among Soviet analysts to exaggerate the efficacy of such appeals.[15] That some members of the technical intelligentsia were deeply offended by the regime's effort to "buy" them is indicated by the famous open letter to Lenin in which Professor M. Dukelsky of the Voronezh Agricultural Institute protested the regime's resort to bribery as a recruitment technique and warned that "without inspiration, without inner fire, without the requirements for creativity not a single specialist will give anything." [16] And the fact that Lenin attached such importance to this letter and felt constrained to write a long, conciliatory answer makes it clear that Dukelsky was not alone in his offended reaction to the change in official wage policy.[17] On the contrary, it seems evident that in many cases this change was at best a necessary rather than a sufficient condition for the adoption of a collaborative approach.

The new wage policy almost certainly played a lesser role than another, complementary, policy change, which was inaugurated at approximately the same time and was implemented with growing vigor and dependability in the following months and years. This change took the form of a sharp curtailment and progressive liquidation of the system of "workers' management" that had sprung up in the aftermath of the revolution.[18] Workers' management had emerged as a more or less spontaneous outgrowth of the revolutionary process. Throughout the country, the revolution had been accompanied by the seizure of plants and factories by local workers' councils and trade-union committees, which promptly set up their own management boards and proceeded to conduct the affairs of the given enterprises according to their own impulsive design. This design rarely bore any relationship to the technological and economic requirements of the situation. In particular, it often involved the exclusion of the former managers and engineers from all positions of authority or influence.[19] The result, of course, was economic chaos and organizational anarchy.

As we have seen, neither of these outcomes was in accord with Bolshevik principles, let alone Bolshevik interests. But after the revolution the regime was powerless to take effective counteraction. Indeed, in order to retain mass support, it even went so far as to sanction the prevailing system, thereby confirming the bourgeois specialists in their belief that Bolshevism was inherently destructive.[20] In fact, though, the regime was merely biding its time until it could accumulate sufficient power to rein in the forces of spontaneity. Already by the spring of 1918 the party leadership had begun to speak out more and more forcefully against the evils of "anarcho-syndicalism" and to place ever greater stress on the need to grant the bourgeois specialists a considerable measure of functional autonomy and executive authority; these themes became more and more prominent with each passing month. Moreover, the leadership backed up its words with increasingly effective action, thereby compelling even the most skeptical bourgeois specialist to take note.

Since it clearly denoted deference to the specialists' expertise and recognition of their "rightful" status, the offensive against anarcho-syndicalist forms of industrial organization could not help but elicit a somewhat favorable response from the technical intelligentsia. And, in a substantial number of cases, it appears to have done much more. For many bourgeois specialists, the forthright rejection of workers' management seems to have gone a considerable way (and, in conjunction with the introduction of a "reasonable" wage policy, a very considerable way) toward meeting all of the demands they had advanced in justifying their participation in the post-October campaign of absenteeism and insubordination. Thus a significant number of "wreckers and saboteurs" had justified their conduct on strictly professional rather than political grounds. As indicated, for example, by the resolutions adopted by the Congress of Officials of Factory, Plant, and Trade-Industrial Enterprises, which convened in Moscow in December 1917, they had explicitly proclaimed their willingness to render diligent and responsible service as soon as the regime undertook to respect at least the most fundamental canons of economic rationality.[21] Moreover, it seems certain that these representations were made in good faith. Despite occasional Soviet claims to the contrary, there is no reason whatever to doubt that the self-proclaimed professionals among the specialists behaved precisely as they had pledged they would once their minimal demands had been satisfied, subordinating political considerations to pride of craft and principles of vocational responsibility.[22]

If professionalism had not developed as highly in prerevolutionary Russia as it had in Western Europe and the United States, it had nonetheless sunk deep roots. In the first place, virtually all members of the technical intelligentsia were at least formally committed to professional codes that prescribed political neutrality as a norm of conduct in the occupational realm.[23] In addition, a significant number had become adherents of full-fledged professionalistic ideologies. To be precise, they subscribed to ideologies that radically denigrated the utility of all political activity and elevated intense participation in professional activity either to a transcendant value in its own right or to a paramount obligation within the framework of a broader ethic of nonpartisan public service or suprapolitical, developmental nationalism.[24] In particular, many engineers and industrial specialists, including a number who subsequently emerged as key figures on the Goelro Commission, subscribed to the views of the eminent scientist D. I. Mendeleev (1834–1907), who had sought to persuade Russia's technical cadres to concentrate on "practical work, making use of existing opportunities" for industrial development.[25]

In urging his colleagues to abjure "politics mongering" and to direct their energies into economically constructive channels, Mendeleev was adopting a distinctly heretical stance. As he was well aware, his advice ran directly counter to the highly politicized tradition of the Russian intelligentsia. At the same time, it was advice peculiarly well calculated to win acceptance from engineers and industrial executives. For one thing, the members of the technical intelligentsia were men whose receptivity to tradition had been weakened as a result of their technical and scientific education.[26] In addition, their special expertise had meant that they could pursue their vocations within tsarist society with relatively few restraints. In this regard they differed markedly from most of their educated compeers who tended, more or less automatically, to be relegated to the status of "superfluous men" — men whose only hope of escaping superfluity was to adopt political opposition as a profession and social radicalism as a way of life.[27]

However much they might have detested the autocratic system — and there is no doubt that they did — the members of the technical intelligentsia had no difficulty in finding "existing opportunities" within the established tsarist order.[28] On the contrary, they constantly encountered opportunities that were immensely satisfying from a professional point of view, and in many cases Mendeleev's doctrine provided a welcome rationale for accepting the rewards and challenges thus offered. Moreover, this doctrine (known as "gradualism" or "realism") had a significant impact even where it did not win full acceptance.[29] And, through a perverse irony, the experience of revolution appears to have convinced some members of the technical intelligentsia in whose outlooks professionalistic themes had not earlier been dominant that Mendeleev's counsel had been sound and that politics was, indeed, a matter of no concern to them.[30]

The revolution's role in precipitating a renunciation of politics in favor of professional service, and the way in which this process redounded to the benefit of the Bolsheviks, is best illustrated by a letter that Pitrim A. Sorokin published in a Bolshevik-controlled newspaper in the fall of 1918. Sorokin, who had been a prominent Right Socialist Revolutionary and up to this point an active foe of Bolshevism, wrote: "The past year of the revolution has taught me one truth: politicians can make mistakes; politics can be socially useful but it can also be socially harmful; work in the fields of science and education is always useful." [31] Then, taking this newfound truth as his point of departure, Sorokin proceeded not only to forswear further opposition to the Bolsheviks but also to promise to become a loyal Soviet employee in the realms of science and education. Whether Sorokin actually reneged on this promise, as the Soviet regime charged when it expelled him from Russia in 1922, is a moot point. Still there is no reason to doubt that the professionalistic sentiments he expressed in 1918 were sincere. And it is clear, in the case of many other men who shared these sentiments, that support for the regime proved stable and enduring. Indeed, it seems virtually certain that the collaborationist "logic" of professionalism became ever more compelling. Not only did the Bolshevik steadily extend their control over existing opportunities but also, and perhaps even more important, they demonstrated an increasing willingness and ability to expand these opportunities. In this way they provided the basis for a progressively more affirmative response to the question — the only question — asked by such true professionals as the future academician, I. P. Bardin: "Do the interests of the Soviet power coincide with my aspirations as an engineer?" [32]

Although it is probably true, as S. V. Utechin has suggested, that professionalism was the outlook of "the majority of . . . 'bourgeois specialists' as they entered into the service of the Bolshevik state," [33] many members of the technical intelligentsia who were neither early adherents of professionalism nor postrevolutionary converts to the faith also made their peace with the regime. These men unquestionably remained ideologically hostile to Bolshevism, but they nonetheless managed to persuade themselves that in the prevailing circumstances active collaboration with the Bolshevik regime was required by the very political principles they professed. This was clearly the case during the Civil War period, when many democratic socialists (especially Mensheviks) and a sizable number of liberals (especially liberal nationalists) concluded that the Bolshevik regime was the sole potentially viable bulwark against the intolerable alternatives of counterrevolutionary restoration or the dismemberment of Russia by foreign powers.[34] And it continued to be the case in the subsequent period. To be sure, as the White peril and the foreign menace receded and it became apparent that the Bolsheviks had no intention of making any major political concessions, it became increasingly difficult to argue the legitimacy, let alone the necessity, of cooperation in terms of liberal or socialist ideology. But many specialists continued (and others now began) to do precisely that.

The liberal variant of the argument is best exemplified by the early writings of the émigré Kadet, N. V. Ustryalov, who was the originator (in 1920) of a doctrine known as *smenovekhism* and the leader of a movement that quickly encompassed "thousands and tens of thousands" of Soviet officials.[35] The socialist variant is best exemplified by the pronouncements of a group of prominent ex-Mensheviks who occupied key posts throughout the Soviet industrial establishment and virtually monopolized professional positions in the central planning agencies.[36] Whichever variant one turns to, however, the central thesis is essentially the same — that the best and probably only way to realize liberal or socialist goals in Russia, given the stabilization of Bolshevik power, was to do everything possible to facilitate economic development. Such development would inevitably engender social and cultural changes of a sort that would render revolutionary Bolshevism historically obsolete, and guarantee its transformation into or replacement by a more "appropriate" liberal or socialist regime.[37]

The risk that the immediate outcome of economic development might be a further entrenchment of the Bolsheviks' dictatorial power was scarcely considered at all; and, if considered, it was quickly dismissed on the grounds that the regime was in any case beyond effective challenge and that the interim involved was bound to be short-lived. This was the import, for example, of an article (self-consciously entitled "To Canossa") in which one of Ustryalov's principal collaborators, S. S. Chakhotin, argued:

> The theory that by strengthening the country's economic position we will "fortify the position of the Bolsheviks" and thereby delay the moment of Russia's return to a normal, peaceful course of development must be decisively rejected. Indeed, the contrary is true: the key to raising the cultural level of the country and restoring its political health lies in the restoration of normal economic conditions.[38]

The very fact that the Bolsheviks were dedicated industrializers would hasten "debolshevization," and the process would be further accelerated if the specialists themselves collaborated with the new regime. In the worst of circumstances loyal collaboration was bound to speed economic development, but it was even more appropriate since the regime had adopted a reasonable management policy. Collaborators were now certain to occupy positions that would enable them to "soften" the regime's policy and canalize it in favorable directions — directions that would facilitate the emergence of the forces of liberalization or socialization inherent in the very dynamics of development.[39]

Needless to say, not all liberals or social democrats subscribed to arguments such as Chakhotin's or views such as those of the Marxist G. A. Solomon, who held that collaboration was essential "in order to serve the people and introduce as many healthy elements as [possible] . . . into the situation," until development could make the Bolsheviks recognize their responsibility and perforce become in the end a popular government." [40] On the contrary, there were many liberals and social democrats who had consistently refused the Bolshevik regime their support or had withdrawn their support after the Civil War. In the eyes

39

of these men, the Chakhotins and Solomons were pure opportunists, and the views they advanced to justify their behavior were wholly illegitimate in ideological terms. In point of fact, however, neither of these charges can be accepted at face value.

As for the charge of opportunism, to accept it as generally applicable would be to impugn the integrity of a large body of men who were rooted, albeit somewhat tenuously, in a tradition that attached exceeding importance to intellectual probity and principaled behavior — the tradition of the Russian intelligentsia. In addition, and even more decisively, it would be to challenge the testimony of a number of extremely well informed and essentially disinterested witnesses.[41] As for the charge of ideological heresy, it is indisputable that the economic determinism of Chakhotin and Solomon was integral to Marxist theory, and it clearly had orthodox status in liberal theory as well. Indeed, it is fair to say that Chakhotin's point of view was merely a practical application of that strand of liberal theory represented by Herbert Spencer, whose conception of the inevitable transmutation of militant political systems into free and open industrial political systems as a direct consequence of economic progress was familiar among educated Russians.[42] But, if their motives were not unduly suspect and their ideological credentials were at least presentable, the liberals and social democrats who chose to collaborate with the regime can be criticized for having had a tragically inadequate understanding of the self-perpetuating, self-aggrandizing nature of political power in general and Bolshevik power in particular. By behaving as if politics were a secondary, derivative phenomenon, they made themselves peculiarly vulnerable to successful manipulation by men for whom politics was a paramount end. And the Bolshevik leaders were precisely such men. Before this leadership could take full advantage of the collaboration offered by the bourgeois specialists, however, it had to overcome considerable resistance within the party itself.

If the regime's willingness to compromise its egalitarian principles and to take the offensive against anarcho-syndicalist forms of economic organization was instrumental in winning over the technical intelligentsia, it was also instrumental in arousing widespread dissension within the ranks of the party. No sooner had Lenin indicated his intention to grant the bourgeois specialists more autonomy than it became apparent that there were many Bolsheviks who shared the anarchistic impulses of the masses — and many party theorists who had *misinterpreted* the patristic management doctrine as a prescription for precisely the sort of anarcho-syndicalist management system that had in fact emerged in the immediate aftermath of the revolution. At the same time, it also became apparent that many party members who had been assigned managerial posts by the regime were strongly opposed to any measures designed to enhance the status of the bourgeois specialists. These "red directors" viewed the specialists as rivals for the offices they now enjoyed, and they had no intention of surrendering without a fight.[43]

It is worth noting parenthetically that this outlook of fear and suspicion was by no means universal. Moreover, in a great many of the cases where it did exist, it was quickly superseded by an attitude of tolerance and respect. Although this change is often overlooked in the pertinent Western literature, there can be no doubt that it was both rapid and extensive. There is, for example, the evidence provided by the previously cited reports of Dzerzhinsky and Krzhizhanovsky. The latter concludes:

It is not necessary to be a particularly acute observer in order to notice the presence of the necessary elements of close cohesion between the technical personnel and the proletarian staff. Here, however, there is not simply cohesion but an extraordinary, original, and necessary process. Before our eyes a merger in friendly work is occurring between the old . . . disciplined technical personnel with its irreplaceable experience and selected . . . workers from the proletarian leadership.[44]

Even more impressive, because it shows official disapproval, is the evidence provided by such men as Trotsky, who complained as early as 1920 that attacks on specialists usually led to conflicts with the victims' Communist superiors, or Shkiryatov, chairman of the party's Central Control Commission, who complained in 1930 that appeals by Communist managers on behalf of bourgeois specialists arrested by the GPU had assumed "epidemic proportions." [45]

This outlook of tolerance once noted, it must be stressed that the commonly accepted picture of the relationship between the bourgeois specialists and the so-called red directors as one of hostility and conflict is valid for the period immediately following the revolution. At this time, most of the red directors did tend to view the bourgeois specialists with intense suspicion and mistrust, thereby aligning themselves with the anarcho-syndicalist elements within the party. Although the two groups were otherwise in sharp disagreement, on this issue they were united and, in combination, they were powerful enough to force Lenin to proceed rather cautiously in promoting the bourgeois specialists.

Not, to be sure, that Lenin failed to move ahead. He was able to achieve the more or less rapid replacement of workers' management by a more centralized administrative system, which secured the bourgeois specialists a considerably stronger place on the management boards of enterprises and higher-level economic organs. Thus official statistics indicate that by 1919 over 50 percent of the top officials of the administrative-productive organs of the VSNKh had achieved high status under the *ancien régime*. An even more graphic picture of "re-establishment" is presented in such unofficial reports as that of a " 'White' professor" who wrote:

at the head of many of the centers and *glavki* sit former employers and responsible officials and managers of businesses, and the unprepared visitor . . . who is personally acquainted with the former commercial and industrial world would be surprised to see the former owners of big leather factories sitting in Glavkozh [the Central Leather Administration], big manufacturers in the central textile organizations, etc.[46]

Nonetheless, despite this steady progress, it was only in January 1920, at the Ninth Party Congress, that Lenin was able to win unqualified endorsement for the sort of thoroughgoing organizational reform he considered necessary. In particular, it was only then that he was able to gain official approval for the replacement of the collegial principle in industrial management by the principle of one-man authority (*yedinolichie*).[47] Moreover, even at the Ninth Congress his views prevailed only after a long and acrimonious debate in which he was required to answer two distinct but interrelated sets of charges: one accused him of abandoning democratic centralism in favor of bureaucratic authoritarianism, and the other accused him of setting the stage for a capitalist restoration by proposing to invest not only Communist managers but also bourgeois specialists with extensive administrative authority. This last set of charges was advanced particularly forcefully by the red directors, who were by no means opposed to one-man authority so long as they, rather than the bourgeois specialists, were its principal beneficiaries.

During the debate at the Ninth Congress, Lenin made a valiant attempt to argue that the principle of one-man authority implied no basic shift in the locus of power within industry, but only a heightening of executive responsibility within the framework of the prevailing administrative system — a system that for all its recent "modifications" still allowed a significant measure of participation in management by the workers and their trade-union organizations. He was obviously being disingenuous, however, and the opposition had an air-tight case when it charged that one-man authority was a euphemism designed to camouflage an attempt to impose on the entire economy the sort of hierarchical and disciplinarian management system that had already (in March 1918) been instituted for the railroads.[48] Although Lenin might claim that the railroad reorganization had merely been a temporary emergency measure dictated by the exigencies of the Civil War, he could not deny that he had justified the reorganization in universalistic terms. He could not escape the obvious connection between his present proposal and his earlier statement that not only the railroads but "every heavy-machine industry . . . demands a [single], unconditional, stern will directing the simultaneous work of hundreds, thousands, and tens of thousands of people." [49] Nonetheless, if the opposition's case against Lenin was irrefutable, it is doubtful that it made any great impression on the party at large. Indeed, though they later regretted having done so, even the anarcho-syndicalist oppositionists were willing to concede that the issue of one-man authority was "not a matter of fundamental principle." [50] And it is almost certain that what these men ultimately conceded was something that most party members had taken for granted from the start.

The situation was quite different when the question of the bourgeois specialists was introduced into the equation. Here the opposition's protests struck a responsive chord throughout the party. How, after all, could one fail to be disturbed at the prospect of a multitude of erstwhile wreckers and saboteurs occupying high posts in a regime which, as Lenin himself acknowledged, they continued to deplore even while they served it? Granted that workers' management was untenable, was it really necessary to move so far in the other direction? Given considerable on-going hostility to the regime on the part of many bourgeois specialists, how could the leadership be so certain that managerial authority could be restricted to the sphere of production and denied expression in the broader political arena? [51] How could it deny the patently un-Marxist character of assurances such as those of Bukharin, who tried to lend theoretical support to Lenin's program by arguing:

> With the dialectical transformation of the bourgeois dictatorship into the proletarian, the technical function of the intelligentsia changes from a capitalistic to a social function of labor . . . Paralleling this, the *basic type of association* changes, *although in the hierarchical scheme the intelligentsia occupies the same "middle" place.* For the highest authority in the state economy is the concentrated social power of the proletariat. Here the technical intelligentsia on the one hand stands above the great mass of the working class, but on the other is in the last analysis *subordinated* to its collective will, the expression of which is found in the proletariat's organization of the state economy. The transformation of the process of producing surplus value into a process of planned satisfaction of social needs finds expression in the regrouping of production relations, notwithstanding the formal retention of the same place in the hierarchical system of production, which in principle assumes as a whole a different character, the character of the dialectic negation of the structure of capitalism and which, insofar as it destroys the social-caste character of the hierarchy, leads toward the abolition of the hierarchy altogether.[52]

Clearly Bukharin was evading (not to mention obfuscating) the issue, and it was legitimate at the time to wonder whether the regime was not in fact, as the opposition suggested, already succumbing to the influence of the bourgeois specialists and setting the stage for a full-fledged bourgeois restoration.[53]

Needless to say, all of these questions raised further questions, and the cumulative impact was powerful enough to shake even the most intellectually subservient and politically sanguine members of the party. As for the impact on those party members who were less confident that Bolshevism was invincible, the evidence leaves no doubt that they were often severely affected. In the end, however, despite grave misgivings, the party bowed to Lenin's will. Although the opposition was able to secure the support of such august bodies as the party organizations of Moscow and the Ukraine, the party fraction of the All-Russian Council of

Trade Unions, and the Third Congress of Councils of the National Economy in the period immediately preceding the Ninth Congress, it was decisively rebuffed by the congress itself.[54] The congress overwhelmingly adopted Lenin's management program as official policy, and there is no reason to doubt that this vote had the approval, however reluctant, of most of the party membership.

In a number of respects, later developments proceeded along the lines that the opposition had anticipated. Already by the end of 1920, 86 percent of all Soviet enterprises were subject to one-man authority, and, in a steadily growing number of cases, this authority was vested in the hands of bourgeois specialists. [55] By 1923, Communists comprised only 23–29 percent of the directors and members of the administrative boards of enterprises, and it seems clear that the vast majority of the non-Communists were bourgeois specialists rather than nonparty workers or trade-union officials.[56] Similarly, the years immediately following the Ninth Congress saw a steady rise in the number of nonparty experts holding responsible posts in high-level management organs. Indeed, within a year of the congress, official sources were able to report that specialists and ex-officials occupied no less than 80 percent of the "most responsible posts" in the VSNKh and comprised 74 percent of the membership of the administrative collegia of industrial glavks.[57] Moreover, the regime saw fit to order those Communists who retained high posts "to command less or, more accurately, not to command." [58] As if this were not enough, the regime simultaneously proceeded to authorize discussion of the need to move beyond one-man authority to full-fledged one-man management (*yedinonachalive*), to end virtually all effective participation by the trade unions in the appointment of managerial personnel, and to transform the specialist-dominated Goelro Commission into a general planning commission with extensive legislative and executive powers.[59]

All of these developments took place under Lenin's aegis.[60]

46

Yet it is clear from the events following his death that they did not stem from his initiative alone. On the contrary, between 1924 and 1928 the prevailing management policy was maintained and in some respects even extended. To cite but one example from each of the years concerned, 1925 witnessed the passage of a Central Committee resolution relieving the bourgeois specialists of a number of the civic disabilities they had been subject to as members of a proscribed class; 1926 brought an industrial reorganization that greatly expanded the rights of engineering personnel; and 1927 saw a noteworthy change in the ideological status of the technical intelligentsia as such.[61] This change occurred when Stalin, in the course of a speech instructing the party that its task was to continue its policy of actively utilizing the bourgeois specialists, identified the latter as members of the "laboring Soviet intelligentsia" whose relationship to the working class was one of union (*smychka*), a highly honorific term that had previously been reserved to describe the relationship between the proletariat and the peasantry.[62] Nonetheless, although these developments, together with those occurring in Lenin's lifetime, clearly substantiated many of the suspicions voiced by the anarcho-syndicalist opposition, they did not entail the sort of political consequences that the opposition had feared.[63]

THE POLITICAL INFLUENCE OF THE BOURGEOIS SPECIALISTS

The opposition was unquestionably on safe ground when it predicted that the regime's management policy would enhance the technical intelligentsia's influence over official policy. Such an increase did occur, and in some areas it assumed substantial proportions. Naum Jasny is almost certainly correct when he asserts that from 1923 through 1927 the group of ex-Menshevik specialists headed by V. G. Groman "dominated . . . current planning and had a profound influence also on the preparation of the First Five Year Plan." [64] Moreover, it is probable that the specialists sometimes utilized their influence to realize "bourgeois" goals, thereby at least partially corroborating another of the opposition's expectations. Thus there seems little reason to dispute the word of A. Gurovich, a high-ranking nonparty official in the VSNKh in 1918–1919, who reports that the efforts of those specialists who sought to soften Bolshevik policy — and they comprised a significant proportion of the total group — were occasionally crowned with success:

It was [always] possible [for the specialists] to be persistent in suggesting different measures designed to "save" or "soften" . . . and this very persistence in and of itself [would often have] . . . a profound effect [on the Bolshevik policy makers] . . . who were constantly full of strong doubts as to the correctness of their decisions regarding concrete questions . . . It was even easier to paralyze the harmful projects of the more hare-brained Communist dreamers. In the majority of cases their plans were easy to subject to devastating criticism . . . and this criticism always made a great impression and often achieved the desired results. Finally, at a minimum, it was almost always possible to introduce [meliorative] changes, corrections, and additions into . . . projects in the guise of editorial revisions, further specifications, or something of a similar order.[65]

Although the forms undoubtedly changed as growing experience made the Communist policy makers more confident of the correctness of their decisions and less vulnerable to the sort of criticism Gurovich describes, there is no reason to believe that "softening" activities ceased after 1919. If anything, the opportunities for such activities probably became more numerous as the bourgeois specialists acquired greater authority in the formal chain of command and consolidated close personal ties with their Communist colleagues — the more so since these colleagues remained dependent on information they could not adequately evaluate and had to accept largely on faith. For, despite the growing critical acumen and practical wisdom of Bolshevik managerial cadres, the bourgeois specialists continued to retain virtually monopolistic control over many of the most fundamental "premises" of policy decisions, the "relevant facts" on which such decisions had to be based if they were to bear any correspondence to the actual capabilities and capacities of the productive system.[66]

It was this last factor to which Lenin called particular attention in 1922 when he observed that "the bourgeois officials are very often better informed than our best Communists." He then went on to ask, "who is directing whom?" and his question clearly suggests that the specialists sometimes made effective use of their "softening" opportunities. However, if Lenin's question was indicative, the answer he offered was absurd: "I doubt very much whether it would be truthful to say that the Communists are directing [the specialists] . . . To tell the truth, they are being directed, not directing." [67] Although such a comment may well have corresponded with a momentary feeling of despair and may have served as a useful tactical device for raising party vigilance, it was defective as a piece of political analysis. Indeed, even where the question of "softening" is concerned, it is virtually certain that what Gurovich asserts to have been true of the period 1918–1919 — that the specialists' ability to exert a moderating influence on official economic policy was marginal at best — remained true throughout the subsequent period.[68] And, where the question concerns the formulation and execution of basic policy, the case is clear. In short, despite Lenin's aberrant admission that his critics had proved right, the opposition's expectations that official management policy would culminate in the "routinization" or "bourgeoisification" of Soviet politics remained unfulfilled. Far from playing a directing role, the bourgeois specialists failed to play any major political role at all.

Among the factors operating to circumscribe the political role of the bourgeois specialists, one of the most imponderable and at the same time one of the most interesting is what might be called the "de-bourgeoisification" of the specialists themselves. Thus we know from the previously cited report of Gurovich that the flow of influence between the bourgeois specialists and the red directors was often reciprocal rather than unidirectional; the result was that the bourgeois specialists often became convinced of the validity of Bolshevik goals and procedures.[69] Moreover, there is a strong probability that the very promotions to high office which provided the specialists with an opportunity to influence policy had the effect of dampening their desire to do so — at least in unauthorized directions. The consensus-generating effects of access to executive privileges and perquisites is relevant in this connection, but the impact of involvement in responsible work was probably even more important. As Inkeles and Bauer have pointed out,

> when the individual is in a responsible position, he must from day to day deal with solving tasks related to the regime's own goals. He is to a greater or lesser degree solving the regime's own problems. To do his job adequately (even from the point of view of his own self-interest) he must address these problems in their own terms. From what we know of psychological processes in general, it seems inevitable that as the individual deals with these problems he must come to accept as legitimate the goals at which they are directed. In effect, he thereby comes to identify himself with the regime and its objectives.[70]

This process once noted, however, a word of caution is in order.

Whereas "de-bourgeoisification" was a real and discernible tendency, the specialists were rarely converted to Bolshevism, and it seems clear that other factors played an equally if not more important role in determining their political behavior.[71] In particular, one must look not only at the changes that occurred in the specialists' political attitudes, but also at the apolitical or politically quietistic character of the original attitudes themselves. Characterized as they were either by a complete disavowal of political activity (professionalism) or else by a sharp devaluation of the importance and necessity of such activity in prevailing circumstances (deterministic liberalism or socialism), these attitudes were clearly designed to encourage accommodation and resignation. By the same token, they were clearly not conducive to the sort of risk taking and calculated perseverance that would have been required in order to parlay technical expertise and managerial authority into political power within the context of the Soviet system. Not only were the basic dynamics of that system such that power accrued only to those who constantly pursued it, but also, and more particularly, the prevailing pattern of political-economic organization was such that only sustained and carefully coordinated action could have counteracted the regime's relentless pursuit of its own distinctive programmatic goals.

In the first place, there was an ever-increasing concentration of authority in all noneconomic spheres in the hands of reliable party cadres, chosen by and responsible to the party Secretariat.[72] The party apparat was itself reconstituted into the principal locus of decision making for a progressively broader range of questions, and there was a conscious effort on the part of the dominant political leadership to render the apparat immune to all outside pressure, especially from the bourgeois specialists. Stalin was well within the bounds of established party principles when he argued, in 1925, that the rise in the number of "nonparty people" in high economic posts, combined with the growth of the industrial establishment itself, posed a serious threat to the party's leadership and required vigorous counteraction in the form of more secretarial control over all facets of party life.[73] Such counteraction was regularly taken, and the organizational measures it entailed served as major barriers to the extension of the specialists' influence beyond the purely economic sphere. Moreover, even in this sphere the specialists had only limited freedom of action.

Despite their great weight in the industrial establishment, the bourgeois specialists never exercised anything approaching a monopoly over the formulation and execution of economic policy. For one thing, general economic strategy was always determined outside the confines of the industrial establishment proper. Indeed, one prominent ex-specialist reports that in the early 1920s even "the two highest organs of the government — the Council of Peoples' Commissars and the Council of Labor and Defense — [only] discussed practical ways to effect measures already decided on by . . . the Political Bureau." [74] Furthermore, within the industrial establishment itself, the bourgeois specialists were by no means free agents. Even during the heyday of the NEP, the "commanding heights" of the economic apparatus were occupied by reliable Old Bolsheviks, and trusted party cadres also continued to fill many of the most strategic posts at the middle and lower levels.[75] In addition, although the main lines of prevailing management policy remained unaltered, after 1925 more and more top policy-making posts appear to have been transferred into the hands of Communists, with the displaced specialists being assigned largely technical or staff functions.[76] Finally, the operations of the industrial establishment in general and the organs in which the bourgeois specialists were dominant in particular were subjected to increasingly ubiquitous surveillance by the party apparat and other affiliated agencies, such as the control commissions, the Workers' and Peasants' Inspection (RKI or Rabkrin), and the secret police. Even prior to Lenin's death a system of control through parallel competing bureaucracies, if not yet through "the institutionalization of mutual suspicion," had begun to emerge, and this system proliferated at a prodigious rate after 1924.[77] Its consolidation provided yet another highly effective barrier against the development of any substantial political potential on the part of the bourgeois specialists, let alone any potential to subvert the forward march of revolutionary Bolshevism.

It is true that the late 1920s and early 1930s witnessed the conversion of all of Soviet industry to the principle of one-man management — a principle that provided not only for the ultimate primacy of managerial authority in a system of institutionalized checks and balances, but also for "the complete subordination of all the workers in the productive process to the will of one person — the leader — and his personal responsibility for the assigned work." [78] Likewise, these years saw the first unqualified *ideological* legitimation of the wage and status system which had grown up in the preceding period and which provided the members of the technical intelligentsia and managerial elite with immense socioeconomic privileges.[79] Finally, the period of the First Five-Year Plan witnessed the first mass enrollment of bourgeois specialists into the party.

Whereas the party had previously issued invitations only to a highly select group of specialists, comprised chiefly of men with revolutionary pasts, it now issued a more or less blanket invitation to the group at large.[80] Moreover, this invitation, which was the logical organizational corollary of Stalin's incorporation of the members of the technical intelligentsia into the "union" of workers and peasants on which Soviet society was theoretically founded, encountered an extremely favorable response. It had not been uncommon during the preceding period for those few specialists who were offered party membership to reject the privilege, but there now occurred an "enormous increase in the enrollment of senior engineers, technicians, and prominent leaders of science into the party." [81] Just how "enormous" is difficult to determine with any degree of precision, but it is indicative that "over 4,000 of the best engineering-technical workers" joined the party in 1930 alone, whereas in 1928 there were only 138 engineers and 751 people with higher technical education in the entire party.[82] Despite this influx, however, and despite the previously noted developments in organizational and social policy, only someone with a highly tenuous grasp of Soviet reality could believe that the period in question marked the beginning of "a new phase in which non-party specialists were allowed a peace of mind [and] an assurance of an unclouded tomorrow." [83] On the contrary, what the "new phase" conclusively demonstrated was that the bourgeois specialists were in a weak political position to start with, and in the process of suffering a rapid decline into complete political impotence.

One of the developments demonstrating the ineffectuality of the bourgeois specialists was the adoption of the Five Year Plan itself, for it cannot be doubted that almost the entire technical intelligentsia was strongly opposed to the Stalinist program of forced-draft collectivization and superindustrialization. Although many specialists were dedicated partisans of central planning, and most were firm believers in a rapid pace of industrial growth, their commitment was to "genetic" or evolutionary rather than to "teleological" or voluntaristic planning; they viewed Stalin's "bacchanalian" approach as the epitome of technical absurdity and economic irrationality, bound to entail not merely extreme human suffering and loss but also a drastic and possibly irreparable decline in production.[84] Almost all of them subscribed to the views of the Gosplan economist V. A. Bazarov, who in November 1928 warned the Eighth Congress of Trade Unions that the adoption of Stalin's plan could entail "the worst results; here you can get such a clearly irrational distribution of resources as will discredit the whole idea of industrialization." [85] And many subscribed to views that made Bazarov's seem pale (and humanly insensitive) by comparison. A substantial number went defiantly on record to this effect, and the temper of the rest can be gauged from a multitude of references in the Soviet press, as well as from such indicators as the remark of the émigré Ustryalov, now too a representative spokesman for the specialists, that "when Bukharin speaks, we can keep silent." [86]

As Ustryalov's remark implies, the position of most of the bourgeois specialists appears to have been virtually indistinguishable from that of the Right Opposition within the party. Indeed, it is even possible that there was some purposeful coordination of oppositionist activity between the leading technical cadres of the VSNKh and Gosplan, on the one hand, and the leading Rightists (especially Bukharin and Rykov), on the other. Although there is no evidence of the existence of any covert organizational ties between the two groups, it is possible that there was a reasonably systematic exchange of information and views.[87] In any event, the crucial point for present purposes is that the opposition of the bourgeois specialists proved wholly ineffectual.

Another development that demonstrated the powerlessness of the specialists was the regime's decision to withdraw the specialists' right to occupy positions of authority without professing total allegiance to the Bolshevik cause. From 1928 on, the Stalinist regime made it unmistakably clear that it no longer subscribed to the old Leninist line, the line that Lunacharsky had summed up by stating that the party's slogan for the technical intelligentsia was "he who is against the bourgeoisie is with us." [88] No longer was the regime prepared to acknowledge Ustryalov's claim that "for a 'specialist' two features are essential: a loyal attitude toward the [governing] power and technical knowledge . . . nothing more can be expected from him." [89] No longer were the bourgeois specialists to be authorized to constitute what had been referred to formerly as "the professional *passif*." [90] Instead, like all other Soviet citizens, they were henceforth to be required to behave as political activists, affirming and glorifying the Stalinist system at every step. Moreover, lest anyone doubt its intentions, the regime proceeded to make the point clear through appropriate organizational measures.

First, the smenovekhite publications that had up to this point enjoyed a unique status as the only avowedly non-Communist organs legally issued in the USSR were banned.[91] In addition, the regime now liquidated the quasi-autonomous All-Russian Association of Engineers — this despite the fact that the association had been instrumental in mobilizing professionalism in the service of the Bolshevik regime and despite the perceived risk that such action would undermine the esprit de corps which had helped to make the technical intelligentsia an enterprising force in production.[92] In Stalin's eyes neither past service nor present economic utility could justify organizational independence, and independence that embodied a measure of historical tradition and was rooted in esoteric knowledge was completely intolerable. What Stalin wanted was nothing less than total control, and he made it clear that professional associations were henceforth to be permitted only where it was absolutely certain that they were nothing more than reliable "transmission belts," completely subject to central direction.

To be sure, Stalin accompanied these measures (and similar ones) with assurances that "we by no means demand that [specialists] . . . renounce their social opinions at once or change them immediately," but it was clear that these assurances were only feeble echoes of the Leninist line.[93] In Stalin's case, "at once" and "immediately" were obviously meant literally, and "renounce" and "change" were the operative terms. This was made explicit two years later (in 1930) when the ostensibly repentant Right Oppositionist, Rykov, summed up the regime's position by asserting that "neutrality toward us is neutrality toward or half-sympathy with our enemies," and warning that "if the old cadres of the technical intelligentsia do not wish to be crushed . . . by the chariot of history and decline to nullity as a useless product, they must restructure themselves." [94] A more graphic statement of the Stalinist perspective is difficult to imagine, and it was to this perspective that the bourgeois specialists were now required to adjust.

A final development that illustrated the true political status of the bourgeois specialists was the extensive purge of the technical intelligentsia conducted between 1928 and 1932. This purge, which proceeded under the slogan, "healthy lack of faith in the specialists," resulted in the arrest of at least two to three thousand engineers and non-Communist managers on the familiar charges of wrecking and sabotage.[95] Its declared purpose, however, was a sham, for despite the full confessions of many of the accused there is little doubt that wrecking and sabotage were virtually nonexistent. This conclusion follows inescapably from the fact that the charges leveled against the specialists were widely disbelieved by those Communists who worked in close contact with the accused, from the fact that most of the alleged (and self-confessed) wreckers and saboteurs were shortly allowed to resume work on highly sensitive projects, and from the innumerable "aesopean" messages, internal inconsistencies, and proven falsehoods in the confessions themselves.[96] The actual objective of the purge was to deflect mass hostility from the regime by providing more or less plausible scapegoats for the immense strains and hardships that inhered in official policies. In addition, the purge was designed to destroy the last remnants of solidarity among the bourgeois specialists and between the latter and the red directors.[97] What was involved, in other words, was arbitrary political terror exercised against completely innocent victims — innocent *and* impotent, for the specialists were powerless to save themselves and could only hope that the regime would permit them to capitulate. Their situation and reaction was graphically described by Karl Radek, who observed at the time: "the broad mass of specialists, stunned by shootings and arrests, dash off in various directions, and frightened by the hostile atmosphere that events have created around them, do not know where to submit, but try in the meantime to hide their heads under their wings, in expectation of better times." [98] A clearer demonstration of the technical intelligentsia's powerlessness would be difficult to imagine. Such a demonstration was scarcely necessary in view of the utter futility of the specialists' opposition to the five-year plan, the withdrawal of their right to all independence of political judgment, and the suppression of their claim to any sort of professional autonomy. But in any case it was now clear beyond all reasonable doubt that the bourgeois specialists had no effective political power.

These developments should have done more than to dispel the illusions of those who believed that technical expertise, managerial authority, and high socioeconomic status would necessarily engender extensive political power. They should also have dispelled the illusions of those who had collaborated with the regime on the assumption that the NEP was irreversible and that industrial development would inevitably lead to the rapid normalization, democratization, or liberalization of the Bolshevik dictatorship. If they did so, however, the ensuing political and economic consequences were marginal, for the available evidence leaves no doubt that most of the bourgeois specialists who were allowed to go on serving the regime (an overwhelming majority) continued faithfully to do so.

Even in 1930, at a time when the wrecker trials were at their height, an official survey showed that 30 percent of all specialists with higher education approached their work with enthusiasm, 46 percent with diligence, and only 24 percent formally; and there is no reason to question the general reliability of these figures.[99] On the contrary, their validity can be inferred from the fact that the bourgeois specialists remained an important element in the Soviet industrial establishment throughout the 1930s. Even as late as 1936, for example, "the technical part of production was still all basically in the hands of the old specialists," and almost half of the heads and deputy heads of heavy-industry glavks who had higher education were pre-1917 graduates.[100] To be sure, thanks to its extremely late start in the training of red or proletarian specialists, the regime had scant choice but to continue to rely heavily on the bourgeois specialists for technical leadership; but it need not have retained so many old-regime cadres or allowed so many of those it did retain to occupy high executive posts.

A further and even more indicative index of the behavior of the members of the old technical intelligentsia is the fact that relatively few bourgeois specialists appear to have fallen victim to the Great Purge.[101] There seems no reason to question official reports to the effect that over 7,000 of the engineers in the Soviet industrial establishment in 1939 were prerevolutionary graduates, and this figure implies a rate of attrition among these graduates that is scarcely above what one would have anticipated in normal circumstances.[102] The circumstances were not normal, however, and the fact that the bourgeois specialists survived them almost as if they were leaves no doubt that they had fully complied with Rykov's demand to "restructure" themselves. They could not have survived otherwise, for the 1936–1938 period witnessed the systematic destruction of anyone who seemed to deviate from the prescribed Stalinist norms of total conformity and total commitment.

Material incentives and sanctions undoubtedly played an unprecedentedly large part in determining the behavior of bourgeois specialists in the period after 1928. Not only were the rewards for cooperation greater and the penalties for noncooperation more severe than before, but also, as we have seen, the onset of Stalinism definitively collapsed many of the specialists' illusions about the nature, dynamics, and durability of Bolshevik power. Yet it seems probable that the specialists' established ideological views often continued to play an important facilitative role — and not only in the negative sense, as effective solvents of political alienation and moral repugnance, but also in the positive sense, as sources of approbation and support.

The example of Ustryalov is especially instructive in this regard, for it is apparent that neither venality nor fear suffice to explain why he saw fit, in 1930, to deny that there could be "any objections in principle to the acceleration of industrialization and reconstruction of agriculture in the USSR." Even less do they suffice to explain why he abandoned his claim to independence of political judgment and announced his acceptance of Stalin's demand for total allegiance, advising his followers among the technical intelligentsia to heed the regime's warnings and to recognize that "It is necessary either somehow to adjust . . . or to lag behind and become a nullity. It is necessary to force oneself actively and conscientiously to serve the state of the revolution . . . The [only] real choice is — with the revolutionary state and against its enemies." [103] Rather, it seems clear that Ustryalov was able to persuade himself that Stalinism, for all its deficiencies, was a fit object of support from an ideological point of view.

On the one hand, Ustryalov appears to have decided that the nationalistic values which had always been prominent in his beliefs had absolute priority over liberal-democratic values. He seems to have concluded, more particularly, that Stalinism's evident contribution to the growth of Russian national power outweighed its equally evident contribution to the destruction of Russian liberty. This conclusion seemed all the more plausible because (after a brief interlude of intensified stress on "pure" Communist ideology) rapid industrialization was accompanied by a marked rehabilitation of nationalistic symbolism and sentiment and could hence still be viewed as the progenitor of "debolshevization." On the other hand, and in a somewhat different vein, Ustryalov apparently managed to persuade himself that the rise of Stalinism could not affect the *ultimate* validity of his earlier prognostications. Ultimately, he continued to insist, industrial development would engender a humane and open society — a society that would conform in basic spirit, if not in specific content or structure, to the one he had earlier envisioned as the outcome of the developmental process. In effect, what Ustryalov did was to reaffirm the essence of smenovekhite ideology, only taking care to fit the beneficent effects of industrial development to a new and slower time schedule.[104]

There is no reason to believe that Ustryalov was the only smenovekhite to make his peace with Stalinism on ideological grounds, although his followers were, of course, no longer free to profess adherence to his views. Moreover it is by no means improbable that many bourgeois specialists of socialist persuasion were able to join Ustryalov's followers in achieving a genuine ideological sublimation of their initial hostility to Stalinism. The rise of Stalinism did, after all, entail the consolidation of certain socialist forms, just as it entailed an increase in national power. And Marxism, like smenovekhism, embodied a set of expectations that could fairly easily survive deferment and "rescheduling." Accordingly, one is led to query the motive behind declarations such as that of the previously mentioned Gosplan economist Bazarov, who declared that he was prepared to accept the Stalinist five-year plan and participate conscientiously in its implementation, even though he violently disapproved of its principle and methods.[105] The fact that neither Bazarov nor the many other Marxist specialists who made similar statements were safe abroad makes it impossible to discount the possibility that the voice in question was one of fear, but the temptation to ascribe an ideological motivation to these statements remains strong.[106]

One recalls in this connection that, in 1925, in a situation relatively free from coercive pressure, the author of one of these statements, the ex-Menshevik planner Groman, had explained his collaboration with the regime on the grounds that, "under the Bolshevik press we are developing culturally and economically." [107] And one wonders whether cooperation with Stalinism was not often justified in similar terms. Certainly no small number of non-Soviet Marxists were led — and even driven — by their ideology to explain away Stalinism as a product of industrial immaturity, while accepting it as an effective vehicle of industrial development and supporting it as such in the belief that socialism could only derive from and was inherent in the developmental process.[108] If the bourgeois specialists were much closer to the brutal reality of Stalinism than even the best-informed non-Soviet Marxists, they also had a much bigger spiritual investment in the Soviet experiment. It seems probable that one consequence of this was a particularly powerful urge to reaffirm the validity of the ideology that had originally called forth this investment.

Finally, it is likely that many adherents of professionalistic ideologies continued to collaborate with the regime as a matter of principle, in the conviction that collaboration was an obligation dictated (or at least fully justified) by vocational responsibility. Indeed, the rise of Stalinism did not confront the truly dedicated professionals with a compelling need to revaluate the ideological legitimacy of continued cooperation with the regime. If the logic of liberal or socialist economic determinism was in principle independent of any particular timetable, it was nonetheless inevitable that the need to affirm this logic in the face of increasing political constraint and repression would evoke many doubts and reservations. The logic of professionalism, however, was timeless. It could apply, in principle, under virtually all conditions and circumstances. Certainly, at a minimum, it applied under the conditions and circumstances of Stalinist Russia, with its new and stimulating opportunities for professional self-fulfillment. To be sure, these opportunities entailed immense human suffering, and this probably weakened their appeal in the cases where professionalism was heavily informed by themes of public service or popular welfare. Still, the case could easily be made now, as it had been earlier, that noncooperation would bring economic ruin and even greater human misery in its wake, whereas cooperation would make it possible to ameliorate some of the most destructive and inhuman consequences of official policy. And, when professionalism was more heavily informed by nationalistic values, the ideological brief for continued cooperation may actually have been strengthened by the heavy-industry orientation of official policy. Be that as it may, technical progress remained technical progress, and this was what was critical from a professionalistic point of view.

The bourgeois engineer Pototsky (in fact a former prince)

struck a politically discordant note when he utilized the occasion of his receipt of an Order of Lenin for outstanding services to declare (in 1931): "Even now I do not quite agree with the Soviet power, but the Bolsheviks are interesting people; one can work with them; they know how to work." [109] At the same time, however, he spoke in the language of true professionalism and revealed a source of support for the regime that lay well outside the realm of material incentives and physical sanctions. And there is no reason to believe that Pototsky was an isolated figure — no more, one thinks almost involuntarily to add, than Albert Speer, whose response to Nazism was virtually identical to Pototsky's response to Stalinism, was an isolated figure among German engineers. That way, though, lies temptation — the temptation to level against the Russian professionals the charge that Trevor-Roper has leveled against Speer and, by implication, the great majority of his German co-professionals — that their ability and willingness to render enthusiastic service to what they knew to be an ethically reprehensible political system burdens them with an inordinate share of moral responsibility for the horrors that followed.[110] But if grave charges are appropriate at all in historical analysis, they must be buttressed by conclusive evidence. And in the case of the bourgeois specialists under Stalinism, all that can be adduced to demonstrate the presence of a significant voluntaristic component in their cooperative behavior is a certain amount of highly suggestive but fragmentary evidence and a measure of more or less plausible speculation.

What is not speculative is the fact of the specialists' continued cooperation. It is misleading to suggest that the First Five-Year Plan marked the beginning of the end of the "ten year alliance between the regime and the non-Communist experts who had helped it to survive." [111] On the contrary, the alliance continued, but with its terms redefined to accord with the political transformation occurring throughout the country. The regime was quite prepared to go on using most of the bourgeois specialists, provided they accommodated themselves to these new terms. And, from whatever motives, the specialists were prepared to accept the regime's conditions and to go on giving diligent and efficient service. Moreover, during the critical first years of rapid industrialization this service was of considerable and possibly even vital importance in enabling Stalinism to survive.[112] This much *political* responsibility the bourgeois specialists must bear.

If the difference between obedience and support is critical from a moral (and psychological) point of view, it is much less critical where politics is concerned. Even if Hannah Arendt's generalization that "in politics obedience and support are the same" is too extreme, it embodies an important insight.[113] For if the difference between obedience and support always retains a certain political salience, it undoubtedly does lose much of its significance in a context where obedience implies compliance with demands that in other political systems could only be realized thanks to intense support, if indeed they are conceivable at all. And it was precisely such demands that Stalin advanced and the bourgeois specialists accepted. In this sense then, if in no other (and, again, it is probable that many members of the technical intelligentsia complied with the regime's demands willingly and with a certain amount of real enthusiasm), it is fair to conclude that the bourgeois specialists gave the Stalinist regime their support. This conclusion may serve as their political epitaph.

★ 4 ★

THE RED DIRECTORS

> The party as it existed earlier, in the period
> of its illegality, when there was a single
> psychology and a single ideology, has split
> into a variety of separate columns . . .
> Military workers, soviet workers, trade
> union workers, and party workers proper
> have organized together among themselves
> . . . The task at present is anew to collect
> the party, to eliminate all deviations, to
> unite the party ideologically.
> Nikolai Bukharin (1921)

> The higher organs of our party are consti-
> tuted almost exactly as they were two de-
> cades ago, but the tasks of the party have
> changed quantitatively and qualitatively. I
> tell you, you are no longer an underground
> party; you are the government of a huge
> country.　　　　Leonid Krasin (1923)

Although their services were indispensable, the bourgeois specialists do not deserve exclusive credit for the rapid industrial
recovery and growth that characterized the first two decades of
Bolshevik rule. Above all, they must share pride of place with
the so-called red directors, the Communists whom the party
assigned to managerial posts in the first years after the revolution.[1] It was this group of perhaps five thousand men which
occupied the "commanding heights" and strategic bluffs of the
industrial establishment during the heyday of the specialist-
regime alliance and which supplied the cadres that were in

charge of most of the major projects associated with the First and Second Five-Year Plans.[2] These cadres, in turn, contributed much of the initiative upon which the success of Soviet economic policy was predicated.

Louis Fischer's report of an encounter with a group of Communist managers who, "instead of extending their hands and saying 'Dybets' or 'Ivanov' or 'Sidorov,' said 'Autostroi' or 'Dneiprostroi' or 'Magnitogorsk,'" and similar reports give graphic evidence of the intensity with which the red directors threw themselves into their work.[3] And even hostile critics acknowledge that their immense energy often compensated for their lack of technical expertise.[4] Moreover, in a great many cases, this energy appears to have been combined with genuine entrepreneurial skills. In particular, the red directors seem to have possessed the skill of "organization-building," which Frederick Harbison has identified as "probably the most critical skill needed for industrial development of a large scale." [5]

That the red directors proved capable of stimulating and co-ordinating innovations, selecting and training subordinates, delegating authority, and mobilizing the enthusiasm and support of the work force is less surprising than might at first appear. For all its appeal to rigidly authoritarian and essentially noninnovative personalities, Marxist-Leninist ideology contained many themes calculated to appeal to the entrepreneurial personality, especially in a cultural milieu that placed a relatively low value on enterprise and efficiency.[6] Adam Ulam is undoubtedly correct when he suggests that one of the chief selective functions of Marxism in Russia was "to draw into the Leninist party the people who, under cover of their revolutionary doctrinarism, possessed in the highest degree the managerial and administrative instincts required to erect the modern industrial state." [7] Marxism made industrial development a primary goal, and the Leninist party always conceived of itself as an "organizational weapon" and consistently sought to train its members in organizational skills. In consequence, the party had a sizable pool of skilled organizers when it seized power, and it rapidly expanded this pool in the postrevolutionary period, when it made a conscious effort to convert itself into what one Soviet historian has aptly called "a colossal . . . apparatus for the recruitment of organizers." [8] Moreover, it took special steps to ensure that a large proportion of its best organizers were assigned to managerial posts. [9]

THE REGROUPING OF THE RED DIRECTORS

Although their backgrounds were not significantly different from the backgrounds of the Bolsheviks who were assigned executive posts in the trade unions or the party apparat, the men assigned to work in the industrial establishment were a diverse lot. In 1923, for example, shortly before Zinoviev announced that the task of recruiting red directors was "in essence completed," 28–30 percent of the party members in responsible management posts were Old Bolsheviks; 68–70 percent were Bolsheviks of Civil War vintage; and 30 percent had belonged to other parties before becoming Bolsheviks. Similarly, 52.7 percent of the cadres at issue were of proletarian origin; 9 percent were of peasant origin; and 37 percent were of official or intelligentsia origin. Finally, to take the one remaining variable on which we have a certain amount of reliable data, 12 percent had higher education; around 10 percent had secondary education; and 78 percent had elementary education. [10] Despite their diverse backgrounds, however, the red directors quickly developed a consciousness of shared interests, a sense of common purpose, and a feeling of mutual solidarity.

One important consequence of this process of group formation was the creation of an effective "management team" capable of the sort of coordinated interaction needed for economic recovery and growth. But there were other consequences as well, including some that the regime found extremely distasteful. In particular, the growth of a sense of managerial esprit de corps gave a yet more ominous cast to a trend that had already begun to occasion the regime considerable concern: the red directors were emerging within the councils of the party as protagonists of a distinctive "managerial" point of view, a point of view that accorded the claims of industry priority over virtually all competing claims. Signs of such a development were discernible even during the Civil War, and by the early 1920s the trend had already become well established.[11]

In and of itself there was nothing heretical in the outlook that led the red directors to "judge the forward movement of life by the construction and reconstruction work" in the economic sector and to see the party's primary raison d'être in the building of plants, the pumping of oil, and the ignition of blast furnaces.[12] Despite official charges to the contrary, few of the men who shared this perspective were guilty of loss of party spirit, "divorce from party responsibility," or abandonment of "the point of view of socialist construction."[13] Indeed, in the case of the leading red directors such charges were almost entirely unwarranted, although the gravest accusations were leveled precisely against "the comrades placed at the summit of industrial construction."[14] The leadership of the industrial establishment was comprised almost exclusively of venerable Old Bolsheviks, who had proved their unqualified devotion to the party during long years of demanding service in the revolutionary underground, and there is no reason to believe that these men suddenly succumbed to a process of political or ideological degeneration.[15] On the contrary, it is apparent that their adoption of a "managerial identity" occurred within the framework of deeply ingrained political and ideological self-conceptions. At the same time, there is no doubt that the process of functional identification did confront the regime with a serious political problem. For, if the red directors did not cease to be committed Communists, they did develop a policy orientation that differed markedly from that of other party members who were caught up in the "logic" of other vocations. The resultant disagreements were often quite severe.

Even where it remained diffuse and unstructured, such internecine conflict could not but be disturbing in a movement that was animated by a passion for unanimity and prided itself in its homogeneity of outlook. And when the red directors and other groups within the party began not only to articulate but to aggregate their respective interests, thereby challenging not only ideological but organizational monolithism as well, the problem became acute. It was, moreover, a problem for which Bolshevik theory provided no answer. Instead it expressed a dilemma that was inherent in Bolshevik theory: the contradiction between the cherished goal of rule by a monolithic party, on the one hand, and the equally cherished goal of thoroughgoing socioeconomic modernization under direct party control, on the other. As the leadership now learned to its dismay, the first of these goals was almost impossible to reconcile with functional specialization on the part of Communists. At the same time, it became increasingly clear that no amount of talk about the redundancy of functional specialization once modernity (full-fledged socialism) was achieved could obviate the fact that such specialization was a prerequisite of modernization. Similarly, it became increasingly clear that, if modernization was to be accompanied by the institutionalization of all-embracing party rule, specialization was even more imperative for Communists than for non-Communists. In the real world, a choice had to be made and certain values had to be compromised.

Once the need to choose was recognized, the choice itself was never in serious doubt. In the short run at least, economic stagnation and loss of control over the administrative machinery of the state presented a graver danger than the disintegration of the party into a series of contentious functional groupings, and the regime responded accordingly. To be sure, in 1921 the Tenth

Party Congress did adopt an official resolution condemning "departmentalism" and ordering the party to introduce a policy of "systematically transferring comrades from one branch of work to another." [16] Even this resolution, however, warned against excessively rapid transfers, and in the event the warning proved to have greater force than the directive. Although the policy of interdepartmental or interfunctional rotation in office was never wholly abandoned, specialization soon became the dominant theme in the official party line.

The signal for a hard turn in the direction of intensive specialization was given in March 1922, at the Eleventh Party Congress. The Central Committee's theses to the congress instructed the party to "group its forces in the economic organs precisely in terms of their economic qualifications," and virtually all of the authoritative speeches at the congress called upon the red directors to commit themselves yet more deeply to their work.[17] In effect, the regime sanctioned a rapid acceleration of the so-called process of managerial regrouping, even though it continued to deplore and excoriate it in theory. Indeed, in the immediate aftermath of the Eleventh Congress, the regime even went so far as to authorize the formation of an independent association of industrial executives, the purpose of which was described as "the coordination of simultaneous political action by the Red industrialists." [18] To be sure, the political action at issue was supposed to be narrowly circumscribed and directed primarily toward the strengthening of labor discipline, but it would nonetheless be hard to find a more graphic illustration of the regime's decisive acceptance of functional specialization at the expense of organizational monolithism. Moreover, at the same time that it undertook to facilitate the institutionalization of the managerial regrouping and its formal organization as a political pressure group, the regime proceeded to increase the red directors' discretionary authority within the economic sector.

Whereas the Tenth Party Congress had expressed concern lest the trade unions completely divorce themselves from industrial management and had called for a decisive strengthening in the economic role of the party apparat, the Eleventh Congress deprived the unions of all but a residual voice in plant administration and ordered party organizations not to "decide economic questions . . . [unless] these questions really demand a solution of a principled character." [19] Nor was it only the lower-level party organizations that were thus enjoined. Lenin himself called for an expansion of the economic jurisdiction of the Council of Commissars at the expense of the Politburo and the Central Committee, while Zinoviev sharply criticized the imperialistic tendencies of the party gubkoms (provincial committees), proclaiming:

if there are excellent workers who have a good understanding of economic affairs in the gubkoms, then we must transfer them to the economic organs. This will represent an economical distribution of forces. Then it will not be necessary to decide questions in passing . . . Now we should . . . introduce the sort of differentiation . . . that will lead . . . not to a situation where everyone does everything and no one is responsible for anything and where there are constant conflicts, but rather to a situation where there is that sound division of labor that we need so badly. [20]

These were strong words, and it is obvious that they were intended to set the course of policy for many years to come. In point of fact, however, they proved to be of only fleeting significance. Within a year of their utterance, none other than Zinoviev himself was proclaiming that "to push aside the gubkoms even a little means to lose everything," and Stalin announced that the goal was nothing less than "a maximal strengthening of the party's leading role." [21] It was these sentiments, in turn, that provided the leitmotif of the three draft resolutions on industrial management that the Central Committee submitted to the Twelfth Party Congress in April 1923.

MANAGERIAL POWER & SOVIET POLITICS

The first of the resolutions called upon all party organizations to become more actively involved in the determination of economic policy:

the party is now in no case able to limit itself only to general propaganda and agitation . . . [and] cannot forget for a moment that the chief responsibility for the economic . . . organs lies on the RKP . . . Still closer to the economy, still more attention to and leadership of the economic organs — this should be the slogan of the party in the next period.

The second proposed to prevent the "economic wing" of the party from losing its party spirit and becoming overcommitted to practicality and effectiveness by merging the regime's two principal control organs, the Workers' and Peasants' Inspection (Rabkrin) and the Central Control Commission (CCC), and providing the new combined organ with an augmented staff, a more centralized system of organization, and a broader mandate. Finally, the third resolution proposed that the party Secretariat's accounting and assignment department be authorized to expand its control over managerial appointments "to encompass all branches of administration and the entire industrial commanding staff without exception."[22]

The widespread managerial protest that these proposals aroused found a particularly vigorous spokesman in the person of the Old Bolshevik engineer, L. B. Krasin, who took as his point of departure three general propositions: that "a rise in production is the urgent necessity," that "the basic task of domestic policy . . . for our party and our state is to dedicate all our . . . forces to this objective," and that all the party's "organization and tactics should be coordinated precisely for the creation and resurrection of production." [23] These propositions led him to dissent from virtually every aspect of the new official line.

While theoretically approving and even welcoming increased party involvement in economic decision making, Krasin made it clear that his approval was contingent upon the elevation of hard-headed and experienced "production leaders and economic executives" to the party's leading organs. Barring such a development, he proclaimed, any increase in the Central Committee's economic authority would be nothing short of disastrous. He even went so far as to dismiss the present membership of the Central Committee as nothing more than a collection of impractical "journalists, literateurs, and professional politicians," thus directing at the topmost party organ a particularly incendiary variant of the cry that many managers in the field were reported to have addressed to provincial party committees: "Comrades, you are not competent in economic questions." Here, indeed, was a challenge, and Zinoviev, whose status as the Central Committee's rapporteur cast him in the role of Krasin's principal antagonist, was so perplexed that his retort took the completely uncharacteristic form of an appeal to Western example and precedent: "Look, Lloyd George is not an agronomist either. Poincaré is not a transport engineer." [24] To which Krasin might well have responded: "His Majesty's Government does not seek to regulate the entirety of British economic life; the *conseil des ministres* does not claim the right to exercise detailed control over French industrial management."

This was, in effect, the answer given by Krasin's colleague in the industrial establishment, the leading Bolshevik economist, Yevgeny Preobrazhensky. Although Preobrazhensky took care to dissociate himself from Krasin's astringent rhetoric, he nonetheless argued that basic changes in the structure and personnel of the leading party organs were essential if the party's present course was to yield other than the direst consequences. After asserting that it was a regular occurrence for economic executives to come away from meetings with the Central Committee full of deep chagrin and even outrage at the ruling elite's ignorance of industrial problems, he urged the Twelfth Congress to create a competently staffed Economic Bureau alongside the

Orgburo and the Politburo. Unless this proposal was adopted, he implied, the only rational course was for the party to abandon its efforts to control all aspects of economic life in its own name and through its own apparat.[25] Clearly, this was but a more restrained and temperate presentation of Krasin's basic case.

If the first of the three draft resolutions proposed by the Central Committee dismayed Krasin, the second and third, pertaining to the expansion of the party's role in industrial personnel policy and to the strengthening of Rabkrin and the CCC, infuriated him. With regard to the second, he bluntly asserted that "all we economic executives await these decisions literally with horror" and defiantly proclaimed that the party's aim should be the barest "minimum of control." Similarly, whereas the Central Committee saw fit to criticize its accounting and assignment department for having played a "passive and insignificant part" in the selection and disposition of industrial personnel, Krasin protested that apparat interference in this area had been excessive. How, he asked, could there be any hope of economic growth when the party insisted on transferring "needed workers" from the industrial apparatus and sending in their stead "some common replacement from the party's manpower fund"? [26]

Once again Krasin's outlook seemed to leave Zinoviev at a loss for a response, and he could only exclaim: "Imagine the psychology of the comrade who wrote such lines!" [27] But this psychology was by no means peculiar to Krasin; it was common to almost all of the leaders of the industrial establishment. To cite but one example, V. P. Nogin, head of the Soviet textile industry and one of Krasin's colleagues on the presidium of the Supreme Council of the National Economy (VSNKh), protested to the Twelfth Congress that broadening the role of the accounting and assignment department would lead to a deplorable situation in which "the comrades who decide the fate not only of the chairmen and members of the boards of trusts but even of factory directors . . . [will] not once have worked in the

74

branches of industry which they in effect lead and will in no way be oriented toward the problems which determine the work of the given branch of industry." [28] What the red directors wanted instead, as the chairman of the VSNKh presidium, P. A. Bogdanov, made clear in his contribution to the Twelfth Congress debate, was a politically responsible but truly professional personnel policy administered by the managerial elite itself. The goal was a situation in which the Central Committee, having appointed the topmost cadres of the industrial establishment in the form of the VSNKh presidium, would leave it to these cadres to appoint and evaluate all lower-echelon managers and would in general place the leaders of industry "in conditions of full independence and responsibility for their work." [29] But, by the time of the Twelfth Congress, such demands were completely unacceptable to the dominant faction within the leadership, and they were decisively rebuffed by the assembled congress delegates.[30]

There is undoubtedly considerable merit in Leonard Schapiro's suggestion that the demands advanced by the red directors at the time of the Twelfth Congress were incompatible with the inherent logic of Bolshevism.[31] Certainly the hallowed Bolshevik principle of the primacy of the party over all other organizations was likely to find its operational expression in the primacy of the party apparat. It was inevitable that the party would become increasingly dependent on its professional functionaries as it acquired a really substantial membership and assumed the heavy burdens of rulership, and the always tenuous line between dependence and subordination was likely to prove more than ordinarily vulnerable in a movement that valued discipline and hierarchy above all else. Certainly, too, the industrial establishment was a particularly unlikely candidate for long-run organizational autonomy, if only because its operations were so directly related to questions of doctrine and problems of power. Yet, if the decisions of the Twelfth Congress were in some sense "logical," it cannot be denied that they represented a radical change from the party line unanimously endorsed by the entire Soviet leadership only a year before.

The contention that official policy in the early and middle 1920s provided for an *uninterrupted* extension of apparat control over management is not borne out by the evidence. It is not true that "at no time was there a particular moment which can be pointed to as the one where a decision was taken to pass from less to more [apparat] control." [32] Rather, as we have just seen, the period of the Twelfth Congress was just such a moment. And this fact makes it almost impossible for any but the most committed dialectician to rest content with an explanation of the Twelfth Congress which is cast exclusively in terms of "logic." Even if one is willing to view the decisions of the Eleventh Congress as aberrant or illogical, it is still necessary to investigate the proximate causes that operated to restore logic to its rightful place precisely at the time of the Twelfth Congress. And it is still necessary to explain why logic, once restored, became so overwhelmingly compelling.

If one takes the leadership's speeches during the Twelfth Congress debate at face value, one must conclude that the shift in official management policy was primarily a defensive response to a sudden large-scale campaign of political self-aggrandizement on the part of the red directors. Such a conclusion, however, would be highly misleading. To be sure, it is likely that the period between the Eleventh and Twelfth congresses did witness a campaign by Krasin and some of his managerial colleagues to secure heavier managerial representation on the Central Committee.[33] It is also likely that Preobrazhensky and some of his close associates continued to press for the establishment of an economic bureau attached to the Central Committee. In addition, the managerial "regrouping" as a whole probably exerted substantial pressure in favor of increased managerial authority in the sphere of labor relations. In particular, the previously mentioned association of industrial executives, the so-called Council of Congresses of Industry, Trade, and Transport, probably played a prominent role in these regards. It seems almost certain, however, that these activities represented the high points of managerial "aggressiveness" during the period between the Eleventh and Twelfth Congresses. There is little reason to believe that in and of themselves they confronted the regime with any ominous threat.

None of the leaders of the managerial regrouping was seriously suspected of excessive personal ambition, and it was becoming increasingly apparent that the red directors were too involved in their work as managers to play any sort of independent political role, let alone to establish themselves as active contenders for power.[34] Most of their demands were directed toward highly particularistic goals, and none of these demands, including even that for increased managerial representation on the Central Committee, could be reasonably interpreted as a sign that the group was acquiring the character of an emergent counter-elite. On the contrary, practically everything we know about the outlook of the red directors clearly suggests that the decisions of the Eleventh Congress satisfied by far the larger and more important portion of their aspirations and left them with few pressing objectives other than to render their newly augmented autonomy fully operational and secure against the threat of outside encroachment. Hence it seems highly probable that the basic line of development between the Eleventh and Twelfth congresses was exactly the reverse of what the leadership alleged: the red directors were not trying to increase their power, but rather to resist a leadership-initiated campaign to abrogate the decisions of the Eleventh Congress.[35]

THE RED DIRECTORS IN THE SUCCESSION STRUGGLE

To explain the shift in official policy, one need look no further than to the radically changed political situation that came into being as of May 24, 1922, the day on which Lenin suffered a stroke that seemed likely (and by early 1923 certain) to foreshadow an early death. From this moment on, the majority of the Central Committee (headed by the troika of Zinoviev, Kamenev, and Stalin) had one overriding goal — to prevent Trotsky, the heir apparent, from assuming Lenin's mantle — and this goal virtually ensured a full-fledged reversal of management policy.[36] To put the point summarily, the party apparat was at once the chief power base of all three of the top figures in the dominant anti-Trotsky coalition; the one major political structure in the Soviet system that did not reckon a significant number of Trotsky's personal followers among its leading cadres; and (for this and other reasons) the one important instrument of rule that promised to remain relatively immune to "Trotskyite" influence as the succession struggle unfolded. These attributes made it almost certain that the apparat would in fact realize its "logical" destiny.

The red directors and the Left Opposition. The leadership was, of course, aware that its efforts to extend the dominion of the party apparat would encounter the resistance of a vigorous managerial "united front" and might well transform the managerial regrouping into something approaching a full-fledged managerial opposition. Similarly it was aware that there would be a natural tendency for any such managerial opposition to gravitate toward the Trotskyite camp, since Trotsky was almost certain to adopt an antiapparat posture, if only in self-defense. For better or worse, though, these were risks the leadership was ready to run. Indeed, it may well have calculated that the red directors would in any case be so strongly predisposed toward Trotsky that there was little to lose by a change in the organizational line. Far from being incidental victims of a general policy of strengthening apparat control, in other words, the red directors may have been singled out by the troika for particularly strict surveillance precisely because they were viewed as in-cipient Trotskyites. Nor was this by any means an implausible view.

In the first place, a substantial number of influential and prestigious red directors, headed by Preobrazhensky and G. L. Pyatakov, were known to be personally devoted to Trotsky, and many others had been directly exposed to Trotsky's charismatic personality during the Civil War, when they had occupied command posts in the Red Army.[37] In addition, during the bitter trade-union controversy of 1920–21, the majority of the red directors appear to have supported Trotsky's view that the trade unions should be "governmentalized" and transformed into agencies whose primary function was the enforcement of labor discipline.[38] Moreover, Trotsky had earned credit with the red directors as a particularly vigorous proponent of the "promana-gerial" organizational decisions of the Eleventh Party Congress.[39] Finally, to the degree — and it promised to be considerable — that the succession struggle assumed the character of a debate over the substance of economic policy, there could be little doubt that Trotskyite appeals would strike a responsive chord among the red directors, who were almost to a man in favor of rapid industrial growth. In the idiom of the period, they were almost all "Americans," and in most cases their Americanism took the form of a glorification of large-scale construction and active commitment to the primacy of heavy industry.[40]

Whatever its calculations on the eve of the Twelfth Congress, the troika was certainly prepared for the worst once it had made its decision in favor of the new organizational line. It must have been pleasantly surprised, therefore, at the actual course of events. For, with the possible exception of a brief period in the winter of 1923–24, when the succession struggle first took on the form of an open competition for power, the red directors do not appear actively to have supported the Trotskyite cause.[41] In fact, with a few important exceptions, they seem to have rallied behind the Central Committee. Thus, if one takes the only reasonably "hard" data that are available, one discovers that of the approximately forty red-director delegates to the Eleventh Party Congress, only six (Alsky, Osinsky, Preobrazhensky, Pyatakov, Smilga, and Ufimtsev) became full-fledged Trotskyites, engaged in open struggle against the Central Committee in the period following the initial intraparty "discussion" of late 1923 and early 1924. As for the behavior of the rest, a low degree of opposition is indicated by these facts: almost none ceased to hold important posts during the subsequent decade; almost half continued to attend party congresses throughout the remainder of the 1920s; the two (Kviring and Sulimov) who were already members of the Central Committee when the succession struggle broke into the open continued to serve in that capacity until the Great Purge; seven others (I. Kosior, Krasin, Krzhizhanovsky, Lobov, Lomov, Rukhimovich, and Tolokontsev) were promoted to the Central Committee in the course of the succession struggle, five (all but Kosier and Lomov) as early as May 1924; and the vast majority of those promoted (all but Krasin who died in 1926 and Lomov and Tolokontsev who were demoted in 1934) retained their posts until at least 1936.[42] Nor is there any reason to believe that the men in this sample were unrepresentative. If anything, it seems probable that they had an unusually high "opposition potential," so that one is forced to conclude that most of the red directors quickly and decisively rejected the Trotskyite temptation. The problem is not so much to establish that such a rejection occurred as it is to identify the causes.

One such cause was clearly the red directors' deep commitment to the principle of monolithic party discipline. Although the red directors were willing to press their claims vigorously before the adoption of an official decision, they were at least as unwilling as other Bolsheviks to break the sacred party rule that, once a decision was adopted, it must be accepted as absolutely binding. The idea of sustained dissent was as repugnant to them as to their fellow party members, and they fully shared the traditional Bolshevik passion for unanimity and subscribed to the view that organized dissent was bound to weaken the party and endanger the socialist cause. If they did not understand the party's constitutional ban on "factions and groupings" as something completely immutable, they nonetheless saw it as an entirely justifiable response to emergency conditions.[43] And they were as susceptible as most Bolsheviks to the argument that the hostile environment surrounding the party required a more or less protracted state of emergency within the party. Lenin's departure from the scene made this argument for unity all the more compelling, for his genius had been one of the most potent weapons in the party's arsenal — so potent, indeed, that the party could afford occasional lapses into internecine conflict. Now more than ever, then, iron discipline was necessary if the party were to survive. And, without the party, there was no salvation. Such were the patterns of thought and the psychological orientation of the true Bolshevik, and they strongly militated against support for or indulgence in any oppositionist activities.[44]

Another reason for the red directors' rejection of Trotskyism was undoubtedly the temporizing and ineffectual character of Trotsky's own leadership, particularly in the critical early stages of the succession struggle. It is probable that many red directors became disenchanted with Trotsky's capacities as a leader as early as the Twelfth Congress, before the succession struggle had even come out into the open. To be sure, Trotsky's report to the congress left little doubt that he was sympathetic to the managerial regrouping and disagreed with the tenor of the new party line. He conspicuously refrained from harsh criticism of Krasin's defense of managerial autonomy; he struck a distinctly discordant note in the proceedings by stressing the importance of strict central planning and emphasizing that "only the development of industry creates an unshakable foundation for the dictatorship of the proletariat"; and he spoke of the role of the party in industrial personnel policy in so reserved a tone that Mikoyan, speaking for the provincial apparatchiki, felt it necessary to protest that his views ran directly counter to the new line.[45] But he did *not* vigorously protest the Central Committee's program, and it seems a fair presumption that not a few of the embattled red directors felt that they had witnessed (and been victims of) an abdication of political responsibility — the more so because it was widely known that Trotsky had submitted to last-minute demands by the troika that he moderate his remarks.[46] Nor can there be much doubt that disenchantment became progressively more widespread, for Trotsky continued to pursue an extremely cautious policy for many months thereafter. And, when he finally did speak out, he made little effort to back his words with effective organizational measures, with the result that his adherents were left defenseless against official pressure and retaliation.

Such pressure was quickly forthcoming and should, of course, be viewed as yet another of the factors responsible for the failure of Trotskyism among most of the red directors. In accordance with the resolutions of the Twelfth Congress, the red directors were in any case slated for particularly intensive screening by the Central Committee's accounting and assignment department and by the CCC and Rabkrin, and this made them even more than ordinarily vulnerable to official sanctions in the form of demotion, diplomatic exile, and expulsion from the party. At the same time, it is probable that their intense dedication to their work made them unusually reluctant to sacrifice themselves for the sake of a movement the success of which became more and more dubious with every passing moment. Further, to turn to more positive arguments, at precisely the instant that the red directors began to despair of the possibility of realizing their objectives under the aegis of Trotskyism, the chances of realizing at least some of these objectives under official auspices began to improve. As soon as the regime realized that there was a real prospect of converting the red directors from disenchanted Trotskyites or reluctant loyalists into active supporters of the Central Committee and its anti-Trotsky majority, it began to moderate its antimanagerial stance. In consequence, many red directors became convinced that they had exaggerated the troika's hostility and that support for the troika would lead to greatly increased official receptivity to managerial demands.

Substantively, the reorientation of official policy entailed a sharp increase in the amount of attention devoted to the needs of heavy industry. Although primary emphasis continued to be placed on the importance of preserving the union between town and country and conciliating the peasantry, from 1924 on more and more stress was placed upon heavy industry. At the Thirteenth Party Congress (May 1924), for example, Zinoviev, speaking as the Central Committee's political rapporteur, announced, "metal is now on the agenda; improvement of the means of production is now on the agenda; the raising of heavy industry is now on the agenda." [47] Similarly, in a report on the work of the Fourteenth Party Conference (April 1925), Stalin sharply criticized the conservatism of Soviet economic policy, while at the Fourteenth Party Congress, which convened in October 1925, he went so far as to proclaim that the party's present task was to ensure "the utmost expansion of our industry." [48] Qualified though they are when read in context — and it is necessary to stress that they were qualified, in view of subsequent Soviet claims to the contrary — these declarations could not have failed to evoke a favorable response from the red directors. And their already great appeal was further enhanced by the fact that they were accompanied by a real spurt in industrial productivity and by a number of promanagerial modifications in the party's organizational line.

In speaking of these organizational modifications as well, one must avoid exaggeration. Above all, the principle of apparat primacy articulated by the Twelfth Congress remained very much in force. Indeed, in 1925 the regime reformulated the principle in a manner that eliminated virtually all hope for official authorization of a fundamental change. Whereas earlier the pretense had at least been maintained that the intensity of apparat control was closely correlated with the relative weight of the bourgeois specialists in the industrial command structure, now it was explicitly acknowledged that the red directors themselves were the primary objects of the regime's suspicion. This was the clear import of a carefully formulated passage in Molotov's report to the Fourteenth Party Congress, in which the speaker first boasted of the rapid increase in the percentage of Communists in top managerial posts and then proclaimed that "in conjunction with this our task in the field of strengthening party leadership over these Communists has increased." [49] However, within the framework of apparat primacy and institutionalized mistrust of the red directors, the regime nonetheless made important concessions to the managers.

For one thing, as we have already seen, a sizable number of red directors were promoted to the Central Committee. These promotions provided the leaders of the industrial establishment not only with symbolic status but also with an opportunity to make their voices heard at the highest stage of the policy-making process. Although it is true that during the mid-1920s decisional prerogatives were being increasingly concentrated in the hands of a narrow stratum of top leaders, the Central Committee was by no means yet a moribund institution, and its members, including its red-director members, were by no means devoid of political influence. Moreover, at the same time that the most prominent red directors were being granted more direct access to the political arena, their less prominent colleagues and subordinates were being granted more discretionary authority in the day-to-day conduct of economic affairs. In fact, a drive to curtail "excessive" interference by lower-level party organs in economic questions began even prior to the Thirteenth Party Congress, and this drive became more and more pronounced in the succeeding months.[50] Consequently, the climate was ripe when Stalin announced in April 1926, "our business executives must be surrounded with an atmosphere of confidence and support . . . The post of builder of industry must be made a post of honor . . . These are the lines along which our party organization must now work." [51] Here was an eloquent testimonial indeed to the red directors' failure to align themselves with Trotsky. But the significance of this announcement is broader than a reference to Trotskyism alone might suggest.

As an index of the past political behavior of the red directors, Stalin's April announcement testifies to their failure to support not only Trotsky but also the Zinoviev-Kamenev Left Opposition that emerged in the spring of 1925 and the so-called United Opposition that crystallized in the late winter and early spring of 1926. It thereby confirms what is implicit in the data already cited regarding the careers of the red-director delegates to the Eleventh Party Congress — that the red directors remained loyal to the Central Committee majority throughout the mid-1920s.[52] The same factors that prevented managerial support for Trotskyism also militated against support for the Left and United Oppositions, and these factors once again proved decisive. Indeed, although their platforms were virtually identical, the Left and United Oppositions almost certainly exercised much less appeal among the red directors than the original Trotskyite opposition. For one thing, Zinoviev and Kamenev had been particularly vociferous in their criticism of the managerial regrouping at the time of the Twelfth Congress, and it is likely that the personal animosity that they then aroused carried over into the subsequent period. In addition, Zinoviev and Kamenev made their debut as oppositionists by excluding a number of prominent red directors from the Leningrad delegation to the Fourteenth Party Congress, thereby rendering highly suspect their subsequent attacks on the Central Committee majority for insufficient solicitude for the rights of the managerial elite.[53] Similarly, their advocacy of a more rapid tempo of industrial development smacked strongly of opportunism and political expediency, the more so because one of their principal allies was G. Ya. Sokolnikov, the highly conservative commissar of finance, who had long since become a *bête noire* in the eyes of the red directors and whose approach to industrial development was considerably more cautious than that embodied in the official party line. Finally, at the very moment when Zinoviev and Kamenev committed themselves most unambiguously to a promanagerial, Trotskyite program, in the late winter and early spring of 1926, signs began to crop out that the official party line was in a state of flux and might change sharply in favor of the managers.

One of the most important of these signs was precisely Stalin's April announcement. Whereas it is true, as I have indicated, that this announcement was in basic harmony with the prevailing party line, in spirit it went beyond the line. It testified above all to the red directors' loyalty in the struggle against Trotsky and his allies, but it was also reminiscent of something approaching Trotskyism. Especially when viewed in conjunction with Stalin's simultaneous announcement that the impending five-year plan should accord initial priority to the development of heavy industry, it confirmed the impression that the general secretary was moving "left" and that the succession struggle was about to enter a new phase.[54]

The red directors and the Right Opposition. There is a strong probability that Stalin's April announcement was designed to foil Mikhail Tomsky's proposal that the party broaden the control functions of the sole remaining vehicles of mass participation in industrial management — the now largely moribund plant production conferences.[55] Although this proposal did not become a matter of public record until the fall of 1926, circumstantial evidence indicates that it had been under discussion within the party for several months before. Hence there is good reason to suggest that Stalin's announcement should be viewed as an exercise in esoteric political communication and interpreted as an effort to capitalize on the intense opposition that Tomsky's proposal aroused among almost all of the red directors.[56] Even if one rejects this suggestion, however, and assigns Stalin's announcement chronological precedence over Tomsky's proposal, there can be little doubt that Stalin sought to exploit the tendency of the red directors to counterpose the one to the other and to conclude that the general secretary was in sympathy with their struggle to prevent any proliferation of industrial control.

Stalin did not openly repudiate Tomsky's proposal (which was ultimately approved by the Fifteenth Party Conference in November 1926), but he conspicuously refrained from endorsing it and made no effort to curtail the managerial opposition it aroused. On the contrary, although he certainly possessed the power to do so, he took no steps either to exclude the members of that opposition from the list of delegates to the Fifteenth Conference or to prevent their engaging Tomsky and his supporters in violent polemical debate of a sort that had not been heard since the Twelfth Party Congress. What is more, in the immediate aftermath of the conference, he sponsored at least two major personnel changes that were certain to be interpreted as confirmation of his tacit adherence to a promanagerial, anti-Tomsky, point of view.[57]

Undoubtedly the red directors were sorely disappointed that Stalin did not give them even more vigorous support. Still it is likely that his behavior in the months preceding and following the Fifteenth Conference went a long way toward establishing Stalin as the figure within the leadership who seemed most receptive to managerial demands. Certainly, at a minimum, his behavior went a long way toward freeing him of the image of supercontroller which almost inevitably attached to him as general secretary of the party and principal apparatchik of the realm.[58] And this image, in turn, seems to have been the one factor that might have cost him the support of the red directors in the critical opening rounds of his struggle against the emergent Right Opposition — for he had already established himself as a vigorous political leader and an advocate of a much accelerated tempo of industrial growth. It is scarcely surprising, therefore, to find that all of the available evidence, including career data of the sort already cited, indicates that he did receive massive managerial support, not least from a number of erstwhile hard-core Trotskyites who now hastened to capitulate and join the battle against the Right.[59]

If Schapiro is correct in his contention that the party apparat, having been molded during the struggle against the left oppositions, was essentially rightist in orientation and hostile to the sharp leftward turn in official policy, the almost inescapable conclusion is that the support of the red directors was of critical importance in enabling Stalin to defeat the challenge of the Right Opposition.[60] Even if this conclusion goes too far, though — and it should be stressed that in numerous instances middle- and lower-level party secretaries had been recruited and evaluated as much in terms of their personal loyalty to Stalin as in terms of their commitment to the prevailing antileftist line — there can be no doubt that managerial support was a major political asset during the early phases of the struggle; it remained politically salient until at least the end of 1928, when Stalin finally succeeded in purging most of the rightists in the apparat. And to say even this much is obviously to assign the red directors a considerable share of "objective" responsibility for the rise and consolidation of Stalinism. Furthermore, this responsibility may have had a substantive dimension as well, for there is a distinct possibility that the red directors played an important part in influencing Stalin's initial decision to adopt a policy of rapid industrialization. It is evident that the main impetus behind the new line came from Stalin's own self-generated conviction that rapid industrialization was the policy best calculated to enlarge his own personal power. But there are indications that V. V. Kuibyshev, who became chairman of the VSNKh in July 1926, played a major role in prompting Stalin to press for a developmental tempo higher than any he had previously considered, and Kuibyshev in turn appears to have been under the influence of the red directors.[61] All this once said, however, and precisely because it has been said, it is important to go on to indicate that the red directors' "subjective" responsibility for the rise of Stalinism was less extensive than this discussion might suggest.

The red directors undoubtedly understood that support for Stalin against the Right Opposition meant acceptance of extensive social dislocation. They undoubtedly understood, too, that it meant acceptance of a considerable curtailment of group autonomy and individual freedom. Finally, they undoubtedly understood that it meant acceptance of a marked increase in the pressure to which they would be exposed as managers. These were outcomes the red directors were prepared to face with relative equanimity. These were costs they were ready to bear (and impose) for the sake of rapid economic growth and socialist consolidation. Nonetheless, it is doubtful that they anticipated the untold suffering, systematic terror, and relentless demands to meet impossible production targets that actually characterized Stalinist industrialization. Indeed, it would have been extremely difficult for them to have done so prior to 1928–1929, for it was only during the later stages of his struggle against the Right Opposition that Stalin became an open proponent of out-and-out Stalinism. And, at this point, many red directors do appear to have become highly critical of the prevailing party line. In effect, they developed a belated appreciation of at least some of the principles that had animated the Right Opposition. By then, however, the cause of the Right Opposition was already hopeless, and the prospect of translating dissent into effective remedial action had become exceedingly remote.

THE RED DIRECTORS UNDER STALINISM

Even before the adoption of the final, unqualifiedly Stalinist variant of the five-year plan, such prominent red directors as G. I. Lomov were engaged in a public campaign against maximalist or "bacchanalian" planning,[62] and their position undoubtedly won increasing support. For all that they were still convinced "Americans," the passing years had taught the red directors to temper their "Americanism" with a certain measure of economic realism and a certain respect for the canons of technical rationality. This was pre-eminently true of those who had been able to acquire a degree of technical training, and it is certainly no accident that the schools and institutes which the regime had recently established to provide red directors with such training proved to be veritable hotbeds of managerial dissidence during the First Five-Year Plan.[63] But it was also true of many less well-trained red directors. Thus there is no reason whatever to query the vast number of authoritative reports that appeared throughout the late 1920s and early 1930s, to the effect that the central economic organs were focal points of resistance to superindustrialization, that economic executives regularly "fought like wild beasts" against the high production targets assigned them by the regime, that "the history of the struggle for the *promfinplan* is rich in examples of how the working class and party organizations have had to overcome the opposition of the economic apparatus," or that many directors and engineers conducted a constant "battle with the party for a lowering of tempos." [64] Nor is it any wonder, in view of the situation these reports depict, that G. K. Ordzhonikidze, who became chairman of the VSNKh in November 1930, felt it necessary to confess to the January 1933 Central Committee plenum that party spirit had become a scarce commodity among the red directors and to acknowledge

that "we [economic executives] cannot particularly pride our-
selves on our discipline." [65] However, as Ordzhonikidze was well
aware, the real problem was not lack of party discipline or party
spirit: it was lack of adequate resources, suitable technical in-
puts, and sufficient plant capacity.

The problem of tempo was rendered more acute by the regime's refusal to accord the red directors a sufficient measure
of discretionary authority or operational autonomy in the conduct of economic affairs. The promise of a moderate, if not an
actively promanagerial, organizational policy which they had
read into Stalin's April 1926 announcement and his conduct during the ensuing period proved largely illusory. To be sure, in
September 1929, the regime did decree the introduction of a
system of full-fledged one-man management, whereby plant
directors were "guaranteed" broad autonomy in deciding production questions, wide-ranging authority in the matter of selecting their subordinates, and complete security against the danger
of having errors of judgment interpreted as manifestations of
criminal intent or political opposition.[66] But these last two pro-
visions remained dead letters, and if the first was sometimes actively enforced, it was nonetheless far more honored in the
breach than in the observance.

To predict the fate of the decree on one-man management
should not have been a difficult task. By 1929 a perceptive
analyst might well have apprehended that the very idea of one-
man management in industry ran directly counter to the main
trend in political development — the centralizing, power-maxi-
mizing trend that entailed a continued effort to politicize all
spheres of action, to destroy all insulated pockets of authority,
and to elevate scapegoatism to a system. Moreover, in addition
to such general considerations, there was no lack of concrete
evidence. In particular, there was the violent and highly authoritative attack directed against the prominent red director, S. P.
Birman, at the Sixteenth Party Conference (April 1929). For

Birman was pilloried precisely because he had dared to assert that the interests of production required a reduction in industrial control, that no specialists or engineers should be removed from their posts without managerial sanction, and that the secret police should stop equating misjudgment with sabotage.[67] On the very eve of its adoption into law, the entire doctrine of one-man management was officially tried and condemned. In effect, then, and almost certainly in intent as well, the regime had forewarned the red directors that under Stalinist conditions no decree, however strongly worded, could bring about an extension of managerial prerogatives that was anything other than strictly circumscribed and highly conditional. Whether this warning was taken to heart at the time it was issued (when the introduction of one-man management had almost certainly been approved in principle), we do not know. But there is no doubt that it was fully validated by subsequent events.

In view of the immediate context of Stalin's April 1926 announcement, the most ironic development in the sphere of industrial control was unquestionably the further strengthening of the plant production conferences. In particular, the production conferences were accorded a key role in the massive self-criticism campaign Stalin introduced in 1929, in a patent effort to transfer responsibility for the dismal plight of the Soviet citizenry from the regime to its administrative cadres. Although Stalin disavowed support for "a witch hunt against our business executives," there was no denying the insight of the oppositionist who wrote that "the slogan of self-criticism is the same sort of lightning rod for Stalin as was the Jewish pogrom for tsarism [only] now it is the economic executives above all who are placed in the position of the unhappy Jews." [68] This "black-hundredization" of the production conferences was, however, merely one of the tribulations that the red directors encountered in the sphere of industrial control.

Just as Stalin reneged on his promise to curtail the control activities of the production conferences, so too he reneged on his promise to curtail the control activities of the party apparat — activities that were particularly objectionable to the red directors since the apparat, unlike the production conferences (or even the secret police), was able to subject management to truly comprehensive operational control on a day-to-day basis. Even during the first and fairest period of one-man management, the regime's efforts to curb apparat control were desultory and highly ambivalent. And from mid-1932 on, the regime directed more and more of its criticism at party committees that did "not concern themselves with concrete details of production" and at managers who persisted in arguing that the party's task was agitation and propaganda "and, as for the rest, don't interfere!" [69] This criticism, in turn, soon gave rise to organizational measures (including the creation of so-called plant party organizers, who were directly responsible to the Central Committee) which made a mockery of the entire concept of one-man management. These measures go a long way toward explaining a phenomenon that Ordzhonikidze professed to find puzzling — that in 1933, over three years after the promulgation of the decree of September 5, 1929, the incessant demand of the red directors was for "one-man management, one-man management!" [70] Demands were one thing, however, and actions quite another.

It is possible that a number of red directors became sufficiently disenchanted with official policy to join the ranks of one or another of the mystery-shrouded opposition groupings that emerged in the period immediately after the defeat of the Right Opposition. Even what little we know of their platforms makes it clear that the Syrtsov-Lominadze "right-left bloc," the Riutin or Riutin-Slepkov "conspiracy," and the "antiparty group" of Eismont, Smirnov, and Tolmachev made rather vigorous efforts to win managerial adherents.[71] Since we also know that several of the men behind these efforts had close personal and career ties with the red directors, it is not unlikely that some adherents were actually recruited.[72] Indeed, the fact that the regime's "unmaskings" of each of the indicated groupings coincided with rather extensive and otherwise inadequately explained personnel shakeups within the industrial establishment suggests that an appreciable number of red directors may have been involved.[73] Nonetheless, the available evidence leaves no doubt that the vast majority of the red directors remained passive in the face of the oppositionists' appeals.

Even where the appeals of the oppositionists struck a responsive chord, such familiar factors as disbelief in the possibility of any opposition's being successful, fear of the severe sanctions that might follow upon failure, reluctance to break the sacred bonds of party discipline, and apprehension lest intraparty strife imperil the Bolshevik regime usually prevented the translation of sympathy into active support. Moreover, in a great many instances, even the sympathy that was proferred was residual and highly qualified, for there were compensations as well as tribulations in the red directors' lives, and the compensations often weighed heavily enough in the balance to make opposition seem not only inopportune but unwarranted.

The most important of these compensations was probably the process of industrialization itself. No long-time protagonist of "Americanism," however chastened, could fail to derive a considerable measure of real satisfaction from the massive economic transformation in which Soviet Russia was caught up. If this transformation was proceeding too rapidly and at too great a cost, it was nonetheless proceeding; the fact that factories and plants were everywhere springing up could not be gainsaid, least of all by the men who presided over their construction. Nor should it be forgotten that the red directors were precisely the presiding officers or, as the phrase went in Soviet parlance, "commanders of production." If they were exposed to ubiquitous surveillance and constant harassment, they also enjoyed immense prestige and status, especially after 1931, when the regime abandoned all pretense of a commitment to egalitarianism in either style or substance.[74] Moreover, the red directors continued to occupy posts of political prominence at both the central and the local levels. Indeed, at the Sixteenth Party Congress an unprecedentedly large number of red directors was elected to the Central Committee, and an analogous promotion policy was pursued where posts on republican central committees and other party committees were concerned.[75] To be sure, these political posts were largely honorific and, even where they entailed more or less direct participation in the decision-making process, they did not provide their occupants with enough influence or power regularly to enforce official responsiveness to managerial demands. But honor can be its own reward. And access to the political arena tends in and of itself to generate procedural consensus and to sustain the hope of securing redress of grievances through established channels. Given such access, men who recognize a system as legitimate in principle are usually slow to despair of the possibility of achieving desired goals through within-system change. It is probable that the absence of this despair was yet another of the factors responsible for the continued refusal of most of the red directors to engage in outright opposition.

The red directors, the Seventeenth Party Congress, and the Great Purge. At first glance, the development of Soviet industrial policy in the middle 1930s appears at least partially to have vindicated the red directors' faith in the possibility of finding within-system satisfaction for their manifold demands. In particular, in 1934 the Seventeenth Party Congress approved a five-year plan (the second) which showed at least a minimal appreciation of the true state of the economy and took at least some account of the intractable actualities of production. However, though this plan was obviously adopted with Stalin's consent, it is questionable whether its adoption can sensibly be interpreted as proof that the red directors were able to secure redress for their grievances within the established framework of the Stalinist system.

At a minimum, close inspection of the record undermines the common assumption that the relatively moderate character of the Second Five-Year Plan was an automatic concomitant of the Soviet economy's passage from the "take-off" stage of industrial development into a stage of economic consolidation. The sources leave little doubt that the decision to proceed at a reduced tempo was the product of a long and bitter intraparty struggle — a struggle in which extremely powerful forces were ranged against the red directors and their newfound spokesman, Ordzhonikidze, who had established extremely close ties with his subordinates in the industrial establishment and shown himself increasingly receptive to their demands.[76]

The antimanagerial forces were so powerful that the official Central Committee theses on the Second Five-Year Plan provided for an extremely high-tempo plan. It was only *after* Molotov and a multitude of secondary spokesmen had received stormy ovations from the Seventeenth Congress, for speeches expounding the view that there could be no significant relaxation in the rate of development, that Ordzhonikidze was able to rise and proclaim that the Politburo was willing to consider certain "correctives" to the Central Committee's proposal.[77] In short, though a lower-tempo plan was ultimately adopted, it is clear that the red directors' victory was snatched from the very jaws of defeat and that, until the last possible moment, Stalin remained at least indifferent and probably hostile to all counsels of economic moderation.[78] More important, it is quite possible that the change in Stalin's disposition was not the result of a last-minute reappraisal of the merits of the case for moderation, but rather the result of a last-minute change in the political stance of the managerial elite. To be precise, it is possible that the Seventeenth Congress witnessed the transformation of many of the red directors into incipient oppositionists, prepared to press for Stalin's removal from the post of general secretary unless he undertook to satisfy their demands.

Soviet sources have recently provided additional support for the long-held suspicion that a number of the more prominent delegates to the Seventeenth Congress, including Sergei Kirov, the powerful and popular head of the Leningrad party organization, were ready to demand Stalin's resignation unless he agreed to a more moderate policy.[79] And in view of the mounting evidence (capped by the presentation of the Central Committee theses on the Second Five-Year Plan) that Stalin was not going to sanction a promanagerial shift in industrial policy except under real duress, it is not unlikely that a number of top-ranking red directors participated in this démarche.[80] If it seems doubtful that even a group comprised of Kirov, Ordzhonikidze, and men of similar stature could actually have defeated Stalin in a direct showdown, it is not unlikely that such a group could have forced Stalin to make significant policy concessions. The general secretary was not so firmly in control by early 1934 that he would not have gone to great lengths to obviate the threat of a sudden declaration of opposition by a substantial group of erstwhile Stalinists. All this once said, however, it must be stressed that Stalin may, in fact, have undertaken a last-minute revaluation of the question of developmental tempo and voluntarily abandoned his former position. There was, after all, an incontestable logic in the argument that maximalist planning would prove less productive in the period of the Second Five-Year Plan than it had in that of the First.[81] And even dictators do change their minds.

Pending access to additional information, it is impossible to choose among these alternative interpretations of the genesis of the Second Five-Year Plan. Also, it seems futile to examine the factors that are likely to have been decisive in enabling Stalin to recover the full plentitude of his power, if he did in fact suffer a major political setback at the Seventeenth Party Congress. Perhaps it is worth noting that such factors would undoubtedly include the presence of strong crossfunctional and interpersonal rivalries within the presumed anti-Stalin coalition, not to mention the inability of the latter to keep close tabs on the operations of the Secretariat while performing managerial and other functions. But there seems little point in further elaboration so long as there is a strong possibility that the question they are designed to answer is purely hypothetical.[82] It is enough to stress that any forthcoming material on the Seventeenth Party Congress warrants close investigation, since it may reveal the existence of a number of interesting and largely unexplored problems. And, in the process, it may well contribute to a better understanding of the fate that overtook the red directors. That fate was mass liquidation in the Great Purge.

The signal for the launching of the Great Purge was, of course, the assassination of Sergei Kirov — a crime whose origins are still obscure but whose perpetration was almost certainly facilitated, if not actually planned, by Stalin. Immediately after Kirov's death, which occurred in December 1934, the regime unleashed a hysterical vigilance campaign, and this quickly developed into a full-fledged paroxysm of terror that convulsed the entire country and wrought unprecedented violence on the central institutions of the system, the industrial establishment prominent among them. Indeed, even during the first wave of arrests and explusions from the party, when the principal victims were former left and right oppositionists, the industrial establishment was probably inordinately hard hit, since many repentant Trotskyites and Bukharinites had been assigned to managerial posts.[83] And, when the secret police received a broader mandate, as they shortly did, the red directors were included in the list of primary purge targets.

If nothing else, the very fact that they had had such close con-

tact with so many former oppositionists was enough to make the
regime especially suspicious of the red directors, and the latter
often reinforced this suspicion by seeking to defend their colleagues and preserve them in their posts. As one authoritative
article put it, "We have Communists working in the trusts and
institutions who have lost their class sensitivity. Not only do
they fail to see that the apparatuses in which they are working
are soiled [*zasoren*] but they even come to the defense of alien
people, calling them 'irreplaceable workers,' etc." [84] Nor did this
article leave any doubt concerning the fate that awaited would-be
patrons of "hidden enemies" and "socially hostile elements." It
specifically cited the example of A. S. Enukidze, the perennial
secretary of the Central Executive Committee, who had just
been expelled from the party and violently denounced in the
public press for his misguided "all-forgivingness." The moral
was thus clearly drawn and, to those in the know, it was apparent that it was not only "Communists working in the trusts" who
were being warned, but rather the entire industrial leadership
and, most particularly, Ordzhonikidze — like Enukidze an old
comrade of Stalin's from the Caucasus and a man whose opposition to the purge was well known. [85]

Despite this warning, Ordzhonikidze continued to intercede
on behalf of his subordinates, and for a time he even enjoyed a
certain measure of success. Although many of his intercessions
failed, and the decimation of the ranks of the red directors proceeded at an ever-accelerating rate, Ordzhonikidze was periodically able to win reinstatement for leading managers who had
been "wrongly" purged. [86] More remarkably, in what was in many
ways a test case, he was for some time able to safeguard the life,
party membership, and governmental position of the ex-Trot-
skyite, G. L. Pyatakov, who had risen to the post of deputy commissar of heavy industry following his capitulation and read-
mission to the party in 1928 and had been one of the guiding
spirits behind the execution of the First Five-Year Plan. [87] By

late 1936, however, it was evident both that Pyatakov was slated for liquidation and that Ordzhonikidze's influence was at an end.

Pyatakov's show trial, the so-called trial of the Trotskyite Parallel Center, which took place in January 1937, was in effect a trial of the entire Communist managerial elite. When the inevitable death sentence was returned against the sixteen defendants, almost all of whom were prominent red directors, it was clear that most of their colleagues and subordinates were doomed as well.[88] Some, like Ordzhonikidze, who committed suicide within a matter of weeks of Pyatakov's trial, anticipated the executioner and took their own lives.[89] A few managed to survive unscathed, thanks to a combination of personal good fortune and official "bad conscience" as expressed in a decision "to leave a few people free in each of the arrest-worthy categories [in order] to demonstrate that membership in one of them did not automatically lead to arrest and to render plausible the personal guilt of each of the accused." [90] Most, however, perished in the dungeons and concentration camps of the GPU.[91] As Lazar Kaganovich euphemistically put it in his report to the Eighteenth Party Congress in March 1939: "In 1937 and 1938 the leading personnel of heavy industry was thoroughly renewed and new people were promoted in place of the exposed wreckers. Thousands of new people were promoted to executive posts . . . In some branches it was found necessary to remove several layers." [92]

If Kaganovich was reticent about the fate of the red directors, he gave a far more adequate account of the motives behind the purge. Indeed, when he introduced the members of the new managerial elite with the boast, "we now have cadres who will perform . . . any task assigned them by Comrade Stalin," he was providing as complete an explanation of the fate of the red directors as any yet devised.[93] In fact, it was above all because he was uncertain that the red directors would bow to his every command that Stalin embarked on his policy of liquidation.

Whether or not this uncertainty had a basis in past experience is at best a moot point, for it depends on the solution to the still insoluble problem of the genesis of the Second Five-Year Plan. However, even if the red directors did not join an anti-Stalin coalition at the time of the Seventeenth Party Congress, it was by no means completely paranoiac to believe that they might turn to opposition under the provocation of the sort of policy Stalin was determined to pursue — not only in industry but also in the political realm where Stalin was now committed to the establishment of an unqualified personal dictatorship.

For all that they had surrendered to the general secretary, the red directors had not surrendered the right to be consulted on major policy questions, or the right to engage in a certain amount of meaningful criticism, or the right to independent status as makers of history and custodians and interpreters of doctrine. And, even if he could have abrogated these rights without provoking the managers to open opposition, Stalin could not reasonably assume that they would feel no sense of loss or abandon all hope of reclaiming what they took to be their due. Many of them were, after all, Old Bolsheviks, who were bound to retain at least some degree of political self-confidence, and few of them were so completely lacking in self-respect and a sense of personal worth that they could be expected to accept the status of politically emasculated state serfs without some defiance or protest. How much better, then, to strike in a manner so unexpected and so unprecedentedly brutal that it destroyed all possibility of effective opposition. How much better to start fresh with men who might not think of themselves as bearers of rights or who might at least be so lacking in self-confidence that they would never dare to assert any claim to independent political status. How much better, in short, to liquidate the red directors and to promote in their stead new men of a more recent political generation, conditioned by exposure to total terror and compelled to earn their promotion to

101

elite status by engaging in hysterical denunciations of their predecessors.[94] Here, I suggest, is the essential motivation behind the "renewal of cadres" that swept through the industrial establishment in the period 1936–1938, the period when Stalin's ominous slogan of 1935 — "everyone can be replaced" — was transformed into a directive — "everyone must be replaced."

If it is fair to state the red directors might not have performed "any task assigned them by Comrade Stalin," it is equally fair to state that in the past, or at least up to 1934, most of them had performed every task that Comrade Stalin had in fact assigned. And it was precisely as a result of this behavior that Stalin was in a position to consolidate total and despotic power. To be sure, the red directors had not been the decisive force behind Stalin's rise to power. Where the struggle between Stalin and his various leftist foes was concerned, the support of the party apparatchiki was of much greater significance and would probably have sufficed to ensure his victory even if the red directors had become oppositionists. With the possibly significant exception of the period 1926–1928, the same point holds with regard to the struggle between Stalin and the Right Opposition. It remains true, however, that the red directors made a substantial contribution to Stalin's rise to power, and took no steps to prevent the definitive consolidation of that power until it was too late, if, indeed, they took such steps at all. In this sense, then, the red directors were architects of their own doom. They were crushed by a juggernaut that they themselves had helped to launch.

★ 5 ★

THE MANAGERIAL ELITE
AFTER THE PURGE

> After the purge colorless people replaced
> the old directors. They were made by the
> party. The old ones were creating the party
> and the Soviet system. The new ones: one
> even talked differently to them. It was
> stressed that they depended on the party.
> True, the possibility to exercise power still
> exists for them. But they lack the willpower
> to do so. A Soviet refugee

> One man is prince and all others are slaves
> who act as ministers and aid in governing
> the country through his grace and permis-
> sion. Machiavelli

Given the circumstances of their rise to elite status, the men
who succeeded the red directors, the "red specialists," could not
have doubted that Stalin was engaged in a ritual propitiation
of the ideological gods when he used the forum of the Eighteenth Party Congress to invite them to become "active participant[s] in the political leadership of the country."[1] They
were well aware that the political system which Stalin had
so diligently established over the course of the past decade and
so ruthlessly consolidated by means of the just completed Great
Purge demanded a sharp restriction of the number of active participants in political leadership. They did not have to be told
that they had been catapulted into the ranks of the managerial
elite only because Stalin was confident that he could confine

their access to the decision-making process within predominantly consultative channels and restrict their authority to essentially instrumental spheres. At the same time, the more sophisticated among them probably realized that, for all its manifest hypocrisy, Stalin's invitation embodied a tacit recognition of an important truth.

In point of fact, it was inevitable that the members of the postpurge managerial elite would play a role in the political leadership of the country. Try as he might, Stalin could not rule alone. However great his autocratic aspirations, he had to delegate some power. And, in an industrialized society with a state-run economy, part of this power would necessarily devolve upon the members of the managerial elite. The real issue, therefore, was not whether the red specialists would be relegated to a position of total political impotence, but rather how much power they would exercise and how they would exercise what power they had.

THE RED SPECIALISTS UNDER STALIN

There can be little question that there was a more or less steady increase in the political influence of the managerial elite, relative to that of other key elite groups, throughout the last decade or so of Stalin's rule. This development has been noted so often that for present purposes it is enough to say that the period 1941–1953 witnessed the transfer of many policy-making functions from the party Secretariat to the Council of Ministers (Council of Peoples' Commissars), an unprecedented expansion of managerial representation on the Presidium (Politburo), and a marked curtailment of party participation in enterprise management.[2] It is important to remember that the Council of Ministers continued to be dominated by nonmanagers, that the managers remained a distinct minority on the Presidium, and that party participation in enterprise management was never completely curbed and was periodically encouraged. But the changes that ensued did entail both a substantial increase in the policy-making role of the top managers and a considerable increase in the operational autonomy of plant and enterprise directors.[3]

The fact that the red specialists clearly achieved a significant measure of political influence makes it all the more frustrating that we know so little about the ways in which this influence was used. Although we possess a considerable amount of information pertaining to the internal group cohesiveness, organizational commitments, socioeconomic outlook, and political orientation of the postpurge managerial elite, most of this information is quite general in character and cannot be directly related to the policy-making process. To put the case summarily, while we can identify the dominant themes that characterized managerial demands, we know relatively little either about the manner in which conflicts among these demands were resolved in the course of particular policy debates or about the actual weight of managerial influence in the determination of any given policy question. These gaps in our knowledge are by no means absolute, but the data are nonetheless too fragmentary and ambiguous to permit a systematic analysis of what might be called the *positive* content of managerial behavior in the last decade or so of Stalin's rule. The situation is quite different, however, if the question is transposed and one asks what the red specialists failed to do.

Viewed in this perspective, the data are quite conclusive: they clearly indicate that the members of the postpurge managerial elite did nothing to belie Stalin's confidence in his ability to subject them to effective control and manipulation. Before discussing these data in any detail, however, it should be stressed that I am not arguing that the postpurge managerial elite was comprised entirely or even largely of paragons of totalitarian virtue, exemplars of the "new Soviet man" with his total and unqualified commitment to every aspect of official policy.[4] Such commitment is exceedingly rare in any political system, and the

Stalinist system was not calculated to resolve all doubts and to eliminate all grievances, even among its leading cadres. What I am arguing, rather, is that the political behavior of the members of the postpurge managerial elite was not characterized by any significant effort to challenge Stalin's will or to prosecute independent policies. To choose but one example, I would suggest that there is not merely an unmistakable ring of truth but a paradigm-like quality to Khrushchev's report of a Council of Ministers' meeting at which Stalin first cowed his industrial ministers into voting approval of a production plan that ran directly counter to their advice and then boasted gleefully about his success in keeping the "industrialists" in their "proper" place.[5] No doubt such scenes were not regular occurrences, in that Stalin was probably somewhat less peremptory most of the time. However, what is of concern here is not Stalin's style of leadership but the fact of his unchallenged leadership, not the tact with which he treated managerial advice but his freedom to ignore or dismiss this advice with complete impunity.

Ironically, the very increase in managerial influence and power previously noted is strong testimony to the managers' political docility, for it is clear that Stalin himself initiated the various organizational measures leading to this increase. To be sure, had Stalin acted otherwise he would have had to forgo major economic and political gains: the measures in question clearly served not only to facilitate the more effective integration of technical expertise into the policy process, but also to reduce Stalin's dependence on the party apparat and secret police, thereby contributing to the consolidation of a system in which the dictator disposed of a multiplicity of instruments of rule and was excessively beholden to none. Yet, though these were gains of real importance, they were not so compelling that Stalin would not have forgone them had he faced any significant political recalcitrance on the part of the managerial elite. In short, the price the managers had to pay for preferment over other groups in society was virtually complete subservience to Stalin's will. If their power loomed large in relation to that of the party apparat, in relation to the dictator it was wholly instrumental and derivative. Indeed, as we shall see, managerial power was so much a reflection of Stalin's favor that it underwent a sharp decline in the immediate aftermath of the dictator's death, when the advantage lay with those who had been least reluctant to seek independent power and to develop enclaves of autonomous authority.

Further and even more conclusive evidence of the managers' political docility is the fact that relatively few of the red specialists were removed from office after 1941. On the contrary, once the liquidation of the red directors and the initial shakedown of the new managerial elite were completed, a quite remarkable stability appears to have reigned along the industrial "cadres front." [6] Thus, of the twenty-one men who held top leadership posts in the industrial establishment in 1942, seventeen continued to serve in high office throughout Stalin's lifetime, two died honorably in office, and only two were purged.[7] Moreover, while there was undoubtedly a somewhat higher turnover rate at the secondary and tertiary leadership levels, even at these levels (where tenure was in any case apt to be more a function of economic effectiveness and administrative efficiency than of political considerations) stability appears to have been the rule. A conservative interpretation of the scattered evidence available suggests that no less and probably considerably more than half of the men who headed Soviet enterprises in 1953 had held directorships or similar posts (for example, heads of ministerial departments) for over a decade, and it seems likely that directors were considerably less secure in their tenure than any other members of the managerial elite.[8]

It might be possible to argue that Stalin had no choice but to persist in his policy of granting the managerial elite increased access to the decision-making process and greater discretionary authority in industrial operations (though later we shall see that Khrushchev radically reversed this policy). But it is impossible to argue that he was not in a position to make extensive personnel changes had he so desired. Hence one is forced to conclude that Stalin did not feel that the members of the postpurge managerial elite had proved deficient in political tractability. And, since the record is replete with evidence that Stalin was in no way inclined to underestimate even the most subtle and amorphous threats to his power, it is highly unlikely that the general secretary's feelings in this matter were much at variance with reality.

There are analysts who accept the main thrust of the preceding argument but who nonetheless contend that shortly before his death Stalin did come to perceive the red specialists as a threat to his total power, and that at the time of his death he was about to subject the industrial establishment to a wholesale purge.[9] However, though there is every indication that Stalin was planning a major blood purge, and there is little reason to believe that the managerial elite would have remained completely untouched, it seems reasonably clear that they were not slated to bear the brunt of the impending blow. On the contrary, it was such stalwarts of the Stalinist Old Guard as Beria, Mikoyan, Molotov, Kaganovich, and Voroshilov, and the members of their immediate entourages, who were to be the chief victims; and it was precisely such managers as Pervukhin, Saburov, Kabanov, Malyshev, and Tevosyan who were slated to replace them as the dictator's top lieutenants. This is the obvious import of the promotion of the latter group to the party Presidium at the Nineteenth Party Congress (October 1952), an act that is otherwise almost inexplicable.[10]

It is possible that Kosygin (who alone among the foremost leaders of the industrial establishment was demoted at this time) was scheduled for liquidation. If so, however, it seems probable that he was to suffer as a particularly close associate of the recently purged planner Voznesensky and a protégé of the deceased party leader Zhdanov — disabilities that were not shared by most of his managerial colleagues.[11] It is also possible that managerial cadres in the field of *light* industry (the field with which Kosygin was particularly associated and which was under the general supervision of Mikoyan) were destined to undergo a thorough scourging. During 1952, several prominent figures in the ministries devoted to light industry disappeared, and there were a number of show trials of light-industry enterprise executives.[12] But even here, there is room for doubt, for the disappearances were never accompanied by accusations of wrong-doing and criminality — as one would expect had they been part of a developing campaign of terror. Also, a great many of the enterprise executives brought to trial were Jews, who may well have been victimized as such (this was the time of the Doctors' Plot) rather than because they were managers. In any case, what is particularly relevant for present purposes is that only one or at most two major heavy-industry figures (a deputy minister of nonferrous metallurgy and perhaps the minister of the communications industry) were removed from their posts, and only a few heavy-industry enterprise executives (of whom some, again, were Jews) were tried.[13] Moreover, it is noteworthy that even those heavy-industry managers who were exposed to criticism during this period were criticized in terms that were comparatively free of terroristic overtones. What was involved was essentially "criticism as usual," although some of the criticism was quite sharp.[14] This was even the case with the strictures leveled at the managers in Stalin's "last testament," the pamphlet "Economic Problems of Socialism," which was issued in October 1952 on the eve of the Nineteenth Party Congress. In "Economic Problems" Stalin did have some harsh things to say about "managers and planners" who, he charged, were prone to forget that "it is essential first to ensure securely not a mythical 'rational organization' of productive forces but the constant growth . . . of all social production, with preponderant growth of the means of production." But the managers and planners were manifestly not the chief targets of Stalin's wrath. They took second place to certain academic economists, and it was against the economists alone that such grave and terroristic charges as "Bukharinism" were leveled.[15] In contrast, the tone used in referring to the managers and planners was more caustic than ominous, more one of chastisement than of excoriation. Insofar as it served to convey a certain animosity against the managerial elite, it seems probable that it was part of a self-conscious effort on Stalin's part to reassure the party ideologues and apparatchiki that his decision to "pack" the Presidium with leaders of the industrial establishment *and* to persist in his policy of granting the managers extensive authority in industrial operations[16] did not signalize a retreat from established Bolshevik doctrines and procedures.

Simultaneously, no doubt, Stalin's critical tone was intended to warn the members of the managerial elite against misinterpreting the regime's on-going and increasingly bountiful favor as a sign of approval of any "deviant" policy orientation they might represent. If my interpretation of the events of the preceding decade and a half is valid, however, this warning was largely redundant, a sign of Stalin's hypercaution. The men to whom this warning was addressed had consistently demonstrated that they were aware of and prepared to abide by the rules of the Stalinist game — rules that required and rewarded political docility and made status and authority directly contingent upon prompt compliance with the dictator's commands. They had demonstrated, in short, that they were prepared to adjure the rule of "active participants in the political leadership of the country" and to serve faithfully instead as diligent executors of "any task assigned to them by Comrade Stalin."

CHANGES AFTER STALIN

There is no reason to doubt that the red directors would have continued to serve in this fashion had Stalin lived. But on March 5, 1953, the rules of the political game automatically changed. Above all, Stalin's death provided almost all segments of Soviet society with an opportunity to advance claims and demands that they had previously had to suppress, thus opening the way for a re-emergence of genuine politics within the Soviet system. The members of the postpurge managerial elite were thereby confronted with what was, for them, an unprecedented situation.

Depressurization. One of the most dramatic and important consequences of the revival of politics following Stalin's death was the introduction of a policy of limited and controlled "depressurization." Thus, the successor regime quickly proceeded (or conveyed its intention) to curb the arbitrary power of the secret police, to authorize greater procedural flexibility in all spheres of state action, and to mitigate the ubiquitous and unrelenting pressure to achieve the unachievable under which all Soviet citizens had been forced to operate. That this policy, the details of which need not concern us here, was welcomed and actively supported by the managerial elite is virtually certain.[17] There is no evidence, however, that the policy was in any meaningful sense a concession to the managers. It seems rather that there was widespread consensus within the elite stratum of Soviet society (and, of course, among the masses as well) that the occasion of Stalin's death should be utilized to ameliorate some of the more flagrant abuses of the past and to disavow some of the more onerous of the late dictator's techniques of domination.

Further — and this is a point of greater immediate relevance — there is no evidence that any significant segment of the managerial elite articulated demands that transcended the boundaries of the broader elite consensus on the scope of depressurization.

More particularly, there is no evidence that a considerable number of managers sympathized with or supported the few distinctly heretical elements within Soviet society that advanced genuinely liberal claims. Certain groups within the cultural and scientific intelligentsia were not content to press merely for greater personal security, the mitigation of the system of "institutionalized mutual suspicion," the curtailment of voluntaristic planning, and the disavowal of some of the more doctrinaire and obscurantist measures of intellectual regimentation. They went even further and advocated the introduction of meaningful civil and political rights, the legitimation of genuine social pluralism, the rejection of the principles of universal socialization and all-inclusive state control in economic life, and the abandonment of the quest for cultural monolithism.[18] But the available evidence suggests that the managers were opposed to any such fundamental reforms.

The first thing to be stressed in this connection is that the members of the managerial elite were charter members of the Soviet "state bourgeoisie," whose growth Stalin had sponsored from the mid-1930s on as a stabilizing element amidst the turmoil of the permanent revolution. The rise of this "new class" has been analyzed in considerable depth elsewhere and need not here occupy us in any detail. It suffices merely to report that, thanks to such measures as the abolition of the "party maximum," the authorization of extensive income differentials, the reintroduction of traditional bureaucratic ranks, the upgrading of the political and ideological status of the intelligentsia, and the imposition of tuition fees for secondary and higher education, a sharply graded stratification system had arisen by the time of Stalin's death. Elite cadres, industrial managers prominent among them, now enjoyed immense official prestige, marked economic preferment, considerable social deference, and a reasonable certainty that, barring failure in their own careers, they could expect to transmit most of their advantages to their children. With this as background, what is of critical importance for present purposes is not the rise of the new class as such but rather the high probability that Stalin's hope was realized — that is, the members of the new class had in fact developed strong vested interests in the maintenance of the status quo.

To stress the vested interests of the new class is not, of course, to suggest that this group was adverse to all change. On the contrary, there can be no doubt that a substantial part of the impetus behind the policy of depressurization derived precisely from a desire on the part of the elite cadres of Soviet society to consolidate and extend their privileges. But it seems probable that most elite cadres, including most of the managers, felt that the realization of this desire was compatible *only* with limited and controlled depressurization. There may be a large measure of truth in the argument that the perquisites of the managerial elite, if not of the new class as a whole, were inherent in a high level of industrial development and were hence unlikely to suffer a sustained eclipse.[19] However, it is highly unlikely that the members of the managerial elite proceeded in terms of any such optimistic perspective. Rather, their conduct was almost certainly dominated by the apprehension that any considerable movement toward full-fledged depressurization would open the way for a basic re-examination of established doctrines and procedures — doctrines and procedures with which their privileges and perquisites were inextricably bound up. Furthermore, their fear on this score was undoubtedly reinforced by an awareness that complete depressurization would permit a significant measure of power to devolve upon the masses. The masses, in turn, were known to resent their own deprived status and it even seemed possible that they were disaffected enough to break out into "disorder and panic," now that Stalin was gone from the scene.[20]

There are other reasons, in addition to the ones just cited, for believing that the overwhelming majority of the managerial elite had a "healthy conservative instinct" and was anxious to keep depressurization within limits. Not least is the fact that few of the men concerned were characterized by the sort of liberal or democratic political orientation which alone might have deterred them from recognizing or seeking to defend their "class" interests. To be sure, some variants of commonsense or of general theory suggest that there should be high positive correlations between such characteristic managerial attributes and experiences as lower-class origin, constant exposure to the writings of Marx, Engels, and the Russian classics, relative familiarity with scientific method, and sustained involvement in technologically sophisticated work, on the one hand, and empathy with the masses, commitment to liberty, respect for criticism and free inquiry, and support for liberal procedures and the rule of law, on the other.[21] But no such correlations seem to have existed in fact. On the contrary, the available sources depict the political outlook of the postpurge managerial elite as highly authoritarian. They reveal precisely the sort of outlook that a more psychologically oriented analyst might anticipate in the case of men who were often raised according to the rigid childrearing practices of the traditional Russian family; who had usually been trained in a narrow technical specialty in an educational milieu rife with Stalinist indoctrination; whose rise to high status was characteristically a consequence of extremely rapid social mobility; who were recruited for, promoted to, and retained in responsible posts by a dictatorial and suspicious regime; and whose occupational socialization occurred in a hypercentralized and highly bureaucratic work environment. This evidence, moreover, derives from a number of quite different sources.

In the first place, depth interviews with former Soviet citizens indicate that the members of the postpurge managerial elite (and postpurge elite cadres in general) tended to be characterized by a high intolerance of ambiguity, acute status anxieties of a sort that were apt to be resolved by stressing hierarchical values, a low level of respect for individual rights, an elitist conception of government, and a low degree of identification with popular demands and aspirations.[22] In addition, official statements and actions in recent years convey a clear picture of widespread and deep-rooted authoritarianism among managerial cadres. To be sure, the regime has focused attention only on certain unwelcome manifestations of authoritarianism, such as the cultivation of home environments in which children are instilled with disdainful attitudes toward the masses, or the perpetuation of a harsh and disciplinarian managerial style at a time when political and economic realities demand the introduction of a more consultative, persuasive style.[23] But the underlying pattern is apparent, and the very operational quality of the regime's concern is testimony to the validity of the picture that emerges from the official criticism.

Finally, we can note that liberally inclined Soviet writers, men who cannot be suspected of merely echoing official statements, have almost unfailingly tended to depict the members of the managerial elite in highly illiberal terms. Of these writers perhaps the most outspoken has been Konstantin Paustovsky, who in 1956 gave the following description of a group of "deputy ministers, very high-placed administrative officials, and very exalted personages" with whom he had recently cruised the Mediterranean:

these people were not content merely to make themselves unbearable by their dismal ignorance, their total indifference to everything except their own position, and their personal vanity. They also amazed us by their crass lack of culture. (Applause) . . .

The problem lies in the fact that in our country there exists — unmolested and to some extent prospering — an entirely new social stratum, a new caste of *petit bourgeois*.

There is a new group of acquisitive carnivores, a group which has nothing in common . . . with socialism. (Voice in the hall: "Quite right!") They are cynics, black obscurantists, the same people who aboard the *Pobeda* [the cruise ship], without any embarrassment or fear, quite openly carried out anti-Semitic talk of a kind worthy of pogrom-makers.

There are thousands of these[24] . . .

Of course, Paustovsky did not intend his criticism to apply exclusively to the members of the managerial elite — it was directed at the entire new class. It is nonetheless significant, though, that he singled out "deputy ministers" and "highly placed administrative officials" for special mention. He would hardly have done so had he viewed the members of the managerial elite as allies or even potential allies in the struggle for full-fledged depressurization that he and his colleagues were waging. In short, it seems clear that he viewed the red specialists not merely as members but as pillars of the new class, actively engaged in that group's effort to reduce its vulnerability vis-à-vis the regime while simultaneously preserving or enhancing its invulnerability vis-à-vis the masses. This effort, in turn, was at once a chief spur to and a chief rein upon the process of depressurization as it actually evolved — not toward political liberty in an open society but toward a somewhat more "rational" or modernized dictatorship.[25]

If it is true, as I have been suggesting, that one of the reactions of the elite stratum of Soviet society to Stalin's death was a tendency toward intraelite coalescence, a second, analytically distinct, and somewhat contradictory reaction can also be observed. This second reaction manifested itself in the sharp intensification of conflict among various elite groups representing divergent and often incompatible views on the organization and distribution of power under the new regime. As we shall see, it seems virtually certain that the members of the managerial elite comprised one such group. Before analyzing the intraelite conflict of the post-Stalin period, however, a more general review of the internal group cohesiveness of the postpurge managerial elite seems in order.

Managerial solidarity. Solomon Schwarz argued, prior to Stalin's death, that the postpurge period had witnessed "an almost complete elimination of friction between industrial and party officials" and, consequently, an almost complete elimination of any distinctive "functional role consciousness" among the members of the managerial elite.[26] However, all three of the major points that Schwarz adduces in support of his argument — and no one else has argued the case so cogently — are open to serious question.

To start with, Schwarz devotes too much attention to the fact that Stalin's postpurge organizational policy altered the "balance of power" between the managers and the apparatchiki, and too little attention to the fact that Stalin remained acutely aware of his own "vested interest in confusion" and was always careful *not* to delimit precise spheres of competence or areas of responsibility.[27] Ambiguity in this regard was the essence of Stalin's carefully nurtured system of parallel, competing bureaucracies, and friction was endemic in this system, although it was now more apt to be resolved in favor of the manager rather than the party official. Indeed, friction was so deep-rooted that a celebrated Soviet war novel could take it for granted that the arrival of a new party organizer at a plant would evoke the following greeting from a top engineer: "Don't put your nose into my affairs. I say this in front of [the plant director] . . . What sort of people are you [party workers]? Right away — blah, blah, Marxism, dialectics. But as regards technology, here you are — and he showed the tip of his little finger. Don't command."[28] Nowhere in the novel is it suggested that this speaker is atypical (indeed, he is a principal "positive hero") or that his assumption of the existence of an occupational "united front" is unjustified, and it is clear that any such suggestion would have been a "lacquering" of reality.

It is true, as Schwarz indicates, that the postpurge period witnessed a campaign to recruit engineers into the party apparat and thereby to ensure that party officials in industry were not technical illiterates. But this recruitment campaign appears to have enjoyed only modest success. The tremendous stress that the Khrushchev regime subsequently placed on the need to staff the apparat with technically trained cadres is indicative in this regard, and what "hard" data are available leave little doubt that the number of engineers-apparatchiki remained small throughout the Stalin period.[29] Moreover, the engineer-apparatchik was likely to lack the highest technical qualifications to begin with (as a result of having devoted himself to politics rather than science while a student) and to become progressively less qualified the longer he remained in the apparat (as a result of inability to keep abreast of technical advances while fulfilling his party obligations).[30] And, to make matters worse, even the best qualified engineer-apparatchik was to a considerable degree impelled to represent (indeed, to assimilate and internalize) an ideologically and politically oriented point of view of the sort that could easily run counter to managerial priorities — this quite apart from the fact that presumed technical expertise was likely to lead him to interfere vigorously in precisely those spheres of production that the managers regarded as an exclusive preserve.

Finally, to take the last of Schwarz's major points, it is unlikely that the practice (by no means new) of assigning members of the managerial elite to party posts did much to mitigate the friction between party officials and industrial executives or to attenuate the managers' tendency to develop a distinctive group identity. Although some managers were assigned full-time party posts for more or less extended periods during their careers, this practice appears to have been very much the exception rather than the rule.[31] In most cases, assignments to party posts seem to have been on a part-time basis and to have been ancillary to career development within the industrial establishment proper. Furthermore, at all but the highest levels these part-time assignments appear to have been more a matter of form than of substance. To be precise, it seems that most of the managers in question were treated purely as expert consultants on matters industrial and otherwise ignored. Moreover, even where this was not the case, the managers were usually assigned relatively inconsequential political tasks of a sort that did not entail sufficient responsibility to induce identification with the apparat as such.[32] Indeed, the available evidence suggests that party assignments were commonly viewed by the managers as useless and debilitating drains on time and energy that they could ill afford to squander. One director, for example, protested against demands that he participate in agitprop work because such work was a "purposeless and unnecessary waste of time," and another "solid" economic executive objected to lengthy party meetings on the grounds that he had "serious business" to attend to and could not afford to "spend his time making idle conversation." [33] Far from being atypical, such behavior exemplified prevailing managerial attitudes — attitudes which, as the party's leading journal put it, failed to recognize that "the labor of a party worker is no less creative than the labor of an engineer, a constructor . . . of any specialist." [34]

During the Stalin era these attitudes and sentiments did not ordinarily find expression in solidary group action. Countervailing pressures regularly intervened, and the pervasive terror that was the hallmark of Stalinism discouraged any sort of organized "interest aggregation." Certainly the friction between the managers and the apparatchiki was never allowed to overflow centrally determined channels or to break out into open political (as opposed to purely bureaucratic or administrative) conflict. Nonetheless, it remained conflict for all of that, and there are indications in the records of the local party conferences preceding the Nineteenth Party Congress that at the time of Stalin's death it had become particularly acute.[35] Accordingly, there seems no cause to treat the emergence of a cohesive managerial group in the post-Stalin period as a particularly startling development. At the same time, however, it is important to stress that such an outcome was neither foreordained nor inevitable. For, if the managerial elite was characterized by strong bonds of solidarity at the time of Stalin's death, it was also characterized by strong internal divisions.

The managerial elite was divided along hierarchical, departmental, and factional lines.[36] Discussing each of these categories in turn, we can note, in the first place, that lower-level managers and especially plant directors clearly felt deep resentment at the "petty tutelage" to which they were regularly subjected by the ministries, whose leaders and officials they were apt to view as distant overlords, woefully uninformed about local conditions and grossly insensitive to the dilemmas involved in trying to bridge the gap between the realities of production and centrally assigned output targets.[37] In the second place, it is evident that there were constant jurisdictional disputes over the allocation of scarce resources among the various "production-branch" ministries into which the postpurge industrial establishment was organized. Indeed, these disputes sometimes became so intense that they led to something approaching mutual sabotage by the competing agencies.[38] Moreover, interdepartmental conflict automatically tended to generate self-perpetuating blocs or alliances. The warring managers regularly sought "outside" backing for their respective interests, and when their quest was successful, as it often was, they naturally tended to reciprocate by backing their erstwhile backers when the latter were embattled. Finally, in the third place, there is no doubt that managerial solidarity was vulnerable to the cross-pressures which resulted from the fact that different managers were the protégés of different members of the top power elite. As such, they were under a heavy obligation to support their particular patrons in the latters' recurring internecine conflicts — conflicts that Stalin encouraged and manipulated in order to maximize his own power.[39]

Needless to say, essentially similar lines of division had existed among the red directors as well.[40] However, internal fragmentation had almost certainly been less marked prior to the Great Purge. Hierarchical tension among the managers appears to have been largely a function of the degree of centralization within the industrial establishment, and extreme centralization was even more characteristic of Soviet economic decision making and administration in the postpurge period than it had been earlier. With regard to interdepartmental friction, at least two interrelated considerations suggest that it too increased. First, it was only during and after the Great Purge that separate and autonomous production-branch ministries were formed in the sphere of heavy industry, and it is likely that institutionalization as such tends to crystallize divergent interests and to reduce the possibility of adjustment and compromise.[41] Second, the members of the postpurge managerial elite were much more likely than their predecessors had been to be experts in one particular branch of production. They usually expected to spend and did spend their entire careers in a given branch and were hence likely to have a much stronger sense of "departmental identity" than the red directors, most of whom had been managerial "generalists," regularly working in diverse branches of production. Finally, with regard to factional conflict, it seems doubtful that patron-client relationships were either as common or as demanding during the prepurge period, if only because the greater scarcity of cadres and the lesser severity of the sanctions attached to official disfavor made sponsorship and protection less essential to survival.[42]

The foregoing points are particularly noteworthy because they cast considerable doubt on the validity of the widely accepted proposition that industrial development brings in its wake a more

121

or less automatic increase in the degree of solidarity and group cohesiveness among individuals performing the same economic function.[43] Other variables relating to modes of organization, processes of training and recruitment, and the character of the political environment must be taken into account before valid correlations can be established between levels of industrial development and degrees of functional solidarity. For immediate purposes, however, the key point is not that the red specialists were less united than the red directors, but merely that the cleavages among the specialists were quite marked.

To explain why the managerial elite emerged as a cohesive group in the period following Stalin's death, it is necessary to stress the fact that the succession struggle turned on issues which directly engaged the managers' basic functional interests and involved those demands which were most incompatible with the demands of the party apparat. Nor is this argument tautological, for it was not the managers but the members of the Stalinist Old Guard who determined the agenda of the succession struggle, and it was by no means foreordained that conflict within the Old Guard would develop in a manner calculated to reinforce managerial cohesiveness and inhibit tendencies toward group formation along crossfunctional lines.

The first phase of the succession struggle. The expansion of managerial representation on the party Presidium at the Nineteenth Congress, and indeed the entire postpurge organization policy of which this expansion was the culmination, might well lead one to anticipate that the leaders of the industrial establishment would emerge as strong contenders for Stalin's mantle.[44] However, the very first step in the succession struggle, the reconstitution of the regime, revealed that such an outcome was most unlikely. In effect, the reconstitution of the regime signified a powerful reassertion of their political primacy by the Stalinist Old Guard, including the men whose influence and perhaps life expectancies had appeared to be sharply in decline in late 1952 and early 1953. Thus, all of the top managers except Pervukhin and Saburov were dropped from the party Presidium; all of the industrial officials who had served as deputy chairmen of the Council of Ministers (Kosygin, Malyshev, Pervukhin, Saburov, and Tevosyan) were removed from their posts; Saburov was replaced as head of Gosplan by a little-known member of the party apparat; and twelve key industrial ministers and many high officials had their offices "reorganized" out of existence.[45] These changes relegated the leaders of the industrial establishment to a distinctly secondary level in the new hierarchy of power and strongly suggested that in the emergent succession struggle, or at least in its first phase, the managers would participate not as an autonomous political force but only as supporters or satellites of one or several of the rival figures in the new "collective leadership."

The antimanagerial changes accompanying the reconstitution of the regime seem to have reflected an initial agreement by the entire collective leadership that the managers should not be allowed to consolidate the political status accorded them at the Nineteenth Congress. However, the conflict within the collective leadership inevitably made this agreement highly precarious. Given this conflict, and the fact that the managers remained in charge of a vital sector of the machinery of state and retained at least some voice in the inner councils of the party, it was almost certain that each of the chief contenders for power would seek to mobilize managerial support, and the ensuing competition was bound to give the members of the managerial elite a significant, albeit subordinate, role in the selection of Stalin's successor. The only question was whether the competition for their support would break down the managers' group cohesiveness, and, as indicated already, this question was soon settled. Malenkov quickly outdistanced his rivals and was able within a relatively brief period to secure the backing of almost all of the top industrial cadres. The only significant exceptions appear to have been men such as Kucherenko, Zasyadko, and Zademidko, who were long-time protégés of Khrushchev's, and men such as Kosygin who had been close associates of Malenkov's erstwhile rival, Zhdanov.[46]

Malenkov undoubtedly had a considerable initial advantage over his rivals in the competition for managerial support. He had begun his career as the party secretary of the Bauman Technical Institute (in which he himself had studied between 1921 and 1925) and thus had an unusually good opportunity to establish close connections with hundreds of young men, among them Malyshev, Pervukhin, and Saburov, who were destined to assume top posts in the postpurge industrial establishment. In addition, he had occupied the chairmanship of the party's cadres department during the Great Purge and so had been in a position not only to promote his already established favorites but also to extend his patronage to thousands of other aspiring young managers. Nor is it likely that Malenkov had allowed these ties to wither during the postpurge period. The fact that the "managerialization" of the party Presidium in 1952 coincided with Malenkov's designation as Stalin's chief lieutenant and heir apparent leaves little doubt on this score.[47]

Although the point is debatable, it does not appear that Malenkov showed any particular bias in favor of "promanagerial" policies in the period prior to Stalin's death.[48] But he had no worse a record in this regard than the other members of the new collective leadership, and in the period after Stalin's death he did advocate programs and policies that had a distinctively "promanagerial" cast. For one thing, his position as *primus inter pares* within the collective leadership probably enabled him to secure much of the credit for the general turn toward depressurization. In addition, he took special pains to identify himself with new measures that had a particularly strong appeal to managers, going out of his way, for example, to indicate that he

was acutely aware of the need for more realistic planning.[49]
Nor was the appeal of his position on planning diminished by
his simultaneous advocacy of greater investment in light industry.

Operationally Malenkov's "new look" in economic policy implied a far smaller withdrawal of resources from heavy industry than the virgin-lands program favored by Khrushchev,
and it is most unlikely that the members of the managerial elite
feared that the new look's partial denigration of the *doctrine*
of the primacy of heavy industry would undercut their authority.[50] At a minimum it is extremely doubtful that any concern
on this score persisted once it became evident that Malenkov was
committed to an organizational policy designed to enable ministries "to decide all important [economic] questions without
reference to others" and to ensure that local party organs would
acknowledge the plant director to be the "supreme boss" in his
enterprise. Certainly, when the promulgation of this policy was
accompanied by the reversal of many of the antimanagerial
changes initiated in the aftermath of Stalin's death and by the
repromotion of most of the top leaders of the industrial establishment to the positions they had lost, all possible doubt must have
been dispelled.[51] In effect, Malenkov's organizational policy
pointed toward a full redemption of the promise of unprecedentedly great influence and authority that Stalin had issued
to the managers at the Nineteenth Party Congress.

It has been argued that this policy had its roots in a belief
that the state apparatus, and more particularly the industrial
bureaucracy, had become the most potent power base in the
Soviet system. According to this interpretation, when Malenkov,
who had been both senior secretary of the party and chairman of
the Council of Ministers, resigned from the Secretariat nine
days after Stalin's death, he did so voluntarily in the sense
that his rivals, while determined to reduce his power, permitted
him (or had to permit him) to choose which of his two posts he

125

would relinquish.[52] Yet it seems highly improbable that Malenkov would have opted to retain his state rather than his party post had he been given such a choice. It it not necessary to read the events of this time in the light of subsequent developments in order to argue that only someone who was less sensitive than Malenkov to the lessons of Soviet history and the fundamental dynamics of Soviet politics would have gambled that the party apparat was no longer the fulcrum of power and the main source of legitimacy (a critical variable in any succession struggle) in the Soviet system. It seems more probable that Malenkov advocated the rights and prerogatives of the managerial elite because, through no choice of his own, the latter had become his principal "constituents." It seems likely, in short, that far from his having done so voluntarily, Malenkov adopted his state-oriented, promanagerial policy in response to the strategic logic of an institutional position that had been forced upon him.[53] Whatever its origins, however, it seems clear that this policy had great appeal for the members of the managerial elite. In terms of my broader argument, it provides yet a third (and, for present purposes, final) reason for concluding that the managers were more powerfully drawn to Malenkov than to his rivals, none of whom was prepared to show comparable solicitude for the bureaucratic and professional interests of industrial cadres. Indeed, at the risk of a slight digression, I would go further and suggest that Malenkov not only outbid his rivals for managerial support but actually cast himself in the role of a full-fledged representative of the managerial elite.

The managers as technocrats. Although the available evidence does not permit any firm conclusions, there is good reason to doubt that the demands (or even the aspirations) of the managerial elite with regard to the distribution and organization of power under the new regime went significantly beyond Malenkov's "platform" of permitting the industrial establishment to

126

decide intramural questions "without reference to others," extending the rights of economic ministers, and acknowledging that the director should be "supreme boss" in his enterprise. To be sure, some managers did undoubtedly go beyond the demand that party workers in industry not "command" to a dismissal of ideology as "blah, blah, Marxism, dialectics," thereby implicitly proposing that Soviet society be more or less thoroughly secularized. Likewise, some undoubtedly went beyond the demand that they themselves be freed from time-consuming party obligations to a denigration of the work of party officials as inherently less creative than the work of "real" specialists, thereby implicitly proposing that the principle of party primacy be rejected in favor of rule by technical experts. However, there are a number of reasons for doubting that many managers went this far, let alone for doubting that the managerial elite as such was truly "technocratic" in its outlook.

In the first place, many postpurge managers were veteran Communists whose party membership antedated not only their rise in the industrial establishment but also their professional training. No small number consisted of former "party thousandites" who, having already "passed through the serious school of party, Soviet, or trade-union work," had been dispatched to institutions of higher education on direct assignment from the party during the period 1928–1933, when the regime had confronted the spectre of an acute manpower shortage.[54] To be sure, few of the former "thousandites" (or other veteran Communists) in the ranks of the postpurge managerial elite were Old Bolsheviks, and it is hence impossible to assume that ideological, as distinct from careerist, motives played the dominant role in their adherence to Bolshevism. It is also true, however, that most of the men concerned joined the party before careers were closed to anyone who lacked a party card and at a time when party membership still entailed a certain amount of material sacrifice.[55] Moreover, motives apart, these were men who had early identified their personal fates with the party, who had frequently already embarked on careers in the party apparat prior to being recruited for technical training, and who had been selected for such training by the Secretariat. When all these factors are weighed in the balance, there seems good reason to conclude that the political outlook of the postpurge managerial elite was characterized by quite real and deep-rooted dedication to the party and its program.[56]

This conclusion is reinforced when one recalls that even those postpurge managers who had received a first-class engineering education had not been trained in the spirit of free scientific inquiry or in the tradition of "free professionalism," but rather according to the tenets of dialectical materialism and the principles of *partiinost* or party spirit. Despite its pressing need for skilled engineers, the regime had constantly demanded that ideological indoctrination occupy a prominent place in all professional education and had, in fact, been particularly unrelenting in this regard during the period of the late 1920s and early 1930s, when most of the top leaders of the postpurge industrial establishment were being trained. Victor Kravchenko, who attended a leading Soviet engineering institute during the period, conveys a good sense of the prevailing educational climate when he reports:

Political education rated even higher in our curriculum than technical subjects . . . Our Leninism Faculty . . . made us toe the mark. Those who could not digest Marx's *Das Kapital*, the dialectics of Engels, the works of Lenin, and above all, the dissertations of Stalin, were thrown out of the Institute more quickly than those who merely had trouble with calculus or blueprints.[57]

Nor should one underestimate the efficacy of such intensive indoctrination in the case of young men living in a closed society, especially when these men have risen to high position with dizzying speed and from culturally deprived backgrounds. Such men are peculiarly likely to feel the need for an unambiguous definition of their environment and their own unfamiliar roles within it; they are peculiarly ill equipped to find a definition that would represent a viable alternative to that provided by the official ideology.[58] To be sure, in many cases ideological indoctrination did not "take" to the extent that the regime would have desired. Official criticism of student attitudes during the 1930s leaves little room for doubt on this score.[59] However, criticism was often used as a prophylactic measure in the Stalinist system, and the regime's criterion was apt to be not merely the well-indoctrinated citizen but the totally indoctrinated "new Soviet man." Moreover, not all students became managers.

The regime's postgraduate recruitment and promotion procedures were explicitly designed to exclude those who succeeded in graduating despite an inability to digest Marx, Engels, Lenin, and Stalin. Molotov described the nature of these procedures with unusual frankness in 1937, when he advised a plenary meeting of the Central Committee: "Where our cadres are [politically] weak, we should decisively promote workers who are politically verified although they are inadequately prepared [from a technical point of view]." [60] To be sure, such absolute stress on the primacy of political criteria in the evaluation of managerial cadres became relatively rare after the Great Purge, but most of the high-ranking red specialists were recruited during the Great Purge, and even in the subsequent period political criteria remained very important.[61] It is clear, at least, that no engineer who was so dedicated to "free professionalism" that he refused to joint the party could hope to rise to a high executive position, and it is likely that the regime took vigorous precautions against being deceived by those for whom party membership was a mere formality.[62] One wonders, indeed, if it was not extreme caution on this score that was responsible for the fact that so many members of the postpurge managerial elite were *not* engineers.[63] This is to suggest, of course, that for no small number of Soviet engineers party membership was something to be shunned or was at best an empty form. But it is also to suggest that entrance into the managerial elite was very carefully controlled from a political point of view and that the screening process was highly sensitized to the threat of a technocratic deviation among the managers.

Finally, the very dynamics of involvement in responsible work tended to reinforce identification with the party and its ideology. Again I cite Inkeles' and Bauer's observation that,

when the individual is in a responsible position, he must from day to day deal with solving tasks related to the regime's goals . . . From what we know of psychological processes in general, it seems inevitable that as the individual deals with these [tasks], he must come to accept as legitimate the goals at which they are directed. In effect he thereby comes to identify himself with the regime and its objectives.[64]

We have already seen this process of identification at work among the bourgeois specialists, and it undoubtedly affected the postpurge managerial elite as well. If anything, its effect should have been much stronger in the later period, for the postpurge managers were much more fully socialized into the Soviet system and much more completely products of that system's recruitment practices. Moreover, by now the ideology had become so deeply embedded in the institutions of Soviet life, and so entrenched in the form of irrevocable policy commitments, that it was less than ever possible to separate the regime and its objectives from the tenets of Marxism-Leninism. These tenets, in turn, were interdependent to a degree that made it extraordinarily difficult to call one into question without at the same time questioning the entire ideology. More particularly, to challenge the key principle of party primacy, one would almost inevitably have to challenge the entire body of doctrine from which the regime derived its policy orientation and its legitimacy. It seems most unlikely that the managerial elite was prepared, psychologically or otherwise, to entertain such a prospect.

130

It is not completely inconceivable, of course, that the successful implementation of Malenkov's policy might have touched off a cycle of rising expectations that would have led to the managers' developing a technocratic self-image and formulating an "imperialistic" political platform. In this sense, there is perhaps some validity in speaking of the members of the managerial elite as latent "technocrats" and of "technocarcy" as the logical end product of their political outlook and program. In the political sphere, however, logic is ultimately dependent on power for its realization, and the managerial elite proved relatively weak. It not only failed to provide the support necessary to enable Malenkov to realize his organizational policy, but was even unable to provide the support necessary to sustain its "representative" in office.

The second phase of the succession struggle. Although it is probable that the members of the managerial elite rallied to his side in increasing numbers and with increasing vigor, Malenkov began to suffer a clear loss of power from the summer of 1954, and on February 8, 1955, he was forced amidst humiliating circumstances to give up the premiership.[65] That Malenkov had been able to survive as the dominant figure in the succession regime for over a year after his resignation from the Secretariat indicates that managerial support was not a completely negligible factor in the political arena, although it should be noted that Malenkov was also aided by continued support from some segments of the party apparat, as well as by a desire on his rival Khrushchev's part to avoid an open split in the leadership until all danger of popular disorder had disappeared.[66] However, if Malenkov's survival demonstrated that the managerial elite had not been reduced to political impotence by the measures directed against it by the initial "collective leadership," Khrushchev's consolidation of power after Malenkov's fall graphically reinforced the lesson that these measures had taught: without the backing of the dominant figure in the regime, the managerial elite was vulnerable in the extreme.

Immediately following Malenkov's removal as premier, the regime launched an exceedingly virulent campaign of criticism against defects in the work of the industrial establishment. Under Khrushchev's direct auspices it also began to encourage personal attacks on key ministers, a number of whom were belabored by name in the press and some of whom were removed from their posts.[67] If my interpretation of the first phase of the succession struggle is valid, there seems little doubt that this campaign of criticisms and denunciation should be viewed in part as retaliation for the managers' support of the defeated Malenkov. Indeed, the campaign's timing and its vituperative character are themselves indications that such support had been rendered on a rather extensive scale.[68] At the same time, however, there seems little doubt that more was involved than a squaring of personal accounts.

It was suspected at the time and is reasonably clear in retrospect that Khrushchev designed the campaign against the leadership of the industrial establishment as the prelude to a basic overhaul of the entire system of economic administration.[69] That such an overhaul was in fact on the agenda was confirmed at the Twentieth Party Congress (February 1956) when Khrushchev, after proclaiming that the industrial apparatus stood in need of "substantial revision," proposed that the central ministries should be stripped of most of their operational functions and perhaps even completely abolished. At the Twentieth Congress, to be sure, Khrushchev left it to Bulganin, his second-in-command, to broach this last possibility, but Bulganin was clearly speaking in his superior's name. In any event, as we know, it was abolition and more particularly the liquidation of the central ministries in favor of a multitude of regional (chiefly oblast) economic councils that was provided for in the actual

"Khrushchev plan of industrial reorganization." It was this plan, which was presented to the public in February 1957 and adopted with only minor revisions shortly thereafter, that became the focal point of managerial political involvement in the period after Malenkov's removal as premier.[70]

A wide range of complex and partly interrelated objectives appears to have lain behind Khrushchev's sponsorship of so radical a plan of industrial reorganization. Among them were: to contain the ever-present threat of "routinization" or "normalization"; to destroy the institutional base and framework of managerial power; to increase the political status and authority of the party apparat; to exacerbate hierarchical tensions within the managerial elite; to facilitate a purge of the managers; to strengthen party control over economic operations; to put an end to the stultifying effects of administrative hypercentralization; to take fuller advantage of the logic of economic geography; to respond to the military-strategic logic of decentralization; and, finally, to minimize the risk of the reorganization's giving rise to administrative chaos. These objectives once noted, however, the challenging task of analyzing and appraising them cannot detain us here.[71] What is more relevant for present purposes is that Khrushchev's reorganization plan was almost certainly opposed by a vast majority of the members of the managerial elite, including many and probably most of the "renegade" managers who had backed the first secretary in his struggle against Malenkov.[72] The fact that he had preceded the introduction of his plan by a campaign to discredit the industrial leadership suggests that Khrushchev had anticipated such opposition, and the available evidence leaves no doubt that his expectation was well founded. Khrushchev himself all but openly acknowledged that he encountered the resistance of "tens of thousands" of highly placed industrial officials, but one could safely infer the existence of such resistance from other data if Khrushchev had been less frank.[73] In particular there is the fact that only a single heavy-industry minister (Beshchev, minister of transport, whose ministry was one of those receiving a temporary reprieve from the sentence of liquidation) spoke in favor of the industrial reorganization when Khrushchev's plan was up for consideration before the Supreme Soviet.[74] In the circumstances there can be no doubt that silence was virtually equivalent to strong dissent. Moreover, despite Khrushchev's vigorous effort to win the support of local industrial officials by presenting his reorganization plan as a vehicle designed precisely to free local cadres from "petty tutelage," it is unlikely that the pattern of overwhelming dissent was confined to economic officialdom at the center.[75]

In the first place, Khrushchev's claims to the contrary notwithstanding, the reorganization plan contained conspicuous elements of economic "irrationality," which undoubtedly diminished its appeal to all dedicated professionals. Not only did it entail a pattern of "decentralization" that in fact bore little relation to the logic of economic geography, but also it threatened to impede the growth of industrial specialization and to slow the rate of technological innovation.[76] In the second place, the level of hierarchical tension within the postpurge industrial establishment was probably fairly low at this time, since central economic officials had shown considerable willingness to abandon the most onerous aspects of petty tutelage in the years since Stalin's death. Substantial flexibility had been introduced into administrative procedures during Malenkov's premiership, when the influence of the ministerial bureaucracy was at its height, and there is no reason to doubt that the top industrial leaders welcomed such measures as the July 1955 Central Committee decree extending the rights of plant directors.[77] Finally, and most important, it is by no means clear that Khrushchev's plan actually pointed toward increased discretionary authority for local ecomic officials. On the contrary, the decision to set up the vast majority of new sovnarkhozes (regional economic councils) in such a way that their boundaries coincided with the boundaries of the oblast committees of the party foreshadowed an increase in party control over production operations. Khrushchev attempted to deny that such an increase was in the offing, but his efforts were half-hearted at best, and the evidence of administrative geography weighed heavily against him. Moreover, the managers were in any event probably disinclined to give him the benefit of any doubt. Khrushchev had virtually ensured their skepticism by accompanying his first public statement of the case for industrial reorganization not only by a strong exhortation to strengthen the role of the party in economic life, but also by the introduction of an exceedingly high-tempo economic plan that showed crass insensitivity to the problems of production.[78]

The operation of all of these factors makes it extremely doubtful that Khrushchev was as successful in "splitting" the industrial establishment as has sometimes been suggested.[79] Rather, as already indicated, it seems probable that most local economic officials perceived the establishment of the sovnarkhozes as incompatible with their basic interests and joined their superiors and colleagues at the center in opposing Khrushchev's reorganization plan. That some enterprise executives did so is clear from the example of Georgy Glebovsky, the director of the Urals machinebuilding plant, who had long been a leading spokesman for the "grassroots" personnel in their quest for freedom from petty tutelage but who saw fit as early as the spring of 1955 to warn against misinterpreting this quest as support for the notion of dismantling the ministries and who subsequently spoke out against Khrushchev's plan.[80] It is true that none of Glebovsky's fellow directors was so courageously outspoken in public, but the Uralmash director had voiced his colleague's sentiments on many previous occasions, and it seems highly probable that he did so now as well.[81] In any event, it is clear that Khrushchev's reorganization plan encountered the resistance of some extremely influential directors (Glebovsky was surely not an isolated figure); and it was violently opposed by almost all of the industrial officials at the center, including most of those who commanded positions of primary or secondary political significance.

The existence of a united managerial opposition was undoubtedly one of the factors responsible for Khrushchev's suffering two serious, albeit extremely short-lived, setbacks between February 1955 and his decisive victory of June 1957.[82] However, the managerial opposition was not primarily responsible either for the major rebuff administered to Khrushchev's economic policy in December 1956, when the Central Committee lowered the production targets in the five-year plan that had been approved by the Twentieth Party Congress and established an economic "superministry" staffed entirely by managers, or for the nearly fatal crisis of June 1957, when the Presidium demanded Khrushchev's ouster as first secretary.[83] Rather, both events must be seen in the broader context of the on-going succession struggle and, more particularly, of the rise of the so-called antiparty group, which consisted initially of Molotov, Kaganovich, and Malenkov and ultimately (by June 1957) of Shepilov, Bulganin, and Voroshilov as well. Although the dynamics of the relationship between the managerial opposition and the antiparty group (a relationship that was probably mediated through the greatly chastened but still influential Malenkov) are almost impossible to fathom, there is little question that the antiparty group, led by men whose political experience, stature, and capacity to mobilize broad support far exceeded those of the managers, constituted the more powerful force. It is indicative both that the issue of industrial reorganization does not appear to have occupied a particularly prominent place in the indictment accompanying the Presidium's demand for Khrushchev's resignation in 1957 and that, once he had weathered the June crisis, Khrushchev dealt much more harshly with the leaders of the antiparty group than with the leaders of the managerial opposition.

It may be going too far to argue that these considerations invalidate Myron Rush's claim that, in the second phase of the succession struggle, the managerial elite was an autonomous political force rather than "merely an instrument of factional intrigue" — but if it was more than an instrument, it was a good deal less than an alternative leadership group.[84] There seems no factual basis whatever for the view that the Soviet Union was on the verge of a "managerial revolution" either in December 1956 or in June 1957.[85] Rather, given the distinctly junior status of the managers in the anti-Khrushchev alliance as well as Khrushchev's ultimately decisive victory, it seems more appropriate to view these events as demonstrations of the limited efficacy of the managerial opposition. What seems to have been involved was not the narrow failure of an effort by the managers to enlarge their power, but rather the not necessarily narrow failure of an effort by the managerial elite to assert itself as a "veto" group where its own most vital interest was at stake.[86] Whatever the nature of their failure, however, one thing seems clear: June 1957 found the managers almost entirely at Khrushchev's mercy.

THE INDUSTRIAL ESTABLISHMENT AFTER 1957: RENEWAL AND RECENTRALIZATION

When Lazar Kaganovich telephoned Khrushchev after the June 1957 Central Committee plenum to plead for his life, he was almost certainly expressing a fear that was common to all those who had supported the anti-Khrushchev opposition over the preceding years.[87] In the case of the managerial elite, however, this fear was wholly unwarranted. Although there is some evidence that Khrushchev hoped to bring the members of the antiparty group to trial on capital charges, there is no reason to believe that the members of the managerial opposition were ever thus endangered.[88] Ironically, the regime's very denunciation of Molotov, Malenkov, and Kaganovich as accomplices in Stalin's criminal activities amounted to a pledge to the managers that

137

they were safe from physical reprisals.[89] And, in the period following the June 1957 plenum, it became increasingly apparent that the majority of high-ranking economic cadres had no reason even to fear for the security of their jobs.

Once he had treated them to a graphic demonstration of his power and deprived them of their established bases of organizational authority, Khrushchev apparently decided that his interests could best be served by retaining the old ministers and top ministerial officials in leading posts. To cite but one representative example, of the twenty members or candidate members of the Central Committee who headed ministries or other economic organs that were liquidated in 1957, six became sovnarkhoz chairmen, nine received new assignments in the central economic apparatus (mostly as deputy chairmen of Gosplan), and two obtained important territorial administrative posts.[90] Moreover, these high-level reassignments proved to have more than purely transitory significance, for most of the men concerned continued to occupy leading posts throughout the remainder of Khrushchev's rule.[91] This point once emphasized, however, it is important to go on and note that the managerial corps as a whole was by no means immune to the process of bloodless "permanent purge" that affected virtually all sectors of Soviet life during the last years of the Khrushchev era. On the contrary, from 1959 on, the middle and lower levels of the industrial establishment appear to have been subjected to an increasingly vigorous "renewal of cadres." Already by 1961, *Pravda* was able to report that the party had recently "dispatched tens of thousands of qualified specialists . . . into agriculture and to lagging enterprises and construction projects. Many able young specialists have been advanced to leading work." And reports to the same effect recurred ever more frequently, especially following the Central Committee plenum of November 1962.[92]

The regime explained the renewal of cadres at the middle and

lower levels of the industrial establishment by a desire to termi-
nate a situation in which managerial cadres frequently failed to
exploit "hidden" production reserves and to encourage technological innovation. Nor is there any reason to doubt that the
purge *was* at least partially inspired by a belief that the replacement of many members of the postpurge managerial elite was a
precondition for rapid economic growth. Khrushchev was obviously using the managers as scapegoats when he asserted that
most of the deficiencies of Soviet industry could be explained
by the fact that the men in charge were "inadequately trained
executives, poorly versed in the economics of management and
production and incapable of properly organizing people." [93] Yet
he may well have felt that the men in charge of Soviet industry
often did behave in a way that compounded structural defects
and failures, and his judgment was probably correct.

The first point to be noted in this connection is that the postpurge managers were often inadequately trained to cope with
the technological and administrative demands posed by the
latest stage of industrial development. In many cases plant
and factory directors were little more than glorified technicians
who had been poorly trained to start with and had long since
ceased to be able to apply what technical skills they had acquired.[94] Furthermore, even where they were better prepared,
their knowledge was becoming increasingly obsolescent. Formal
training apart, almost all of their career experiences (and perhaps their precareer experiences as well) had been such as to inhibit initiative and enterprising behavior of the sort now required.[95] Sustained involvement in a hypercentralized and authoritarian bureaucracy had tended in and of itself to make
them cautious and formalistic in their approach, and this tendency had been powerfully reinforced by ubiquitous terror.[96] As
Khrushchev put it in his secret speech to the Twentieth Party
Congress, terror led to a situation in which "many workers began
to work uncertainly, showed overcautiousness, feared everything

that was new, feared their own shadows, and began to show less initiative in their work." [97]

To be sure, this was but part of the story and, judging by his subsequent decision to engage in such neo-Stalinist activities as the restoration of harsh penalties for vaguely defined "economic crimes," Khrushchev himself was well aware that this was so.[98] Terror had also been a spur to initiative, and, under Stalin, no manager survived long who was not able to meet most of the unrelenting demands made up him. Nevertheless, in the circumstances prevailing then, these demands could usually be better met by the skillful use of coercion than by supporting or initiating technological innovation and cultivating harmonious labor relations. But now the old framework of sanctions — the infamous laws on lateness, absenteeism, work transfers, as well as the general terror — had been largely dismantled, and a new managerial style was essential.[99] However, adaptation to the post-Stalin atmosphere was not easy for men who were no longer young and whose attitudes had been shaped by Stalinism.[100] As one official spokesman put it in a statement that suggests the orientation behind the renewal of cadres: "the cult of personality made workers forget about independence and initiative and led to intellectual atrophy. And, despite the fact that all of this has been struck a decisive blow, the habits which were formed in the course of decades cannot completely disappear in a moment." [101] What the regime feared was that such habits of dependence and caution would in fact never disappear, and the fear was certainly justified. The postpurge managerial elite was now a tired and dispirited group whose energy and enthusiasm had in fact been largely spent.

While the managers undoubtedly welcomed the various measures of liberalization associated with de-Stalinization, their response tended to take the form of massive relaxation rather than an upsurge of zeal and rededication. Moreover, among the most ideologically committed and politically conscious members of the group, Khrushchev's revelations about the "crimes of the Stalin era" often led to extreme disorientation. These men were compelled to call their entire pasts into question, and the accompanying confusion probably served even further to inhibit bold action and to encourage adherence to routine. This factor also may help to explain the existence of a situation that Khrushchev described in the following terms:

> We still have many officials . . . who fear everything that is new and advanced. An old fossil of an official argues: "Why should I become mixed up in all this? There will be a lot of bother and it might even lead to unpleasantness. They talk about improving production! . . . Let the high-ups worry! Let the top men do the thinking. When a directive comes we'll see about it!" Another official, after he has received instructions, directs his energies largely to evading a vital job or merely going through the motions of tackling it.[102]

In sum, it seems probable that in a number of critical respects, many members of the postpurge managerial elite were deficient in the kind of enterprise that was necessary for successful economic leadership in the post-Stalin era. Accordingly, Khrushchev may well have been correct in his conviction that without a thoroughgoing renewal of cadres, the sort of "rational" entrepreneurial stimuli that some Soviet economists and economic officials had begun to advocate would be of doubtful efficacy. But, whether correct or not, Khrushchev appears to have been acting on the basis of just such a conviction, and this was one of the major factors behind his sponsorship of the new (bloodless) purge. At the same time, there can be no doubt that other factors also played a role, including a desire on Khrushchev's part to achieve two complementary political goals: the prevention of social routinization or "normalization" and the consolidation of his personal power.

Khrushchev was obviously greatly concerned over the widespread indulgence by the new class of various "bourgeois instincts," including the accumulation of private property, the abuse of official positions for personal profit, and the pampering and overprotection of children.[103] Though these "retrograde" practices were not new to the Soviet scene, the curtailment of terror had probably made them more common and heightened the danger that they would culminate in the transformation of the new class from a service elite or state bourgeoisie into an autonomous upper class. This development was one that Khrushchev was determined to prevent, and he apparently decided that the specific remedial measures he adopted — a reduction of income differentials, a ban on the construction of private homes, and so on[104] — would be nothing more than palliatives unless they were accompanied by increased "circulation" within the elite. In the party apparat, he introduced the "permanent purge" as a constitutional provision, and the "renewal of cadres" in the industrial establishment was a manifestation of the same basic approach.[105] In both cases what Khrushchev was seeking was a functional analogue of or surrogate for Stalinist terror, for he, no less than Stalin, was committed to eternal warfare against the ever-present danger of "bourgeoisification." Far from wanting an autonomous society to develop alongside the polity, Khrushchev was determined to extend the already overwhelming hegemony of the political system over all facets of social life.[106] Moreover, within the framework of this all-embracing political system, he was bent on consolidating absolute personal power. This last desire, in turn, was yet another of the motives behind the continuing renewal of managerial cadres.

In terms of its direct political significance, the purge of the managerial corps was designed to fill the industrial establishment with men who were untainted by association with the anti-Khrushchev opposition and completely beholden to Khrushchev for their promotion to elite status. Clearly, such men could only be recruited from among the younger members of the technical intelligentsia, and, to borrow a phrase from the Soviet lexicon, it was not accidental that Khrushchev's speeches incessantly stressed the need to promote young specialists and engineers:

142

fresh, forward-looking cadres of recent academic vintage and a post-Stalinist "party stage." [107] This accent on youth goes a long way toward explaining why Khrushchev began his purge of the industrial establishment at the bottom rather than the top, for the immediate advancement to top leadership posts of men who had only recently risen to executive rank would have entailed immense economic costs.

To be sure, as the example of Stalin's own renewal of managerial cadres indicates, such costs need not have acted as an absolute deterrent. Khrushchev, though, was neither as all-powerful nor as unconcerned with economic cost accounting as his predecessor, and his policy was more restrained. Whereas Stalin had been willing to risk a radical drop in productivity in conjunction with the liquidation of the red directors and promotion of the red specialists, Khrushchev was prepared to hold off the definitive "Khrushchevization" of the industrial establishment until the men he had in mind for top leadership posts had accumulated a reasonable amount of experience. And in the interim, he was willing to leave the old leading cadres in their posts. His decisive triumph at the June 1957 Central Committee plenum greatly lessened the risks that attached to their retention, and the option of replacing them with the second-echelon cadres who comprised the only available pool of experienced personnel had no great appeal. In many cases the members of the middle-management elite were themselves erstwhile oppositionists, and most of them were probably considerably less well endowed than their superiors with entrepreneurial skills. However, if the ex-ministers, top ministerial officials, and first-rank directors had much to recommend them in Khrushchev's eyes, it was only for the time being.

In the not too distant future these cadres were also slated for renewal, and, during the next several years it became increasingly apparent that the time of reckoning would not be long delayed. By the end of 1962 and beginning of 1963, it seemed clear that Khrushchev was ready to apply his oft-repeated principle on "the need to avoid retaining oldtimers too long" to the leading managers.[108] The "young, literate people" whom he had been pushing ahead for the past five years were now ready for high-level posts, and their promotion was now on the agenda. Moreover, this promotion was to take place in a highly favorable organizational context.

If Khrushchev's renewal of managerial cadres was similar to Stalin's in that it was designed to place industrial leadership in the hands of men who were free of any taint of opposition and wholly indebted to the man in power, for their rise, it was also similar in that it was associated with a policy of reducing the authority of the party apparat relative to that of the state bureaucracy. In both cases, moreover, this policy was initiated by the ruler's decision to assume the office of premier in addition to the office of first secretary of the party. But the changes in organizational policy that followed Khrushchev's assumption of the premiership in March 1958 were even more radical and discontinuous than those introduced by Stalin in the period after 1941.[109] Indeed, it is not too much to say that the established organizational policy did a virtually complete about-face in the last five years of Khrushchev's rule.

With regard to industrial organization, for example, Khrushchev celebrated his accession to the post of the ousted Bulganin by launching a vigorous policy of economic recentralization — so vigorous, in fact, that the subsequent period witnessed what was in effect, if not in name, the almost complete reconstitution of the old ministerial system. Only the final step remained to be taken, and it seemed clear that it would be taken as soon as the renewal of cadres was completed. Economic recentralization, though, was only the lesser part of the story, for at the same time that Khrushchev reorganized the industrial establishment along lines that ran directly counter to the "spirit of 1957," he reorganized the party apparat along lines that were inimical not only to the spirit of 1957 but even to the "spirit of 1917." These two processes of reorganization, in turn, were mutually reinforcing, and their development made it clear that what Khrushchev had in mind with regard to party-state relations was not merely a restoration of the pre-1957 status quo ante, but a substantial downgrading of the traditional status of the apparat.

Although Khrushchev had previously sponsored a number of significant measures of economic recentralization, the first point at which the full scope of his intentions was revealed was the Central Committee plenum of November 1962.[110] Only then did he seek and gain Central Committee approval for such far-reaching measures as the formation of an All-Russian Council of the National Economy, the creation of a single interrepublic sovnarkhoz for the Central Asian republics, a massive consolidation of regional economic councils, and the establishment of a multitude of new production-branch state committees with broad supervisory powers over the conduct of local economic operations — thereby making it clear that he was ready to write off the 1957 economic reorganization altogether. Similarly, while he had indicated a willingness to curtail the overwhelming primacy of the apparat from 1958 on, it was only in November 1962 that Khrushchev revealed a willingness radically to reduce the apparat's power. Nor is there any doubt that this was precisely what the decisions of the November plenum in regard to party organization revealed.

To take the most important of these well-known decisions, it is obvious that the bifurcation of the party along territorial production-branch lines, with the establishment of separate party committees for agriculture and industry at all subnational levels, implied a wholesale emasculation of the apparat's power. At a single blow, the politically critical obkoms were transformed into specialized administrative "transmission belts" devoid of almost all significant policy-making authority; and the strategic elite of obkom secretaries, the dominant group within the Cen-

145

tral Committee, was doubled in size and reconstituted as a corps of glorified low-level economic controllers.[111] No amount of official rhetoric could conceal the fact that these changes dealt the entire party apparat a potentially crippling blow. And the concurrent changes in industrial organization clearly indicated that it was the state bureaucracy which had been singled out as the principal repository of the authority being wrenched from the obkoms and their staffs. Indeed, in the circumstances, no alternative repository could have been selected, for Khrushchev was not prepared to reconstruct the bureaucratic empire of the secret police, and he was not yet powerful enough to establish an ubiquitous personal secretariat.

As these last remarks suggest, Khrushchev's radical downgrading of the party apparat was undoubtedly motivated by a desire for political self-aggrandizement. More particularly, it was motivated by Khrushchev's wish to free himself from the need to rely excessively on any single instrument of rule, to reduce his dependence on the "constituency" from which the bulk of his power had derived, and to undercut the power of a number of Presidium members whom he himself had elevated to the ruling elite but who nonetheless possessed a significant measure of independent support within the party. Of these three closely interrelated purposes, it was almost certainly the last which loomed largest in Khrushchev's calculations, for the Presidium members in question had demonstrated a periodic willingness to join forces and to utilize their independent power to balk a number of the would-be autocrat's major policy initiatives.[112] It was this phenomenon that above all else inspired Khrushchev to give the 1962 party reorganization so radical a cast.

That a substantial number of Khrushchev's colleagues on the Presidium and almost all leading apparatchiki were opposed to the 1962 party reorganization was strongly suggested at the time and has been amply confirmed by subsequent events.[113] In November 1962, however, the oppositionists were confronted with an alignment of forces which made overt resistance hopeless, and the Central Committee plenum bowed to Khrushchev's will without significant public protest or dissent. Khrushchev had marshaled his support with care, and it seemed likely that the next months would witness rapid progress toward his goal of autocratic power. But appearances were deceptive. In early 1963 a number of the programs that Khrushchev had previously advocated without success were implemented, but the same year provided clear signs that Khrushchev's opponents had not been so weakened by the reorganization of the party apparat as to be incapable of effective rear-guard action and occasional counterattack.[114] They still kept their seats in the country's leading political organ, and Khrushchev's obvious reluctance to use terror emboldened them to maintain their struggle rather than to acknowledge defeat and plead for mercy. Moreover, a number of Khrushchev's erstwhile allies seem to have had second thoughts about the implications of his moves for their own status and security, particularly in the summer of 1964 when Khrushchev indicated a desire to establish a far-flung personal secretariat, headed by his son-in-law Adzhubei. Finally, still other members of Khrushchev's camp became disillusioned with the increasingly obvious failure of many of their mentor's economic programs and foreign-policy initiatives. In short, Khrushchev's own forces began to disintegrate and desert him before he succeeded in crushing the residual power of those who had shown independence in the past; his position underwent a rapid deterioration at the very moment it seemed on the verge of becoming unassailable. This deterioration, in turn, set the stage for the palace revolution of October 1964, the carefully planned conspiracy that ended in Khrushchev's sudden deposition.

THE FALL OF KHRUSHCHEV AND ITS CONSEQUENCES

That the leaders of the industrial establishment played any significant part in Khrushchev's ouster is extremely doubtful. It is possible that Kosygin drew a few of his former managerial colleagues into the final stages of the anti-Khrushchev conspiracy — but the circle of conspirators appears to have been limited to members of the Presidium until the very last moment, and even at the end it appears to have been confined primarily to high-level apparatchiki. Moreover, the satisfaction that the hold-over managers felt at being avenged for past defeats was undoubtedly tempered by the new regime's first policy initiatives: almost all of them, particularly the immediate revocation of the party reorganization of November 1962, bespoke an overriding concern for the welfare of the party apparat and its leading cadres.[115] Even the new premier, Kosygin, was a peculiarly "unmanagerial" manager who had always enjoyed the special trust of apparat-dominated factions, and, apart from his promotion, the principal personnel changes sponsored by the new regime showed minimal concern for managerial prestige.[116] Thus, of the four men promoted to the Presidium following Khrushchev's ouster, three (Shelepin, Shelest, and Demichev) were men whose careers had been associated almost entirely with the party apparat.[117] However, if these signs of apparat resurgency somewhat dampened the enthusiasm with which the leaders of the industrial establishment greeted Khrushchev's ouster, subsequent developments have probably enhanced their satisfaction.

If the new regime made it clear that its first concern was the vitality of the party apparat, its initial policy was in no sense antimanagerial, and it has since begun to show increasing receptivity to managerial claims and demands. It has extended Khrushchev's commitment to realistic planning and taken unprecedented steps in the direction of enterprise autonomy. Simultaneously it has carried forward Khrushchev's policy of economic recentralization, thereby alleviating any fear that the reunification of the party apparat signaled a return to the sort of apparat-dominated administrative system that prevailed (though to a diminishing extent) in the period 1957–1962.[118] In addition, by appointing Kosygin premier and allowing him considerable freedom of action, the new regime has indicated a willingness to accord the leaders of the industrial establishment high symbolic status and a pledge of continued receptivity to managerial demands. If Kosygin has not been a vigorous champion of managerial interests in the past, he is nonetheless the first full-fledged member of the managerial elite to be elevated to the premiership. Further, the fact that his prestige and authority are now vested directly in the state machine virtually ensures that he will prove a more consistent representative of his colleagues. Indeed, the leaders of the industrial establishment may well anticipate that Kosygin will emerge as the protagonist of a more or less unqualifiedly "promanagerial platform," the realization of which would secure them a decisive voice in the policy process. With the experience of the post-Stalin succession struggle behind him, Kosygin is likely to be especially wary of supporting policies that could lead his colleagues in the Presidium to see him as a new Malenkov, trying to use the state machine as a basis for political self-aggrandizement. But the managerial elite is nonetheless his natural political constituency. To the degree that he is personally ambitious or becomes involved in power-political conflict, the logic of his institutional position dictates that he try above all to mobilize managerial support. Moreover, even if Kosygin were not directly involved or were once again to play a "renegade" role, a new succession struggle would almost certainly find the principal rivals for power engaged in an active quest for managerial support, thereby providing the industrial leaders with substantial political leverage and new opportunities to propel policy in directions highly favorable to their interests.

At this writing it is too early to tell whether the leaders of the industrial establishment will in fact reap any sizable share of the political benefits that could accrue to them in consequence of the events of October 1964. The situation is still in a state of flux, and it is not my intention here to trace the various power-political outcomes that might ultimately take place. Rather, for present purposes, it suffices to register two less speculative points.

In the first place, it seems reasonably clear that the current leaders of the industrial establishment will not attempt to use whatever increment of power they may achieve to effect fundamental changes in the structure of the Soviet system. As already indicated, their basic outlook is overwhelmingly conservative, and their response to any new opportunities for the exercise of influence and power will almost certainly continue to reflect this outlook. If it is true, as some analysts have suggested, that the "failure" of Khrushchevism shows that the Soviet system has advanced to the point where fundamental changes are unavoidable, it is nonetheless likely that the leader of the industrial establishment will seek to hold such changes to a minimum.[119] Thus, while continuing to press for greater operational autonomy within their own sphere, the managers will resist any extensive decentralization of authority outside that sphere. Similarly, while continuing to press for greater realism in economic planning, they will resist any large-scale shift of resources from heavy to light industry. In Khrushchev's words, they will remain "steel eaters" par excellence.[120] Finally, while continuing to demand freedom from political and ideological constraints in the enjoyment of their socioeconomic privileges, they will resist any social relaxation that might call the legitimacy of their advantaged status into question. In sum, the leaders of the industrial establishment will be a retrograde force, seeking to hold change within narrowly circumscribed channels, if not actually to restore the status quo ante of the period 1953–1956. Their rise to a position of significant influence or power might eventually lead to a "degeneration" of the political system, but it would almost certainly not lead to a vigorous and purposeful reorientation of the system to accommodate new demands and solve new problems. It seems unwarranted, however, to discuss the role of the current leaders of the industrial establishment in long-run terms.

Although they were very young when they made their debuts as members of the managerial elite, the leaders of the industrial establishment are now approaching old age. Most of them are in their sixties, and age alone will suffice to keep their tenure in office relatively brief. Moreover, it is by no means certain that they will not be retired prematurely, albeit according to a more dilatory schedule than the one Khrushchev had in mind.[121] Unless they can accumulate a considerable amount of power, in fact, they are likely to be retired in the relatively near future. For one thing, any reasonably stable regime that does not depend heavily on managerial support is likely to be anxious to turn over the leadership of the industrial establishment to men of its own choosing. In addition, the cadres that now fill the middle ranks of the managerial elite have had their expectations of rapid advancement aroused, and any regime that can afford to calculate in other than strictly short-run terms is likely to weigh the danger of frustrating these expectations at a heavy premium — the more so because there is no reason to suspect that these cadres retain any personal loyalty to Khrushchev, and every reason to believe that they will prove more effective economic entrepreneurs than their present superiors.[122] In any event, it is certain that these younger men will dominate the industrial establishment before too much time has passed, and it is clearly they rather than the remaining red specialists who will primarily determine the future contribution of the managerial elite to Soviet political development.

★ 6 ★

THE EMERGING MANAGERIAL ELITE

> After the death of Stalin we entered
> upon a period of destruction and re-evalua-
> tion. It is a slow and inconsistent process,
> it lacks perspective, and the inertia of both
> past and future lie heavy on it. Today's
> children will scarcely be able to produce a
> new God, capable of inspiring humanity
> into the next historical cycle. Maybe He
> will have to be supplemented by other
> stakes of the Inquisition, by further "per-
> sonality cults," and by new terrestial labors,
> so that after many centuries a new Purpose
> will rise above the world. But today no one
> yet knows its name.
> > Abram Tertz, *On Socialist Realism*
> > (trans. Dennis)

> I really think that what we are discussing
> boils down to the Party's future recruiting
> program; if the Party can enlist enough
> people whose ideas and opinions coincide
> with its own, then perhaps it can last for a
> very long time. But is this actually possible?
> > George Kennan (in Aron, ed.,
> > *World Technology*, p. 86)

In 1964 *Izvestia* published a profile of L. M. Filyukov, the
newly appointed director of the Bryansk machinebuilding plant,
thereby introducing its readers to a more or less typical representative of the cadres that will soon displace the red specialists
as the dominant group within the Soviet industrial establishment.[1]
Like Filyukov, most of the members of the emerging managerial

152

elite are men in their thirties or forties, who received their technical training in first-class schools and institutes, and there is every reason to believe that they are highly skilled engineers with a thorough grasp of technological processes and a genuine commitment to technical innovation.[2] Moreover, if they are not so already, most of these men will probably soon become as skilled as Filyukov is alleged to be in the use of a persuasive or consultative managerial style.

Although many young Soviet engineers appear to have had difficulty in disengaging themselves from a purely technological perspective and adjusting to the larger problems of "human engineering" that executive responsibility entails, much of this difficulty derives from the rapidity with which the new managers have been promoted and is hence likely to prove short-lived. This is the more probable because the regime, in a striking new departure, has introduced a number of Western-type training and retraining programs in "business administration" and the "sociology of industrial management."[3] Given access to such programs and additional experience in their new roles, it is virtually certain that the men concerned will become much more adept than the red specialists in the modern executive arts of coordination, consultation, negotiation, and persuasion. Unlike the red specialists, the "Filyukovs" are neither so insecure in their status nor so habituated to "commandism" as to make the adoption of a democratic managerial style a psychological or operational impossibility. And they undoubtedly possess a real intellectual and professional appreciation of the technical and social developments which make the adoption of such a style imperative. In sum, insofar as the problem of lack of entrepreneurialism is a function of the training, outlook, and orientation of the cadres who occupy the strategic posts in the industrial establishment, it is probable that the promotion of men such as Filyukov will prove an effective countermeasure.[4]

If the members of the new managerial elite do prove to be

more effective entrepreneurs than the red specialists, they will automatically make an important contribution to the Soviet system's capacity for maintenance and growth. The question remains, however, whether their more explicitly political behavior will contribute to the same end. Will the history of the post-Khrushchev era at long last confirm the expectations of those who look to the Soviet managerial elite as the vanguard of rapid political change? This is the question to be investigated in the following pages. Before proceeding, however, it seems advisable to point out that any pressure for rapid political change that is applied by the emerging managerial elite is much more likely to be directed toward the establishment of a technocratic order than toward the creation of a liberal democracy. Technocrats are far more numerous than democrats among the young engineers and industrial specialists of the Filyukov generation, and, even on a man-for-man basis, they are far more likely to become caught up in the managerial recruitment process.

That there are men of liberal disposition among the young engineers and industrial specialists of the Filyukov generation is certain. The presence of these men is implicit in the various statements in which Yevtushenko, Voznesensky, and other "literary rebels" have identified the young technical intelligentsia as the group most responsive to their "dissonant voices." [5] And it is amply confirmed by my own firsthand observations.[6]

To be sure, many of the men in question think of themselves as neo-Marxists or neo-Leninists. Their liberalism often takes the form of a commitment to a system of tutelary democracy rather than one of popular self-government and institutionalized protection for civil rights. But they are nonetheless animated by the vision of an open society on Western lines. If their imagery is that of "the Revolution betrayed" and their goal is to recover the purity they believe to have been present in early Bolshevism, they nonetheless interpret Marxism-Leninism in radically revisionist terms. Thus they reject not only the cult of personality

154

and the use of terror, but also the principle of monolithic unity and the total subordination of the individual to the collective will. Moreover, as contact with the West increases, they will undoubtedly become more genuinely democratic in their outlook. They are highly responsive to "alien" influences, and their critical temper is such that norms of tolerance and freedom will acquire progressively greater importance in their scheme of values as they see such norms in operation. Even now the young engineer who identified himself to the author as a Jeffersonian and professed his commitment to the inalienable rights of man is not alone, and his views are likely to find even more supporters in the near future. However, if liberalism is neither unknown nor without a certain potentiality for growth, technocratism is far more common and is likely to grow at an even faster pace. The criticism in official media leaves little doubt on this score, and contact with the men concerned suffices to dissolve what doubt remains.

Although Western writings on the Soviet technical intelligentsia often fail to distinguish between liberals and technocrats, the two groups are in fact quite distinct. Thus, though the technocrats sometimes sympathize with the "literary opposition" on particular issues, their basic vision is anything but liberal. On the contrary, their ultimate outlook was well described by *Komsomolskaya pravda* when it complained that

there are in our country many [members of the younger technical intelligentsia] . . . for whom there is a gulf separating the work of an engineer from that of an ordinary worker and who have nothing but contempt for those who are engaged in production . . . [believing that] it is the exclusive task of the engineer to make plans and that of the workers to carry them out.[7]

Far from feeling a sense of solidarity with the cultural intelligentsia, the technocrats frequently reject literature and the arts altogether and set themselves up as apostles of a self-contained and superordinate "scientific culture." They are the physicists whom the novelist Tendryakov has in mind when he speaks of the "physicists" and "lyricists" as two contrasting and contentious types within the ranks of Soviet youth.[8] Similarly, in a dichotomy articulated by a young engineer during the course of an attack on Yevtushenko "and his ilk," they are the *tekhniki* (technicians) as opposed to the *gumanshiki* (humanists).[9] To the degree that the technocrats really identify with any literary tendency, it is with the one represented by writers such as Granin and Dudintsev, who are themselves technocratically inclined.[10] If they have a literary hero at all, he is the engineer Lopatkin, the hero of Dudintsev's *Not by Bread Alone*, who, having finally managed to win reluctant acceptance for his important new invention, remembers the words of a close friend who had once said to him, "Listen well, one day you'll enter politics."[11] Like Lopatkin, many of them are fascinated by the notion that their technical expertise implies special political rights — rights that attach to them as members of a self-perpetuating elite ("upper-story men," in Dudintsev's phrase) who are predestined to rule the world in accord with the dictates of scientific rationality. This rationality, in turn, implies comprehensive economic planning and all-embracing social control.

As I indicated in my second chapter, this technocratic vision is not in principle as far removed from Bolshevik ideology as one might at first suppose. In this connection it is worth recalling Lenin's remarks to the Eighth Congress of Soviets regarding "the happy era when [pure] politicians will grow ever fewer in number . . . and engineers and agronomists will do most of the talking." It is worth remarking too that Khrushchev explicitly reaffirmed the legitimacy of this image in 1959, in his report to the Twenty-First Party Congress.[12] Still, principle is one thing, practice another. And, in practice, the disparity between the vision of the young technocrats and the "happy era" of Lenin and Khrushchev is immense. For the technocrats not only fail to recognize Marxism-Leninism as the master science, they refuse to recognize it as science at all. As party ideologist L. F. Ilichev has put it: "Among some part of our intelligentsia an incorrect attitude toward the social sciences has grown up. Some reason approximately as follows: Now, technical science — that's important; but social science — what has it to offer; only theories; nothing concrete." [13]

Clearly, this outlook is no less ominous than liberalism is from the point of view of the regime. Were it to be widely represented within the ranks of the emerging managerial elite, it would undoubtedly foreshadow radical political change. In point of fact, however, neither liberalism nor technocratism nor any close approximations thereof are likely to bulk large in the political outlooks of the new managers. Any other conclusions seems almost inconceivable when one considers the socialization and recruitment experiences of the men who will soon dominate the Soviet industrial apparatus.

THE POLITICAL SOCIALIZATION AND RECRUITMENT
OF THE NEW MANAGERIAL ELITE

The technical intelligentsia of the Filyukov generation is comprised of men who were exposed during their formative years (during the 1930s) to an unprecedentedly intense and thoroughgoing process of totalitarian political socialization. Most of them were reared in "new-class" homes in an atmosphere informed by genuine support for the regime and active commitment to official goals and policies.[14] Moreover, even those of their parents who were themselves alienated from or hostile to the regime were usually anxious to enhance their children's career prospects and hence made a concerted attempt to inculcate a proper political outlook.[15] In all cases, the effort to inculcate "pro-regime" values and attitudes that was begun in the family was reinforced and carried forward at an ever-accelerating tempo in the schools.

By the time the Filyukov generation entered school during

the 1940s, educational indoctrination was both ubiquitous and systematic. Students at all levels received a rigorous and intensive ideological "molding" in accord with a carefully designed program of "political upbringing." [16] In order to imbue them with "Soviet patriotism," their very first readers and songbooks proclaimed that "everywhere in all spheres . . . the Soviet people march in the forefront of other nations," and their primary-school teachers tried to make certain that they realized "not only with their minds but with their hearts" that "capitalism is hunger, unemployment, and eternal fear of tomorrow." [17] It was expected that an emotionally charged juxtaposition of the glories of Soviet life and the horrors of life elsewhere would "foster a hatred for the exploiters" and give rise to a feeling on the part of the students that they stood in debt before their own society and were obliged to repay its beneficence with endless and unstinting service.[18] To indicate the type of service that was desired, primers and grade-school texts were replete with hagiographic biographies of famous political leaders, valiant soldiers, and outstanding scientists, whose lives embodied such proletarian virtues as love of labor, "personal self-sacrifice with the aim of bringing victory to the fatherland," and "devotion to revolutionary and scientific ideas." [19] And, once again, as in the case of the picture of the world at large, graphic examples of negative heroes were juxtaposed to the portraits of positive heroes in order to reinforce assimilation of the correct character traits. The dichotomous image of the world was complemented by a dichotomous image of human nature, and every effort was made to inculcate a radical intolerance of ambiguity.

At the secondary levels of the educational system, the indoctrinational themes were essentially the same, although the approach became more sophisticated and progressively greater amounts of time and energy were devoted to the development of proper orientations toward the regime and governmental levels of the political system. The quest was now for a "convictional certainty," which was to rise out of but also transcend the emotional predispositions built up in the earlier grades, so that the students' emotional revulsion against the West and love for the Soviet Union would be complemented by a "conviction in the inevitable victory of socialism."[20] In addition, increasing attention was devoted during these years to cultivating a "class point of view" and training students to unmask and expose the class essence of ideas.[21] But what was sought was total loyalty to the party rather than ideological finesse. Indeed, there was an implicit recognition that, until the students had been subjected to an all-out attempt to socialize them into party loyalty, familiarity with the niceties of historical and dialectical materialism could lead to "confusion" and provide a standard by which to judge the party and resist changes in the party line.[22] Accordingly, it was only in the institutions of higher education that the formal study of Marxism-Leninism was introduced.

It was only at this stage that the regime could be reasonably sure that students had acquired not only discipline — officially defined as "submission to the will of a leader" — but also self-discipline — officially defined as spontaneous "conformity and obedience."[23] It was only now that the regime could tell whether or not it had begun to achieve its goal of educating students who had "no interests opposed to the collective interests" and training young people who were at once "people of initiative" and people who were prepared to restrict the exercise of this initiative to the purely instrumental level, where it would find expression as "an independent search for the best way to fulfill a command."[24] Having reached its decision and admitted the young people to its institutions of higher education, however, the regime wasted no time in introducing formal training in official doctrine. Although higher education was otherwise strictly specialized, all university students were required to take several courses in Marxism-Leninism and other related subjects. These courses in turn were explicitly designed to consolidate the world view of that segment of Soviet youth from whose ranks would come the elite cadres of Soviet society and to ensure that these cadres would approach their future assignments from a "party-spirited" point of view, making the proper choice — the choice in conformity with the regime's current schedule of priorities — among the conflicting alternatives that would confront them as they moved up the ladder of success and were accorded more and more operational autonomy.

That these socialization experiences did not always produce perfect examples of the new Soviet man was obvious even before Stalin's death. It is evident that only the existence of a genuine problem could have impelled the aging general secretary to make the startling admission that a generation which had lived virtually its entire life under Stalinism and had received its education in the finest Soviet schools contained "thousands of . . . cadres who . . . [lack] an adequate Marxist education, [are] uninformed of many truths . . . and [are] thus obliged to wander in the dark." [25] This problem, of course, was the product of many factors. In the first place, many parents whose political orientation was completely orthodox proved unwilling or unable to prevent their children from becoming complacent "white hands," taking their privileged status for granted and lacking any sense of intense political obligation or dedicated commitment to the regime's chiliastic goals.[26] In addition, still other parents, with a more qualified loyalty to the Bolshevik cause, found it impossible to avoid transmitting certain reservations to their offspring. The latter were thus predisposed to approach their formal political education with considerable ambivalence, if not outright skepticism, and the school system often proved unable to overcome this heritage of doubt. Indeed, in many cases political education was conducted in so crude and rigid a fashion that it provoked profound emotional revulsion and intellectual dissent in its own right.[27] Moreover, even where it was more successful from an official point of view, its successes often proved short-lived.

Under Stalinism the disparity between the textbook description of reality and reality itself was so great that even exemplary students sometimes fell into cynical disillusionment at their first contact with the adult world. As one university graduate put it, "When we graduated . . . we had no idea what a complex joke life could sometimes be. We walked into it with eyes shut. Many of us got our heads bloodied, and that first painful collision turned into something of a moral crash." [28] And, to bring the story up to date, many youths whose faith survived the shock of contact with the actualities of full-fledged Stalinism were badly shaken by the subsequent demolition of the Stalin cult. Even Soviet sources acknowledge that de-Stalinization tended to produce "a trauma in impressionable young souls." [29] But, though all these points are undeniable, they give a distorted picture of the political outlook of the emergent managerial elite.

Even when they left much to be desired from the point of view of the regime, the combined efforts of parents and teachers to socialize the members of the Filyukov generation usually yielded significant returns. At the very least, these pressures usually left those who experienced them with a strong conviction of the underlying legitimacy of the Soviet system and a predisposition in favor of within-system change as opposed to systemic change. [30] Similarly, while contact with the adult world sometimes brought disillusionment in its wake, it often brought the fulfillment of expectations of elite status, access to a wide range of gratifying privileges and perquisites, and involvement in the consensus-generating dynamics of responsible work. Also, while the process of de-Stalinization sometimes produced a trauma, the changes introduced after Stalin's death frequently eradicated major sources of discontent, dissolved serious doubts, and reinforced loyalty to the system.

The cumulative impact of these stabilizing pressures should

161

not be underestimated. Refugee interviews and data collected on the scene by later Western scholars leave little doubt about the basically conservative political outlook of the majority of the young engineers and industrial specialists of the Filyukov generation. That there are many exceptions is impressive testimony to the capacity of the human spirit to overcome indoctrination and to resist the temptation of compromising fundamental values for the sake of material benefits and careerist goals — but, for all that, the exceptions remain exceptions.

THE POLITICAL OUTLOOK OF THE NEW MANAGERIAL ELITE

My own contact with the younger generation of the Soviet technical intelligentsia has left me strongly convinced that this group contains a substantial number of individuals who qualify for all practical purposes as full-fledged new Soviet men.[31] Nor should one think of these men, who might also be characterized as ideologically committed political activists, as fanatics whose political activism assumes forms that are incompatible with managerial effectiveness. On the contrary, most of them are relatively strong-minded realists, well aware of the "imperatives" of economic and technical rationality and anxious to see that these imperatives are taken into account in the policy process. At the same time, however, their realism is confined within a broader ideological orthodoxy and finds its principal expression in implementation of the established party line. Although they are prepared to engage in some "creative interpretation" of traditional doctrine, they are genuine true believers who are convinced that progress can and must be attained without departure from the fundamental tenets of Marxism-Leninism or deviation from doctrinally sanctioned goals or procedures. In short, though the young men in question show significant individual differences in the way in which the various components are mingled, none of their evaluations of the present or aspirations for the future transcends the limits inherent in a blend of

Marxist idealism, Leninist fanaticism, Stalinist authoritarianism, and Khrushchevean pragmatism. The net effect is a political outlook characterized by unwavering devotion to the Soviet system and to almost all of the basic principles of social, economic, and political organization that it embodies.

As I have already noted, unqualified loyalty and self-sustaining activism are relatively rare commodities in any political system, and the foregoing discussion is not intended to suggest that the ideologically committed political activists are typical representatives of the younger Soviet technical intelligentsia. However, these activists are far more numerous than is ordinarily recognized in the West, and there is every reason to believe that they will attain positions of great prominence in the near future. Moreover, if the majority of their compeers are unworthy of the title "new Soviet man," they are infinitely less deserving of the title "gravediggers of Communism."

If most young Soviet engineers are not paragons of official virtue, they nonetheless display a marked tendency to view Soviet reality through the glow of their own contentment — a contentment that derives from their having been raised in affluent and privileged families, educated in the best Soviet schools, and launched by the regime upon promising careers. Similarly, if their orientation toward life is more contemporaneous than chiliastic, their basic Weltanschaunng is firmly rooted in Marxist-Leninist doctrine and their policy views are permeated with ideological content. Again, if they favor a more relaxed policy of social control and are restive because of the total politicization of Soviet life, they fully accept the principle of collectivism and the doctrine of single-party rule, and are largely unconcerned with individual rights and civil liberties. And so on and so forth, for the basic pattern is already quite familiar from my earlier discussion of the political outlook of the post-purge managerial elite. To put the case in summary form, if the grievances of the majority of the younger technical intelligentsia are not entirely inconsequential, they are nonetheless circumscribed by a framework of consensus and are characterized by too high a degree of specificity, too low a level of intensity, and too great a lack of programmatic integration to portend any effort to initate rapid or extensive political change.

If statistical probability alone points to the conclusion that the number of political dissidents or near-dissidents in the emerging managerial elite will be strictly limited, analysis of the regime's managerial recruitment process makes this conclusion even more compelling. Before turning to such an analysis, however, it is worth noting that many of the liberals and technocrats within the ranks of the younger technical intelligentsia consciously try to avoid assignments that might require them to compromise their most cherished principles and to assume the onus of responsibility for the very policies that alienate them from the regime. Among other things, this is one of the factors behind the "flight" from production to research which characterizes the behavior of many young engineers and industrial specialists — but it probably finds its most graphic expression in refusal to join the party.[32] Since party membership remains a virtual prerequisite for promotion to high executive rank, such refusal constitutes a practically foolproof method of withdrawing oneself from the list of managerial candidates, and it is one to which the political dissidents among the young engineers and industrial specialists frequently resort. But, by the same token, the political reliability of the manpower pool from which the regime draws its managers is considerably enhanced.

When self-selection ceases to operate, restrictive selection takes over, and these two processes are complementary. Although there is no doubt that professionalistic and achievement-oriented criteria have recently assumed increasing priority over political criteria in the recruitment of managerial personnel, political criteria continue to play a prominent role. Among other things, the previously noted exclusion of virtually all non-Communists from the recruitment process is clear evidence that this is so. Nor can the regime's requirements be satisfied by merely formal membership in the party. On the contrary, the regime demands that candidates for high executive posts be active and dedicated Communists, wholly committed to the Marxist-Leninist cause. As the editors of *Pravda* put it:

In order to conform to the profile of a real Communist leader it is necessary to be not only a good practical worker, possessed of appropriate technical qualifications, but also a politician who views things in the perspective of the party and the state, knows how to look ahead, and is able to lead the masses with conviction, inspiring them with faith in the victory of our common cause . . . This means above all [that one must] know and understand the party line and the course that the country must follow in order successfully to fulfill the party's decisions.[33]

And there is no doubt that the regime makes strenuous efforts to put such demands into effect.

Even a cursory examination of the current Soviet press reveals that personnel review boards are under orders to place heavy emphasis on the degree to which candidates for executive posts have proved willing to assume extensive social obligations and to participate actively in agitation and propaganda work among the masses, as well as in the activities of the various public organizations whose proliferation has been so marked a feature of the recent Soviet scene. Moreover, in view of the fact that the part played by the party apparat in review procedures has not diminished and may actually have increased in recent years, there is no reason to doubt that the regime's orders are faithfully observed.[34] Since even those political deviants who are willing to join the party are often either unwilling to become party activists or unable to perform the role in a manner that satisfies the personnel officers in the party apparat, the odds against the new managerial elite's containing any substantial number of dissenters are correspondingly enhanced. To be sure, "mistakes" have occurred in the recruitment process, and they will undoubtedly occur again. But they will almost certainly be confined to the lower echelons of the managerial elite, and even there they will be infrequent. At a minimum, the overwhelming majority of the new managers will be comprised of men who are basically loyal organization men, with a well-developed tendency toward political conformity. And there is a high probability that the most strategic managerial posts will be occupied by committed political activists of the sort already described.

That ideologically committed political activists will dominate the post-Khrushchev industrial establishment is strongly suggested not only by our knowledge of official recruitment policy as such, but also by the evidence that is available on individual career patterns. Thus, of the activists known to me, most are men whom the regime identified as potential leaders early in their lives and whose careers to date have been characterized by an ever more comprehensive initiation into the rites of executive responsibility. In the universities and institutes, for example, they were regularly selected to serve on the Komsomol committees of their schools, and their postgraduate careers have witnessed a series of rapid promotions within the industrial bureaucracy, interrupted on occasion by short-term assignments in the party apparat.[35] In addition, not a few of them have been posted to booster courses in special party-state schools, whose programs are designed to prepare carefully selected cadres for upper-echelon command posts. All of these considerations leave little doubt that the outlooks of the new leaders of the industrial establishment will be fairly orthodox, and there is every reason to believe that it is they rather than their less exemplary colleagues and subordinates who will determine the main direction of managerial politics in the decades to come. Moreover, to reiterate what was said above, these colleagues and subordinates will themselves embody a set of values, attitudes, and beliefs that is essentially supportive of the established political order and of the system of social and economic organization on which it rests.

The foregoing analysis is not intended to suggest that the emerging managerial elite will fail to advocate any changes in established practices once it achieves real scope for independent action. On the contrary, it is practically certain that the new managers will press for operational autonomy and procedurally stabilized access to the policy process within their own spheres. Pursuit of these goals is virtually a corollary of involvement in a managerial career, and here even those of the new managers whose basic outlooks qualify them as paragons of political orthodoxy will undoubtedly run true to form. Further, there is every reason to believe that their quest will be both active and persistent. Unlike their predecessors, the members of the emerging managerial elite are politically self-confident and have a well-developed sense of mastery over their own fates. Their political style has not been shaped by sustained exposure to arbitrary terror, and their willingness to articulate their claims and to engage in a forceful defense of their own interests is not restrained by pervasive insecurity and habitual fear. In this respect, they bear a closer resemblance to the red directors than to the red specialists, and they will probably rival the former in the diligence with which they try to win official recognition for the principle, so clearly stated by the chairman of the VSNKh at the time of the Twelfth Party Congress (1923), that economic executives should be placed "in conditions of full independence and responsibility for their work."

Whether this effort will be more successful in the case of the new managers than it was in the case of Bogdanov and his colleagues, time alone will tell. That it will encounter the uncompromising resistance of certain segments of the party apparat seems certain. And, at the margins, where it becomes uncompromising in its own right, this quest for full economic responsibility will probably be opposed by the entire apparat as such, including those apparatchiki who are themselves members of the technical intelligentsia. Although the number of such apparatchiki is steadily growing and their rise may portend a significant reduction in party-state tension, even they, not to mention the "pure" politicians and ideological functionaries who will continue to figure prominently in the party's "leading nucleus," are likely to have only limited sympathy for managerial demands.[36]

Although these engineers-apparatchiki frequently tend to adopt what their more "verbocratic" colleagues consider an excessively pragmatic approach to economic questions, their pragmatism is informed by intense political activism and often finds expression in particularly niggling "petty tutelage" over economic operations and especially imperious interference in the conduct of economic affairs.[37] Moreover, the longer these cadres remain in the apparat, the less likely they will be to underestimate the importance of ideological and political considerations in the formulation of economic policy. Not only official recruitment and promotion procedures but also the natural human tendency toward self-justification and institutional identification will ensure that this is the case. In brief, the more the industrial cadres become wedded to party careers — and after a few years of work in the apparat a return to economic work becomes exceedingly difficult, if only due to loss of technical expertise — the more likely they are to develop a self-conception similar to that of the hero of a recent Soviet novel who is described as "an engineer by education . . . but a party worker by profession." [38] And, having developed this distinctive self-image, they are likely to behave in the same manner as their fictional prototype, who is depicted as a relentless protagonist of apparat primacy against a somewhat recalcitrant managerial elite. At a minimum, as already indicated, it seems safe to assume that these technically trained apparatchiki will oppose the more comprehensive and unqualified demands of the managerial elite as a threat to their personal and institutional prerogatives.

Since the apparat is still the principal custodian of the symbols of legitimacy and the chief fulcrum of organizational power within the Soviet system, the prospect that the new managers will be able to carry the full range of their claims and demands must be considered rather remote. At the same time, there is an ever-present possibility that conflict within the top leadership will put the managers in a position where they will be able to exercise a decisive influence on the direction of economic policy. Moreover, even apart from this possibility, there seems little question that an unprecedentedly large number of apparatchiki will be sufficiently attuned to managerial problems that they will favor some concessions to the managerial elite. Such concessions are more than ever likely to be forthcoming if it is in fact true, as many have argued, that popular support for the Soviet system has become increasingly dependent on economic effectiveness as distinct from doctrinal and institutional continuity.[39]

A shift of this sort could scarcely fail to increase official receptivity to managerial claims, and it is highly probable that such a shift has actually occurred. Certainly, at the very least, it will become progressively more dangerous and progressively more expensive for the regime to pursue an aggressively antimanagerial policy, and there seems no reason to anticipate a train of developments that would tempt the leadership to court such risks or absorb such costs. On the contrary, the very fact that the emerging managerial elite is characterized by such a high degree of political reliability points strongly in the opposite direction, although any turn to a vigorously promanagerial policy would encounter serious obstacles.

These considerations noted, the question of whether the emerging managerial elite will meet success or failure in its quest for greater latitude in the determination of economic policy and the conduct of economic affairs will not be subjected to further scrutiny here. At best, the question could only be answered in a tentative fashion and on the basis of an analysis that would far transcend the limits of the present study. Rather, the questions to be answered are, first, whether or not the new managers are likely to press for additional freedom or power in the event that their goals of greater operational autonomy and policy discretion are achieved and, second, whether or not sustained failure to achieve these goals through authorized channels is likely to lead the new managers to press for radical change in the system. The answers to these questions, I would suggest, will depend less on situational contingencies than on the already established political outlooks of the men concerned. And, if my analysis is correct so far, it seems probable both that the new managers will accept failure rather than turn to illegitimate means of struggle if they are unable to attain the autonomy they desire through authorized channels and that they will become active defenders of the status quo if they succeed.

This argument is in no sense a denial of the view that the Soviet Union is currently in a state of flux. It is an argument on behalf of the proposition that only the most improbable concatenation of circumstances could engender a pattern of behavior on the part of the new managers that would justify the expectations of those who look to the managerial elite as protagonists of radical political change. Although the new managers will favor appreciable changes in current political practices, their demands will not be directed toward the transformation of the Soviet system as such. What they desire bears little resemblance either to political freedom and civil liberty in an open society or to rule by engineers in the name of pure science and technical rationality. Rather, their composite image of the good society is and is likely to remain one in which such cardinal attributes of the system as the dictatorship of the party, the primacy of the party apparat, the canonization of Marxist-Leninist ideology, the comprehensive institutionalization of collectivist forms of social and economic organization, and extensive central planning are combined with such "new" attributes as stabilized policy-making procedures, a substantial devolution of authority to specialized functionaries of proven political reliability, and reliance on material and honorific incentives as the principal means of social and economic mobilization. This vision is undoubtedly far removed from Stalinism, and it stands a good distance from Khrushchevism as well. On balance, however, it smacks at least as much of continuity as of change, and it certainly cannot be characterized as either democratic or technocratic in any reasonably precise sense. Moreover, there is no inherent reason why the realization of this vision should portend the establishment of a democratic or technocratic order.

There is no doubt that political change tends to have a self-sustaining momentum of its own and to entail a wide range of unanticipated consequences. But it is also true that every social system is subject to what can be called, in the vocabulary of Mosca and Michels, "the law of social inertia" — a law stating that all social and political forces "have a tendency . . . to remain at the point and in the state in which they find themselves" or, more elaborately, that change always encounters powerful countervailing pressures which, if they do not stop the process altogether, tend to slow its tempo, deflect its energy into the revitalization of traditional forms, and restrict its innovative impact to what are, from the point of view of the system, tangentials rather than essentials.[40] History provides a multitude of examples that demonstrate the "victory" of this latter law over the law of self-sustaining change, and there seems no self-evident reason why the good society of the emerging managerial elite could not furnish yet another. Indeed, as I have already indicated, there seems no reason why the law of social inertia cannot operate to sustain the present system in the face of managerial demands for change. Nevertheless, even if it is true that the Soviet system is highly unstable, it is likely that the same basic system reconstituted along the lines desired by the emerging managerial elite would be considerably better endowed for the task of self-maintenance and within-system growth.

As is true of the present system, this reconstituted system would be characterized by the dominance of a politically self-conscious, reasonably cohesive, and essentially satisfied ruling elite, having comprehensive and firmly institutionalized control over the principal instruments of power and influence. But, at the same time, it would also be characterized by greater institutional flexibility, a less rigid and authoritarian political culture and style, and a better balanced and more productive economy. These changes in turn all point toward increased stability, and the odds seem high that the resultant system would prove viable and effective. Be that as it may, however, the decisive point for present purposes is that the members of the managerial elite would almost certainly do everything in their power to preserve such a system. In sum, any development beyond the confines of what some have labeled "rational" totalitarianism would find the managers engaged on the side of the law of inertia. The law of change might nonetheless prevail, but the managers would be its opponents, not its vanguard.

★ 7 ★

CONCLUSION

> By settled habit the technicians, engineers,
> and industrial experts are a harmless and
> docile sort, well fed on the whole and some-
> what placidly content with the "full dinner
> pail" which the . . . Vested Interests ha-
> bitually allow them.
>
> Thorstein Veblen, *The Engineers*
> *and the Price System*

The fact that the renowned aeronautical engineer A. N.
Tupolyov designed one of his best planes while confined in a
Stalinist prison may or may not symbolize the irrepressible
creativity inherent in the Soviet system.[1] It certainly symbolizes
the docility and political impotence that have characterized the
role of the technical intelligentsia and managerial elite in the
development of that system. Although theories of political development which cast the engineers and managers in the role of
foreordained "gravediggers of Communism" have been common
for over fifty years, they have found little confirmation in events.
At almost every step, the technicians have bowed to the dictates
of the ruling elite, and, in those cases where they have proved
somewhat recalcitrant, their resistance has ultimately been futile.
What political influence they have had has been primarily a
function of their unquestioning acceptance of an instrumental
and dependent role, and the only periods during which they
have acquired a certain independence have been those in which
the central leadership has been internally split. Far from growing at a progressive and ever-accelerating rate, in other words,

managerial power has been both marginal and contingent, and there is little doubt that it will remain so for some time to come. And the probability is high that this power will be used in the future, as it has in the past, for essentially functional, system-supporting goals.

That the "gravedigger" interpretation of the political role of the Soviet managerial elite has remained so widespread and so intellectually respectable in the face of such overwhelming counterevidence is graphic testimony to the powerful hold that economic determinism exercises over modern political analysis. To be sure, the protagonists of this interpretation often fail to acknowledge their underlying theoretical orientation and sometimes even explicitly deny it. But their analyses are in fact almost invariably informed by a conviction that politics is a reflection of economics. Although they are usually prepared to recognize that a variety of short-term disparities and asymmetries are possible and even likely, they nonetheless view the forms and content of political life as essentially derivative phenomenon, which must ultimately conform to the "logic" of the production process. This logic, in turn, is held to find particularly forceful expression in the outlook of the men who direct the economy, and it is these men, whose functional indispensability is assumed to increase with time and to endow its possessors with progressively more compelling power, who are viewed as the immediate source of the pressure that drives the political system irresistibly toward a state of perfect articulation with the economic "base." [2] Whether the predestined outcome of this process is democracy or technocracy remains a subject of contention among the analysts concerned. Yet all are agreed that the resultant polity must embody norms and procedures that sharply restrict the role of traditionalistic and ideological-charismatic components in political behavior and ensure the dominance of a dispassionate and cosmopolitan political culture that ac-

knowledges the claim of the managerial elite to an extensive policy-making role.

The Soviet Union's persistent deviation from this scenario
clearly suggests the advisability of adopting a less rigid and
unilinear approach to political development and economic modernization. At a minimum, there is need for an approach which
recognizes that occupational specialization can attain a high level
without giving rise to social or political pluralism; that engineers
and managers can be governed at least as much by transfunc-
tional ideological and political commitments as by their "objective" interests as incumbents of economic roles; that these interests can be largely, if not completely, satisfied within the
framework of a political system that is neither democratic nor
technocratic; and that men who are oriented toward the maxi-
mization of political power can successfully maintain a position
of dominance over men who are oriented toward the optimiza-
tion of economic utilities, although their doing so may require
important sacrifices. Only when these factors are duly recognized
and studied will it be possible to construct a genuinely empirical
theory of political development — the sort of theory that will at
once account for the available data, provide a coherent structure
for synthesis and generalization, and point the way toward fruit-
ful new hypotheses. Needless to say, this task of theory construction cannot be far advanced within the confines of the present
study.[3] But, to generalize what was said above, it seems clear
that no substantial theoretical progress is likely without an
initial recognition that the primacy of politics is a phenomenon
no less "natural" and no less "inevitable" than the primacy of
economics.

To deny that the primacy of politics has so far been the rule
in the development of the Soviet system is to fly in the face of
the available evidence, and, if my analysis is correct, this rule
is likely to hold in the future as well. Not, to be sure, that there

will be no significant differences between the next stage of the developmental process and its predecessors, for the opposite is clearly the case. The environment confronting the present Soviet leadership is undoubtedly characterized to a greater extent than ever before by a high level of technological complexity, an educated and highly skilled labor force, a considerable range of well-entrenched professionalisms, a more or less stabilized system of social and economic stratification, and many of the other well-known attributes of an industrial order. And there is no doubt that this environment will pose unprecendented challenges and require many revisions in the regime's traditional techniques of domination — revisions far surpassing those introduced in the years since Stalin's death. At the same time, however, economic modernization has put an unprecedentedly wide variety of refined instruments of control and mobilization at the regime's disposal, and the data now available suggest that the leadership is rapidly assimilating the skill required to use them effectively. Modern society also has vulnerabilities, and skillful exploitation of these weaknesses should allow the leadership to retain the ability to shape substantial segments of reality in accord with ideological principles, thereby validating its established beliefs, reaffirming the legitimacy of its quest for total power, and perpetuating its own position of unchallenged political eminence.[4] At least this outcome seems probable unless there is a sharp decline in the quality of top leadership cadres or a sustained and all-consuming succession struggle — and neither of these eventualities seems immediately in prospect.

In advancing this prognosis, it is not my intention to suggest that the Soviet system is about to become an absolute political monolith. My discussion of the post-Khrushchev managerial elite should dispel any doubt on this score, and a broader examination of the major groups and strata in Soviet society would undoubtedly reinforce the conclusion that monolithism will prove at least as unattainable in the future as it has in the past. The question, however, is not whether monolithism will prove elusive, but whether it will prove so elusive that the hope of achieving it will itself come to seem illusory. Only in the latter case would there be a good probability that Soviet politics would lose its superordinate position and revolutionary character. The point, in short, is not that politics will attain a position of absolute sovereignty and become the exclusive prerogative of a homogeneous ruling elite, but rather that politics will continue to dominate economics and will remain largely in the hands of committed technicians of power.

These considerations obviously have a direct bearing on the hotly debated question of whether or not the Soviet system should be viewed as representative of a unique and *sui generis* political type — the totalitarian system.[5] In the first place, since the question of typology is inextricably bound up with the question of "model building," the foregoing points serve to reinforce an argument raised in the Introduction: that most of the currently available models of totalitarianism are of dubious utility for any thoroughgoing operational or developmental analysis of the Soviet system. Not only do these models tend to be excessively structural and static in character, but also, and more important, they place such heavy emphasis on political monolithism that they tend to deflect attention away from such aspects of Soviet politics as interest articulation and aggregation, alliance formation, bureaucratic bargaining, and so on.[6] These processes have never ceased to operate within the Soviet system, and it is essential that they be recognized and systematically analyzed. Otherwise the relevance of the Soviet political experience to other political systems will be obscured, and evaluations of the process of political change in the USSR will be badly distorted. Too often studies that show a keen awareness of the complexity of present-day Soviet politics mistakenly assume that developments in the past conformed almost perfectly to the guidelines laid down in ideal-type models. As a

177

consequence, change is evaluated in an essentially ahistorical perspective, which is bound to lead to an overestimation of its rate and is likely to lead to a misperception of its content. To be sure, these dangers need not apply if we remember that the models in question are precisely ideal-types, intentionally simplified for heuristic purposes and designed to exaggerate the dominant features of a given empirical configuration. But the risks are nonetheless so nearly intrinsic that it seems advisable, for the time being at least, to use a more open-ended and empirical approach to the study of Soviet politics.

What, though, of the concept of totalitarianism as such? Or, more accurately, since the concept cannot be completely detached from the models its authors have elaborated, what of the utility of the current models of totalitarianism for purposes other than systematic analysis of the internal dynamics of Soviet politics? Here I suggest that for certain purposes even an inadequate model may be better than no model at all. And I would argue that there are good reasons for recognizing totalitarianism as a distinct political type of which the Soviet system is a close though, in terms of the available models of the type, highly imperfect approximation.[7] In particular, this is the case where the goal is the comparative analysis of whole systems — and, we should recall, it was this goal, above all, that the original studies of totalitarianism were designed to serve. Here the theorists of totalitarianism have pointed out a vital truth that was apt to be obscured by earlier political typologies and that retains its validity, despite the deficiencies of particular models for the analysis of the dynamics and development of the Soviet (or any other) system. To be precise, the theorists of totalitarianism have called attention to the important differences between authoritarian systems which are oriented toward the preservation of the status quo, or are bent on nothing more than rapid socioeconomic modernization, and systems, such as the Soviet, which are directed toward the creation and maintenance of a state of permanent revolution.

It is only in systems of the second type where all restraints on the exercise of central power are subjected to perpetual assault; where an effort is made to restructure all of society in the image of a chiliastic ideology; and where an unceasing attempt is made to produce new men who are not merely "civic men" or "industrial men" but "Soviet men," completely socialized into a monolithic and homogeneous political culture. These distinctive attributes, in turn, have a direct bearing on the accountability and responsibility of leadership, the availability of opportunities to choose among politically meaningful alternatives, the scope of group autonomy, the range of private initiative, the accessibility of information and knowledge, the efficacy of protest, the degree of tolerance for diversity and dissent, and the extent of personal security. And it is precisely such variables that have always been of central concern to serious students of political life.

Needless to say, all of these variables are inextricably bound up with the problem of individual liberty and human freedom. The essence of the preceding argument, then, can be reformulated to read that the operations of the Soviet system result in massive repression of man's capacity for self-determination and autonomous choice. Whether men have ever been less free is perhaps a moot point, but it is doubtful that any other system has been characterized by so low a correlation between its level of actual freedom and what might be called its level of potential freedom, as measured by economic resources, educational capacity, technical capabilities, and such.[8] Potentially, the Soviet Union compares favorably with other industrialized societies and outranks most nations of the world. But the opportunities that might have been used to expand the arena of liberty have been used to keep it narrowly restricted and subject to constant encroachment. That a nucleus has still been preserved, and that efforts to expand it from within have never ceased, cannot fail to be sources of immense gratification to all who respect the integrity of the human personality. Such gratification, however, must be tempered by a realistic awareness of the background against which it exists. If history teaches anything, it is surely that freedom is as precarious as it is precious, and freedom in the Soviet Union is at best residual and highly vulnerable.

WORKS CITED
NOTES
INDEX

WORKS CITED

Abramovitch, Raphael R. *The Soviet Revolution, 1917–1939.* New York: International Universities Press, 1962.

Achminow, German F. *La Puissance dans l'ombre: ou, le fossoyeur du Communisme.* Paris: Les Iles d'Or, 1952.

Alexandrov (Michaelson), Alexander S. *Kto upravlyaet Rossiei?* (Who Rules Russia?). Berlin: Parabola, 1933.

Almond, Gabriel A., and James S. Coleman, eds. *The Politics of the Developing Areas.* Princeton: Princeton University Press, 1960.

The Anatomy of Terror: Khrushchev's Revelations about Stalin's Regime. Washington, D.C.: Public Affairs Press, 1956.

Andronnikov, S. *Rost i vospitanie bolshevistskikh kadrov* (The Growth and Education of the Bolshevik Cadres). Leningrad: Gazetno-Zhurnalnoe i Knizhnoe Izdatelstvo Leningradskovo Soveta, RK i KD, 1939.

Anti-Soviet Trotskyite Center, Report of Court Proceedings. Moscow: People's Commissariat of Justice of the USSR, 1937.

Arakelian, A. *Industrial Management in the USSR.* Washington, D.C.: Public Affairs Press, 1950.

Arendt, Hannah. *On Revolution.* New York: Viking Press, 1963.

———— *The Origins of Totalitarianism,* New York: Harcourt, Brace, 1951.

Armstrong, John A. *The Politics of Totalitarianism: The Communist Party of the Soviet Union from 1934 to the Present.* New York: Random House, 1961.

———— *The Soviet Bureaucratic Elite: A Case Study of the Ukrainian Apparatus.* New York: Frederick A. Praeger, 1959.

Aron, Raymond. "Soviet Society in Transition," *Problems of Communism,* VI (November–December 1957).

———— ed. *World Technology and Human Destiny.* Ann Arbor: University of Michigan Press, 1963.

Avtorkhanov, Abdurakhman. "Possible Effects of Khrushchev's Overthrow," *Analysis of Current Developments in the Soviet Union,* no. 10. Munich: Institute for the Study of the USSR, 1964–1965.

———— "Soviet Decentralization," *Bulletin,* IV, no. 3. Munich: Institute for the Study of the USSR, 1957.

Azhaev, Vasily Nikolaevich. *Daleko ot Moskvy* (Far from Moscow). Moscow: Gosudarstvennoe Izdatelstvo Khudozhestvennoi Literatury, 1952.

Azrael, Jeremy R. "The Educational System as an Agency of Political

Socialization in the U.S.S.R.," in James S. Coleman, ed., *Education and Political Development*. Princeton: Princeton University Press, 1965.

———— "An End to Coercion?" *Problems of Communism*, XI (November–December 1962).

———— "The Party and Society," in Allen Kassof, ed., *Prospects for Soviet Society*, forthcoming, 1966.

———— "Political Profiles of the Soviet Technical Intelligentsia and Managerial Elite." Unpub. diss., Harvard University, 1961.

———— "Politics and Management," *Survey*, no. 49 (October 1963).

Babich, Andrei V. "Measures to Deal with Ubiquitous Corruption in Leading Soviet Circles," *Analysis of Current Developments in the Soviet Union*, no. 16. Munich: Institute for the Study of the USSR, 1962–1963.

Bardin, I. P. *Zhizn inzhenera* (The Life of an Engineer). Moscow: Molodaya Gvardia, 1938.

Barghoorn, Frederick C. *Soviet Russian Nationalism*. New York: Oxford University Press, 1956.

Barmin, I. P. "Borba party Lenina-Stalina za podgotovku inzhenerno-tekhnicheskikh kadrov dlya promyshlennosti v pervoi stalinskoi pyatiletke" (The Struggle of the Party of Lenin and Stalin for the Preparation of Engineers and Technical Cadres for Industry during the First Stalinist Five-Year Plan). Unpub. diss., Moscow State University, 1950.

Barmine, Alexander. *One Who Survived*. New York: G. P. Putnam's Sons, 1945.

Bauer, Raymond A. *The New Man in Soviet Psychology*. Cambridge: Harvard University Press, 1959.

———— "The Psychology of the Soviet Middle Elite," in Clyde Kluckhohn and Henry A. Murray, *Personality in Nature, Society, and Culture*, 2nd ed. rev. New York: Alfred A. Knopf, 1956.

Baykov, A. *The Development of the Soviet Economic System: An Essay on the Experience of Planning in the USSR*. New York: Macmillan, 1947.

Beck, F., and W. Godin. *Russian Purge and the Extraction of Confession*, London: Hurst and Beackett, 1951.

Beilin, A. E. *Kadry spetsialistov SSSR, ikh formirovanie i rost* (Cadres of Specialists in the USSR, Their Formation and Growth). Moscow: TsUNKhU Gosplana SSSR, 1935.

Bell, Daniel. *The End of Ideology*. Glencoe: Free Press, 1960.

Bereday, George Z. F., and Jaan Pennar. *The Politics of Soviet Education*. New York: Frederick A. Praeger, 1960.

Berliner, Joseph S. *Factory and Manager in the USSR*. Cambridge: Harvard University Press, 1957.

WORKS CITED

——— "Marxism and the Soviet Economy," *Problems of Communism*, XIII (September–October 1964).

Bienstock, Gregory, Solomon M. Schwarz, and Aaron Yugow. *Management in Russian Industry and Agriculture*. Ithaca: Cornell University Press, 1948.

Binder, Leonard. *Iran: Political Development in a Changing Society*. Berkeley: University of California Press, 1964.

Black, Cyril E. "Revolution, Modernization and Communism," in Cyril E. Black and Thomas P. Thornton, eds., *Communism and Revolution: The Strategic Uses of Political Violence*. Princeton: Princeton University Press, 1964.

Blake, Patricia, and Max Hayward, eds. *Dissonant Voices in Soviet Literature*. New York: Pantheon Books, 1962.

Boffa, Guiseppe. *Inside the Khrushchev Era*, trans. Carl Marzani. New York: Marzani and Munsell, 1959.

Bolshaya sovetskaya entsiklopedia (Great Soviet Encyclopedia), 2nd ed., XLIV. Moscow: Gosudarstvennoe Nauchnoe Izdatelstvo *Bolshaya sovetskaya entsiklopedia*, 1956.

Bonch-Bruevich, V. D. *Izbrannye sochinenia* (Selected Works), III: *Vospominania o V. I. Lenine, 1917–1924 gg* (Reminiscences of V. I. Lenin, 1917–1924). Moscow: Izdatelstvo Akademy Nauk, 1963.

Brzezinski, Zbigniew. "Communist Disunity and the West," *New Republic*, December 18, 1961.

——— *Ideology and Power in Soviet Politics*. New York: Frederick A. Praeger, 1962.

——— "The Soviet Political System: Transformation or Degeneration," *Problems of Communism*, XV (January–February 1966).

Bubnov, A. *VKP(b)*. Moscow: Gosudarstvennoe Sotsialno-Ekonomicheskoe Izdatelstvo, 1931.

——— and Ye. Preobrazhensky, eds. *Za pyat let, 1917–1922* (For Five Years, 1917–1922). Moscow: Izdatelstvo *Krasnaya nov*, 1922.

Burg, David. "Observations on Soviet University Students," *Daedalus*, Summer 1960.

Callaghan, Tim (J. R. Azrael). "Studying the Students: Between Conformity and Dissent," *Soviet Survey*, no. 33 (July–September 1960).

Cantril, Hadley. *Soviet Leaders and Mastery over Man*. New Brunswick: Rutgers University Press, 1960.

Carr, Edward Hallet. *The Bolshevik Revolution, 1917–1923*, 2 vols. New York: Macmillan, 1951, 1952.

——— *The Interregnum, 1923–1924*. New York: Macmillan, 1954.

——— *Socialism in One Country, 1924–1926*, 2 vols. New York: Macmillan, 1958, 1960.

Churchill, Winston. *The Second World War, IV: The Hinge of Fate.* London: Cossell, 1954.

Ciliga, Anton. *The Russian Enigma.* London: George Routledge and Sons, 1940.

Communist Party of the Soviet Union, conferences and congresses. (See also *Direktivy KPSS*; Gruliow, ed., *Current Soviet Policies; Kommunisticheskaya partia v rezolyutsiakh.*)

VIII Syezd rossiiskoi kommunisticheskoi party (b), mart 1919 goda, protokoly (Eighth Congress of the Russian Communist Party [Bolshevik], March 1919, Protocols). Moscow: Gosudarstvennoe Izdatelstvo Politicheskoi Literatury, 1959.

IX Syezd RKP(b), mart-aprel 1920 goda, prot. (Ninth Congress). *Moscow:* Gos. Izd. Pol. Lit., 1960.

X Syezd RKP(b), mart 1921 goda, stenografichesky otchyot (Tenth Congress . . . Stenographic Report). Moscow: Gos. Izd. Pol. Lit., 1963.

XI Syezd RKP(b), mart-aprel 1922 goda, sten. otch. (Eleventh Congress). Moscow: Gos. Izd. Pol. Lit., 1961.

XII Syezd RKP(b), sten. otch (Twelfth Congress). Moscow: Izdatelstvo *Krasnaya nov,* Glavpolitprosvet, 1923.

XIII Syezd RKP(b), sten. otch. (Thirteenth Congress). Moscow: Gos. Izd. Pol. Lit., 1963.

XIV Konferentsia vsesoyuznoi kommunisticheskoi party (b), sten. otch., 27–29 aprelya 1925 g. (Fourteenth Conference of the All-Union Communist Party [Bolshevik]). Moscow: Gosudarstvennoe Izdatelstvo, 1925.

XV Konferentsia VKP(b), sten. otch. (Fifteenth Conference). Moscow: Gos. Izd., 1927.

XV Syezd VKP(b), dekabr 1927 goda, sten. otch. (Fifteenth Congress). Moscow: Gos. Izd. Pol. Lit., 1962.

XVI Konferentsia VKP(b), aprel 1929 goda, sten. otch. (Sixteenth Conference). Moscow: Gos. Izd. Pol. Lit., 1962.

XVI Syezd VKP(b), sten. otch. (Sixteenth Congress). Moscow: Ogizdat Moskovsky Rabochy, 1931.

XVII Syezd VKP(b), sten. otch. (Seventeenth Congress). Moscow: Partizdat, 1934.

XVIII Congress: *The Land of Socialism Today and Tomorrow: Reports and Speeches at the Eighteenth Congress of the Communist Party of the Soviet Union (Bolshevik).* Moscow: Foreign Languages Publishing House, 1939.

Conquest, Robert. *Power and Policy in the USSR: The Study of Soviet Dynasties.* New York: St. Martin's Press, 1961.

Counts, G. S., and Nucia P. Lodge, trans. *I Want to Be Like Stalin.* New York: John Day, 1947.

Croan, Melvin. "The Politics of Marxist Sovietology: Otto Bauer's Vision," *Journal of Politics,* XXI (1959).

Dahrendorf, Ralf. *Class and Class Conflict in Industrial Society.* Stanford: Stanford University Press, 1959.

Dan, F. (F. D. Gurevich). *Dva goda skitany, 1919–1921* (Two Years of Wandering, 1919–1921). Berlin: H. S. Herman, 1922.

Daniels, Robert Vincent. *The Conscience of the Revolution: Communist Opposition in Soviet Russia.* Cambridge: Harvard University Press, 1960.

———— ed. *A Documentary History of Communism from Lenin to Mao.* New York: Random House, 1960.

Davies, R. W. "Some Soviet Economic Controllers, II," *Soviet Studies,* XI (April 1960).

———— "Some Soviet Economic Controllers, III," *Soviet Studies,* XII (July 1960).

Denicke, G. *Links with the Past in Soviet Society.* Washington, D.C.: Department of State External Research Paper, March 21, 1952.

Deutscher, Isaac. *The Prophet Outcast, Trotsky, 1929–1940.* London: Oxford University Press, 1963.

———— *Russia in Transition,* 2nd rev. ed. New York: Grove Press, 1960.

Dicks, Henry V. "Observations on Contemporary Russian Behavior," *Human Relations,* V, no. 2 (1952).

Dinerstein, Herbert Samuel. *War and the Soviet Union: Nuclear Weapons and the Revolution in Soviet Military and Political Thinking.* New York: Frederick A. Praeger, 1959.

Direktivy KPSS i sovetskovo pravitelstvo po khozyaistvennym voprosam (Directives of the CPSU and the Soviet Government on Economic Questions), 4 vols. Moscow: Gosudarstvennoe Izdatelstvo Politicheskoi Literatury, 1957–1958.

Djilas, Milovan. *The New Class: An Analysis of the Communist System.* New York: Frederick A. Praeger, 1957.

Dudintsev, Vladimir. *New Year's Tale,* trans. Gabriella Azrael. New York: E. P. Dutton, 1960.

———— *Not By Bread Alone,* trans. Edith Bone. New York: E. P. Dutton, 1957.

Dzerzhinsky, F. E. *Izbrannye proizvedenia* (Selected Works), 2 vols. Moscow: Gosudarstvennoe Izdatelstvo Politicheskoi Literatury, 1957.

Ebon, Martin. *Malenkov, Stalin's Successor.* New York: McGraw-Hill, 1953.

Ehrenbourg, Ilya. *Out of Chaos.* New York: Henry Holt, 1934.

Ehrlich, A. *The Soviet Industrialization Debate, 1924–1928.* Cambridge: Harvard University Press, 1960.

Elkin, B. "The Russian Intelligentsia on the Eve of the Revolution," *Daedalus,* Summer 1960.

Engels, Frederick. *Anti-Dühring: Herr Eugen Dühring's Revolution in Science,* 3rd ed. Moscow: Foreign Languages Publishing House, 1962.

———— "Novy dokument F. Engelsa" (Letter to von Benigk, August 21, 1890), *Voprosy istory KPSS* (Problems in the History of the CPSU), no. 2 (1964).

———— *Socialism: Utopian and Scientific,* trans. Edward Aveling. New York: International Publishers, 1935.

Erickson, John. *The Soviet High Command: A Military-Political History, 1918–1941.* London: St. Martin's Press, 1962.

Erikson, Erik. *Childhood and Society,* 2nd ed. rev. New York: W. W. Norton, 1963.

Fainsod, Merle. *How Russia Is Ruled,* rev. ed. Cambridge: Harvard University Press, 1963.

———— "Khrushchevism in Retrospect," *Problems of Communism,* XIV (January–February 1965).

———— "The Twenty-Second Party Congress," *Problems of Communism,* X, special supplement (November–December 1961).

Fedyushkin, Sergei A. *Privlechenie burzhuaznoi tekhnicheskoi intelligentsy k sotsialisticheskomu stroitelstvu v SSSR* (Recruitment of the Bourgeois Technical Intelligentsia to Socialist Construction in the USSR). Moscow: VPSh, 1960.

Feldmesser, Robert Allen. "Aspects of Social Mobility in the Soviet Union." Unpub. diss., Harvard University, 1955.

———— "The 'Classless Society,'" *Problems of Communism,* IX (March–April 1960).

Fetscher, Irving. "Marx, Engels and the Future Society," in W. Laqueur and W. Labedz, eds., *The Future of the Communist Society.* New York: Frederick A. Praeger, 1962.

Feuer, Lewis S. "Marx and the Intellectuals," *Survey,* no. 49 (October 1963).

———— ed. *Marx and Engels: Basic Writings on Politics and Philosophy.* Garden City, N.Y.: Anchor Books, 1959.

Fischer, Louis. *Machines and Men in Russia.* New York: Harrison Smith, 1932.

Friedrich, Carl J., ed. *Totalitarianism: Proceedings of a Conference held at the American Academy of Arts and Sciences, March, 1953.* Cambridge: Harvard University Press, 1954.

—— and Zbigniew K. Brzezinski. *Totalitarian Dictatorship and Autocracy.* Cambridge: Harvard University Press, 1956.

Garthoff, Raymond L. "The Role of the Military in Post-Stalin Politics," RAND Corporation Research Memorandum P-937. Santa Monica, September 12, 1956.

Gerschenkron, Alexander. *Economic Backwardness in Historical Perspective.* Cambridge: Harvard University Press, 1962.

Gerth, Hans H., and C. Wright Mills. "A Marx for Managers" in Robert K. Merton, et al., eds., *Reader in Bureaucracy.* Glencoe: Free Press, 1952.

—— eds. *From Max Weber.* New York: Oxford University Press, 1946.

Gladkov, Feodor. *Energia* (Energy). Moscow: Sovetsky Pisatel, 1952.

Gladkov, I. A., ed. *K istory plana elektrifikatsy sovetskoi strany* (Toward a History of the Plan for the Electrification of the Country of Soviets). Moscow: Gosudarstvennoe Izdatelstvo Politicheskoi Literatury, 1952.

Goure, Leon. *The Seige of Leningrad.* Stanford: Stanford University Press, 1962.

Granick, David. *Management of the Industrial Firm in the USSR: A Study in Soviet Economic Planning.* New York: Columbia University Press, 1955.

—— *The Red Executive: A Study of the Organization Man in Russian Industry.* Garden City, N.Y.: Doubleday, 1960.

Granin, Danil. "Idu na grozu" (Into the Thunderstorm), *Znamya* (Banner), nos. 8, 9, 10 (August–September–October 1962).

—— *Iskateli, roman* (The Seekers, a Novel). Leningrad: Sovetsky Pisatel, 1960.

Groth, R. J. "The 'Isms' in Totalitarianism," *American Political Science Review,* LVIII, no. 4 (1964).

Gruliow, Leo, ed. *Current Soviet Policies,* 4 vols. Vol. I: *Documentary Record of the 19th Congress, CPSU;* New York, Frederick A. Praeger, 1953. Vol. II: *Documentary Record of the 20th Congress, CPSU;* New York, Frederick A. Praeger, 1957. Vol. III: *Documentary Record of the 21st Congress, CPSU;* New York, Columbia University Press, 1960. Vol. IV: *Docmentary Record of the 22nd Congress, CPSU;* New York, Columbia University Press, 1962.

Gurovich, A. "Vysshy sovet narodnovo khozyaistva" (Supreme Council of National Economy), *Arkhiv russkoi revolyutsy* (Archive of the Russian Revolution), VI. Berlin, 1922.

Haas, Ernst B. "Technocracy, Pluralism and the New Europe," in Stephen R. Graubard, ed., *A New Europe?* Boston: Houghton-Mifflin, 1964.

Hagen, Everett E. *On the Theory of Social Change: How Economic Growth Begins.* Homewood, Ill.: Dorsey Press, 1962.

Haimson, Leopold H. "The Solitary Hero and the Philistines: A Note on the Heritage of the Stalin Era," *Daedalus,* Summer 1960.

—— "Three Generations of the Soviet Intelligentsia," *Foreign Affairs,* XXXVII (January 1959).

Harbison, Frederick. "Entrepreneurial Organization as a Factor in Economic Development," *Quarterly Journal of Economics,* LXX (August 1956).

Harper, Samuel N. *Civic Training in Russia.* Chicago: University of Chicago Press, 1929.

Hayek, Friedrich A. *The Counter-Revolution of Science.* Glencoe: Free Press, 1952.

Heller, A. A. *The Industrial Revival in Soviet Russia.* New York: Thomas Seltzer, 1922.

History of the Communist Party of the Soviet Union (Bolshevik), Short Course. New York: International Publishers, 1939.

Hoeffding, Oleg. "The Soviet Industrial Reorganization of 1957," *American Economic Review,* XLIX (May 1959).

Hough, Jerry Fincher. "The Role of the Local Party Organs in Soviet Industrial Decision Making." Unpub. diss., Harvard University, 1961.

Hyman, Herbert. *Political Socialization: A Study in the Psychology of Political Behavior.* Glencoe: Free Press, 1959.

Inkeles, Alex. "Social Change and Social Character," *Journal of Social Issues,* XI (1955).

—— and Raymond A. Bauer. *The Soviet Citizen: Daily Life in a Totalitarian Society.* Cambridge: Harvard University Press, 1959.

Ipatieff, V. N. *The Life of a Chemist.* Stanford: Stanford University Press, 1946.

Itogi obyedinyonnovo plenuma TsK i TsKK VKP(b), 17–21 dekabrya 1930 (Results of the Joint Plenum of the Central Committee and the Central Control Commission of the All-Union Communist Party (b), December 17–21, 1930). Leningrad: Ogiz Priboi, 1930.

Itogi partiinoi raboty za god 1922–23 (Results of Party Work for 1922–23). Moscow. Krasnaya Nov. 1923.

Ivanov, V. M., and S. N. Kanev. *Na mirnoi osnove* (On a Peaceful Basis). Leningrad: Lenizdat, 1961.

Jasny, Naum. *Soviet Industrialization, 1928–1952.* Chicago: University of Chicago Press, 1961.

Joravsky, David. "Soviet Scientists and the Great Break," *Daedalus,* Summer 1960.

Kalinin, M. I. *On Communist Education: Selected Speeches and Articles.* Moscow: Foreign Languages Publishing House, 1949.

Kassof, Allen H. "The Administered Society: Totalitarianism without Terror," *World Politics,* no. 16 (July 1964).

Katuntsev, N. M. "Rol rabochikh fakultetov v sozdany kadrov narodnoi intelligentsy v SSSR" (The Role of the Workers' Faculties in the Creation of a Peoples' Intelligentsia in the USSR), *Vestnik istory mirovoi kultury* (Herald of the History of World Culture), no. 6 (November–December 1958).

Kautsky, John, ed. *Political Change in Underdeveloped Countries: Nationalism and Communism.* New York: John Wiley and Sons, 1962.

Kautsky, Karl. *The Social Revolution.* trans. A. M. and May Wood Simons. Chicago: Charles H. Kerr, 1907.

Kennan, George F. *Russia, the Atom and the West.* New York: Harper, 1958.

Kerr, Clark, John T. Dunlop, et al. *Industrialism and Industrial Man: The Problems of Labor and Management in Economic Growth.* Cambridge: Harvard University Press, 1960.

Key Officials of the Government of the USSR and Union Republics (Research Section, Series II, no. 81, February 1962). Munich: Institute for the Study of the USSR, 1962.

Khrushchev, N. S. "Educating Active and Conscious Builders of a Communist Society," *School and Society,* February 14, 1959.

Kim, Maxim P. *Kommunisticheskaya partia-organizator kulturnoi revolyutsy v SSSR* (The Communist Party — Organizer of the Cultural Revolution in the USSR). Moscow: Gosvdarstvennoe Izdatelstvo Politicheskoi Literatury, 1957.

Klyuchnikov, Yu. V., N. V. Ustryalov, et al. *Smena vekh: Sbornik statei* (Landmarks: Collection of Articles). Prague: 1922.

Kolbenkov, Nikolai F. *Sovershenstvovanie rukovodstva promyshlennosti SSSR, 1956–1960* (The Improvement of the Leadership of Industry in the USSR, 1956–1960). Moscow: Izdatelstvo Sotsialno-Ekonomicheskoi Literatury, 1961.

Kolontay, A. *The Workers' Opposition in Russia.* Chicago: Industrial Workers of the World, n.d.

Kommunisticheskaya partia sovetskovo soyuza v rezolyutsiakh i resheniakh syezdov, konferentsy, i plenumov TsK (The CPSU in the Resolutions and Decisions of the Congresses, Conferences, and Plenums of the Central Committee), 4 parts. Moscow: Gosudarstvennoe Izdatelstvo Politicheskoi Literatury, 1954–1960.

Krassin, Lubov. *Leonid Krassin: His Life and Work*. London: Skeffington and Sons, n.d.

Kravchenko, Victor. *I Chose Freedom: The Personal and Political Life of a Soviet Official*. New York: Charles Scribner's Sons, 1946.

Kritsman, L. *Geroichesky period velikoi russkoi revolyutsy* (The Heroic Period of the Great Russian Revolution), 2nd ed. Moscow: Gosudarstvennoe Izdatelstvo, 1926.

Krylenko, N. V., ed. *Ekonomicheskaya kontrrevolyutsia v Donbase* (Economic Counterrevolution in the Donbas). Moscow, 1928.

Krzhizhanovsky, Gleb Maksimilianovich. *Izbrannoe* (Selected Works). Moscow: Gosudarstvennoe Izdatelstvo Politicheskoi Literatury, 1957.

Kuzminov, I. "Soviet Productive-Technical Intelligentsia," *Problemy ekonomiki* (Problems of Economics), no. 5, 1936.

Labedz, Leo. "Deutscher as Historian and Prophet," *Survey*, no. 41 (April 1962).

———— "The New Soviet Intelligentsia," *Survey*, no. 29 (July–September 1959).

Land of Socialism Today and Tomorrow. See Communist Party, XVIII Congress.

Lange, Oskar. "On the Economic Theory of Socialism," in Benjamin E. Lippincott, ed., *On the Economic Theory of Socialism*. Minneapolis: University of Minnesota Press, 1948.

Laqueur, Walter A., and George Lichtheim, eds. *The Soviet Cultural Scene, 1956–1957*. New York: Frederick A. Praeger, 1958.

Laskovsky, N. "Reflections on the Soviet Industrial Reorganization," *American Slavic and East European Review*, XVII (1958).

Leites, Nathan. *A Study of Bolshevism*. Glencoe: Free Press, 1953.

Lenin, V. I. *Polnoe sobranie sochineny* (Complete Collection of Works), 5th ed., 55 vols. Moscow: Gosudavstvennoe Izdatelstvo Politicheskoi Literatury, 1958–1963.

———— *Selected Works*, 12 vols. New York: International Publishers, 1935–1938.

Leonhard, Wolfgang. *The Kremlin since Stalin*, trans. E. Wiskemann and M. Jackson. New York: Frederick A. Praeger, 1962.

Lerner, Daniel. *The Passing of Traditional Society: Modernizing the Middle East*. New York: Free Press of Glencoe, 1958.

Letter of an Old Bolshevik: The Key to the Moscow Trials. New York: Rand School Press, 1937.

Liberman, Simon I. *Building Lenin's Russia*. Chicago: University of Chicago Press, 1945.

———— "Narodny komissar Krasin" (People's Commissar Krasin), *Novy zhurnal* (New Journal), VIII. New York, 1944.

Lichtheim, George. *Marxism: An Historical and Critical Study.* New York: Frederick A. Praeger, 1962.

———— "Reflections on Trotsky," *Commentary,* January 1964.

Lied, Jonas. *Sidelights on the Economic Situation in Russia.* Moscow: Khrushchev Printing Works, 1922.

Linden, Carl. "Khrushchev and the Party Battle," *Problems of Communism,* XII (November–December 1963).

Lowenthal, Richard. "The Revolution Withers Away," *Problems of Communism,* XIV (January–February 1965).

———— "Totalitarianism Reconsidered," *Commentary,* June 1960.

Lunacharsky, A. V. *Ob intelligentsy* (On the Intelligentsia). Moscow: Izdatelstvo *Krasnaya nov,* 1923.

Machajski. "On the Expropriation of the Capitalists" in V. F. Calverton, ed., *The Making of Society.* New York: Modern Library, 1937.

McClelland, David S. *The Achieving Society.* Princeton: D. Van Nostrand, 1961.

McLean, Hugh, and Walter N. Vickery, eds. *Year of Protest, 1956.* New York: Vintage Books, 1961.

Marcuse, Herbert. *Soviet Marxism: A Critical Analysis.* New York: Columbia University Press, 1958.

Markham, F. M. H., ed. *Henri Comte de Saint-Simon: Selected Writings.* Oxford: Basil Blackwell, 1952.

Marx, Karl. *Capital: A Critique of Political Economy.* trans. S. Moore and E. Aveling. New York: Modern Library, 1906.

———— *Capital: A Critique of Political Economy,* III. Moscow: Foreign Languages Publishing House, 1959.

Marx and Engels, Correspondence, 1846–1895, trans. Dona Torr. New York: International Publishers, 1936.

Massachusetts Institute of Technology Study Group. "The Transitional Process," in Roy C. Macridis and Bernard E. Brown, eds., *Comparative Politics: Notes and Readings,* rev. ed. Homewood: Dorsey Press, 1964.

Maynard, John. *The Russian Peasant and Other Studies.* New York: Collier Books, 1962.

Mehnert, Klaus. "Changing Attitudes of Russian Youth," in Cyril E. Black, ed., *The Transformation of Russian Society.* Cambridge: Harvard University Press, 1960.

———— *Soviet Man and His World.* New York: Frederick A. Praeger, 1962.

Mendeleev, D. I. *K poznaniyu Rossy* (Toward an Understanding of Russia). St. Petersburg: Izdanie A. S. Suvorina, 1907.

———— *Zavetnye mysly* (Cherished Thoughts), 9 parts. St. Petersburg: Izdanie M. P. Frolovoi, 1904–1905.

Merton, Robert K. "Bureaucratic Structure and Personality," in Clyde Kluckhohn and Henry A. Murray, eds., *Personality in Nature, Society, and Culture.* New York: Alfred A. Knopf, 1948.

Meyer, Alfred G. "USSR Incorporated," in Donald W. Treadgold, ed., *The Development of the USSR.* Seattle: University of Washington Press, 1964.

Michels, Robert. *Political Parties: A Sociological Study of the Oligarchical Tendencies of Modern Democracy,* trans. Eden and Cedar Paul. Glencoe: Free Press, 1949.

———— "Sulla scadenza della classe media industriale antica sul sorgere di una classe media industriale moderna nei paesi di economia spiccatamente capitalistica," *Giornale degli economisti,* XXXVIII (1909).

Milosz, Czeslaw. *The Captive Mind.* New York: Vintage Books, 1955.

Milyutin, V. P., et al. *Kondratevshchina.* Moscow: Izdatelstvo Kommunisticheskoi Akademy, 1930.

Molotov, V. M. "Na dva fronta" (On Two Fronts), *Bolshevik,* no. 2 (January 31, 1930).

Moore, Barrington, Jr. *Political Power and Social Theory.* Cambridge: Harvard University Press, 1958.

———— *Soviet Politics: The Dilemma of Power.* Cambridge: Harvard University Press, 1951.

Mosca, Gaetano. *The Ruling Class,* trans. Hannah D. Kahn. New York: McGraw-Hill, 1939.

Mosely, Philip E. "Khrushchev's New Economic Gambit," *Foreign Affairs,* no. 36 (July 1958).

———— *The Kremlin and World Politics: Studies in Soviet Policy and Action.* New York: Vintage Books, 1960.

———— "Some Vignettes of Soviet Life: 1930–32," *Survey,* no. 55 (April 1965).

Neuwald, Mark. "The Origin of the Communist Control Commission," *American Slavic and East European Review,* XVIII (October 1959).

Newth, J. A. "The Soviet Population: Wartime Losses and the Postwar Recovery," *Soviet Studies,* XV (January 1964).

Nicolaevsky, Boris. "The Party Men and the Managers," *The New Leader,* July 29, 1957.

Nomad, Max. *Aspects of Revolt.* New York: Noonday Press, 1961.

Nove, Alec. *Economic Rationality and Soviet Politics, or Was Stalin Really Necessary?* New York: Frederick A. Praeger, 1964.

———— "The Industrial Planning System: Reforms in Prospect," *Soviet Studies,* XIV (July 1962).

———— "The Soviet Industrial Reorganization," *Problems of Communism,* VI (November–December 1957).

WORKS CITED

———— "The Uses and Abuses of Kremlinology, *Survey,* no. 50 (January 1964).

"Ocherki nashikh dnei: Tri dnya v Kremle" (Sketches of Our Times: Three Days in the Kremlin), *Novy mir* (New World), no. 7 (July 1955).

Ogarkov, A. I. *Borba kommunisticheskoi party za sozdanie inzhenerno-tekhnicheskikh kadrov tyazholoi promyshlennosti v period pervoi pyatiletki, 1928/29–1932/33* (The Struggle of the Communist Party for the Creation of Engineers and Technical Cadres in Heavy Industry during the First Five-Year Plan, 1928/29–1932/33). Unpub. diss., Moscow State University, 1956.

Ordzhonikidze, G. K. *Stati i rechi* (Articles and Speeches), 2 vols. Moscow: Gosudarstvennoe Izdatelstvo Politicheskoi Literatury, 1956.

Ovalov, Lev. "Partiinoe poruchenie" (A Party Mission), *Moskva,* no. 7 (1959).

Paloczi-Horvath, George. *Khrushchev: The Making of a Dictator.* Boston: Little, Brown, 1960.

Panferov, Feodor I. *Borba za mir* (The Struggle for Peace). Moscow: Gosudarstvennoe Izdatelstvo Khudozhestvennoi Literatury, 1945.

———— *Volga-matushka reka* (Mother River Volga). Moscow: Sovetskaya Rossia, 1958.

Partia v borbe za vosstanovlenie narodnovo khozyaistva, 1921–1925 gody (The Party in the Struggle for the Reconstruction of the National Economy, 1921–1925). Moscow: Gospolitizdat, 1961.

Pashukanis, E., ed. *15 let sovetskovo stroitelstva* (Fifteen Years of Soviet Construction). Moscow: Gosudarstvennoe Izdatelstvo Sovetskoe Zakonodatelstvo, 1932.

Pethybridge, Roger. *A Key to Soviet Politics: The Crisis of the Anti-Party Group.* New York: Frederick A. Praeger, 1962.

Petrovsky, D., ed. *Kadry tyazholoi promyshlennosti v tsifrakh* (Cadres of Heavy Industry in Figures). Moscow: Sektor Obshchikh Izdany, NKTP, 1936.

Pipes, Richard., "The Forces of Nationalism," *Problems of Communism,* XIII (January–February 1964).

Pistrak, Lazar. *The Grand Tactician.* New York: Frederick A. Praeger, 1961.

Plenum Tsk KPSS, 24–29 iyunya 1959 stenografichesky otchyot (Plenum of the Central Committee of the CPSU, June 24–29, 1959, Stenographic Report). Moscow: Gosudarstvennoe Izdatelstvo Politicheskoi Literatury, 1959.

Plenum Tsk KPSS, 24–26 marta 1965 goda, stenografichesky otchyot (Plenum of the Central Committee of the CPSU, March 24–26,

1965, Stenographic Report). Moscow: Gosudarstvennoe Izdatelstvo Politicheskoi Literatury, 1965.

Ploss, Sidney I. "A New Phase of the Soviet Policy Debate." Princeton: Center of International Studies, October 16, 1963.

————— "Recent Alignments in the Soviet Elite." Princeton: Center of International Studies, March 16, 1964.

————— "Some Political Aspects of the June 1963 CPSU Central Committee Session." Princeton: Center of International Studies, August 28, 1963.

————— "Soviet Politics since the Fall of Khrushchev." Philadelphia: University of Pennsylvania, Foreign Policy Research Institute, 1965.

Pogodin, Nikolay. *The Chimes of the Kremlin,* in *Soviet Scene, Six Plays,* trans. Alexander Bakshy. New Haven: Yale University Press, 1946.

Popov, N. *Outline of the History of the Communist Party of the Soviet Union,* II. New York: International Publishers, n.d.

Price, Morgan Philips. *My Reminiscences of the Russian Revolution.* London: G. Allen & Unwin, 1921.

Project on the Soviet Social System: Series A, 37 vols. Cambridge: Russian Research Center, Harvard University, 1950–1951.

Project on the Soviet Social System: Series B, 24 vols. Cambridge: Russian Research Center, Harvard University, 1950–1951.

Prokofyev, V. V. *Industrial and Technical Intelligentsia in the USSR.* Moscow: Co-operative Publishing Society of Foreign Workers in the USSR, 1933.

Protsess kontrrevolyutsionnoi organizatsy Menshevikov (The Trial of the Counterrevolutionary Organization of Mensheviks). Moscow: Izdatelstvo Sovetskoe zakonodatelstvo, 1931.

Pye, Lucian W. *Politics, Personality, and Nation-Building: Burma's Search for Identity.* New Haven: Yale University Press, 1962.

Rezunov, Mikhail Denisovich. *Sovetskoe gosudarstvo i sotsialisticheskoe obshchestvo* (The Soviet Government and Socialist Society). Leningrad: Gosudarstvennoe Sotsialno-Ekonomicheskoe Izdatelstvo, 1934.

Riesman, David. *Thorstein Veblen: A Critical Interpretation.* New York: Charles Scribner's Sons, 1953.

Rigby, T. H. "How Strong Is the Leader?" *Problems of Communism,* XI (September–October 1962).

————— "Traditional, Market, and Organizational Societies," *World Politics,* no. 4 (July 1964).

Riutin, M. "Rukovodyashchie kadry VKP (b)" (Leading Cadres in the All-Union Communist Party (b)), *Bolshevik,* no. 13–14 (July 31, 1928).

Rogers, J. A. "The Russian Populists' Response to Darwin," *Slavic Review*, XXII (September 1963).

Rostow, W. W. "Rostow on Growth: A Non-Communist Manifesto," *The Economist*, CLXXXXII (August 15 and 22, 1959).

Rothstein, Andrew. ed. *Wreckers on Trial: A Record of the Trial of the Industrial Party Held in Moscow, November–December, 1930.* New York: Workers' Library Publishers, 1931.

Rozenfeld, Ya. S. *Promyshlennaya politika, SSSR, 1917–1925 gg* (Industrial Politics, USSR, 1917–1925). Moscow: Izdatelstvo *Planovoe khozyaistvo,* 1926.

Rush, Myron. "Economic Managers: Russia Five Years after Stalin — Part 7," *The New Leader*, May 12, 1958.

——— "The Khrushchev Succession Problem." Santa Monica: U.S. Air Force Project, RAND, RM-2763, May 1, 1961.

——— *Political Succession in the USSR.* New York: Columbia University Press, 1965.

Saint-Simon, Comte de. *Oeuvres de Saint-Simon et L'Enfantin,* XXXVII. Paris, 1875.

Sbornik pyatiletki, ezhegodnik za 1930 g (A Collection on the Five-Year Plan, A Yearbook for 1930), II. Leningrad: Izdatelstvo *Krasnaya gazeta,* 1930.

Schapiro, L. *The Communist Party of the Soviet Union.* New York: Random House, 1960.

——— *The Origin of the Communist Autocracy: Political Opposition in the Soviet State, First Phase, 1917–1922.* Cambridge: Harvard University Press, 1956.

——— "The Party and the State," in W. Laqueur and L. Labedz, eds., *The Future of the Communist Society.* New York: Frederick A. Praeger, 1962.

Schenck, Fritz, and Richard Lowenthal. "Soft Goods vs. Hard Goods: Politics and Planning in the Soviet Empire," 3 parts. *The New Leader,* January 5, 12, and 19, 1959.

Schlesinger, Rudolf. "A Note on the Context of Soviet Planning," *Soviet Studies*, XVI (July 1964).

Schumpeter, Joseph A. *Capitalism, Socialism and Democracy.* New York: Harper, 1950.

Schwarz, Solomon M. "Heads of Russian Factories: A Sociological Study," *Social Research*, IX (September 1942).

de Schweinitz, Karl, Jr. *Industrialization and Democracy: Economic Necessities and Political Possibilities.* New York: Free Press of Glencoe, 1964.

Selznick, Philip. *The Organizational Weapon: A Study of Bolshevik Strategy and Tactics.* New York: McGraw-Hill, 1952.

Sherman, George. "Soviet Youth: Myth and Reality," *Daedalus,* Winter 1962.

Shils, Edward. "The Intellectuals in the Political Development of New States." *World Politics,* XII (April 1960).

Shmelev, V. A. *Voprosy podgotovki inzhenerno-tekhnicheskikh kadrov* (Questions on the Preparation of Engineers and Technical Cadres). Leningrad: Gosudarstvennoe Sotsialno-Ekonomicheskoe Izdatelstvo, 1931.

Simon, Herbert. *Administrative Behavior: A Study of Decision-Making Processes in Administrative Organization.* New York: Macmillan, 1958.

Slusser, Robert, ed. *Soviet Economic Policy in Postwar Germany: A Collection of Papers by Former Soviet Officials.* New York: Research Program on the USSR, 1953.

Solomon, Georgy Alexandrovich. *Sredi krasnykh vozhdei* (Among the Red Leaders). Paris: Michen, 1930.

Sorel, Georges. *Reflections on Violence,* trans. T. E. Hulme and J. Roth. Glencoe: Free Press, 1950.

Sorokin, Pitirim A. *Leaves from a Russian Diary.* New York: E. P. Dutton, 1924.

Sostav rukovodyashchikh rabotnikov i spetsialistov soyuza SSR (The Composition of the Leading Workers and Specialists in the Soviet Union). Moscow: Soyuzorguchyot, 1936.

Souvarine, Boris. *Stalin: A Critical Survey of Bolshevism.* New York: Longmans, Green, 1939.

Soveshchanie khozaistvennikov inzhenerov, tekhnikov, partiinikh i profsoyuznikh rabotnikov tuazholoi promyshlennosti (Conference of Industrial Managers, Engineers, Technicians, Party, and Trade-Union Workers in Heavy Industry). Moscow, 1934.

Sozinov, E. M. *Kommunisticheskaya partia v borbe za perekhod ot rabochevo kontrolya k rabochemu upravleniyu i natsionalizatsiu krupnoi promyshlennosti, 1917–1919* (The Communist Party in the Struggle for the Transition from Workers' Control to Workers' Management and toward the Nationalization of Large-Scale Industry, 1917–1919). Unpub. diss., Moscow State University, 1953.

Spencer, Herbert. *The Principles of Sociology,* II. New York: D. Appleton, 1900.

Stalin, Joseph V. *Leninism,* 2 vols. New York: International Publishers, 1933.

—————— *Works,* 13 vols. Moscow: Foreign Languages Publishing House, 1952–1955.

Sukhomlinsky, V. A. *Vospitanie sovetskovo patriotizma u shkolnikov*

(Teaching of Soviet Patriotism to Schoolchildren). Moscow, 1959.

Swearer, Howard. "Khrushchev's Revolution in Industrial Management," *World Politics*, XII (October 1959).

Tendryakov, Vladimir. *Chrezvychainy sud* (An Extraordinary Court). Moscow: Moskovsky Rabochy, 1962.

Tertz, Abram. *On Socialist Realism*, trans. George Dennis. New York: Pantheon Books, 1960.

Tevekelyan, V. "Za moskovskuyu reku" (Beyond the Moscow River). *Moskva*, nos. 2,3,4 (1959).

Timasheff, Nicolas. *The Great Retreat: The Growth and Decline of Communism in Russia*. New York: E. P. Dutton, 1948.

Tokaev, G. A. *Betrayal of an Ideal*. Bloomington: Indiana University Press, 1955.

Trevor-Roper, H. R. *The Last Days of Hitler*. New York: Berkley Publishing Corp., 1947.

Trifonov, I. *Ocherki klassovoi borby v SSSR v gody NEP, 1921–1937* (Sketches of the Class Battle in the USSR during the NEP, 1921–1937). Moscow: Gosudarstvennoe Izdatelstvo Politicheskoi Literatury, 1960.

Trotsky, Leon. *My life*. New York: Grosset and Dunlap, n.d.

——— *The New Course* (with *The Struggle for the New Course* by Max Shachtman). New York: International Publishing Company, 1943.

——— *Terrorism and Communism*. Ann Arbor: University of Michigan Press, 1961.

Trud v SSSR, 1924–1926 gg, diagrammy (Labor in the USSR, 1924–1926, Diagrams). Moscow: VTsSPS, 1926.

Truman, David B. *The Governmental Process: Political Interests and Public Opinion*. New York: Alfred A. Knopf, 1953.

Tucker, Robert C. "Towards a Comparative Politics of Movement-Regimes," *American Political Science Review*, LV (June 1961).

Ulam, Adam. "Another Crisis," *Problems of Communism*, XIV (May–June 1965).

——— "The New Face of Soviet Totalitarianism," *World Politics*, XII (April 1960).

——— *The Unfinished Revolution*. New York: Random House, 1960.

Undrevich, V., and M. Kareva. *Proletarskaya revolyutsia i gosudarstvenny apparat* (The Proletarian Revolution and the State Apparat). Moscow: Izdatelstvo *Vlast sovetov*, 1935.

Ustryalov, N. V. *Na novom etape* (At a New Stage). Shanghai: Tipografia *Tsenturion*, 1930.

——— *Nashe vremya, sbornik statei* (Our Era, Collection of Articles). Shanghai: 1934.

———— *Pod znakom revolyutsy* (Under the Sign of the Revolution). Harbin: Izdatelstvo *Russkaya zhizn*, 1925.

Utechin, S. V. *Russian Political Thought.* New York: Frederick A. Praeger, 1963.

Valentinov, N. (N. V. Volkov). "De Boukharine au Stalinisme," *Le Contract social*, VII (March–April 1963).

———— *Doktrina pravovo kommunisma, 1924–1926 gody: Istory sovetskovo gosudarstva* (The Doctrine of Right-Wing Communism, 1924–1926: A History of the Soviet Government). Munich: TsOPE, 1960.

———— "Sut bolshevisma v izobrazheny Yu. Pyatakova" (The Essence of Bolshevism in the Conception of Yu. Pyatakov), *Novy zhurnal* (New Journal), no. 52 (March 1958).

Veblen, Thorstein. *The Engineers and the Price System.* New York: Viking Press, 1936.

———— *Essays in Our Changing Order.* New York: Viking Press, 1934.

———— *Imperial Germany and the Industrial Revolution.* New York: Viking Press, 1942.

Volfson, S. Ya. *Intelligentsia kak sotsialno-ekonomicheskaya kategoria* (The Intelligentsia as a Social and Economic Category). Moscow: Gosudarstvennoe Izdatelstvo, 1926.

Volkov (N. V. Valentinov). "Memoirs." Unpub. manuscript, Archive of Russian and East European History and Culture, Columbia University.

Von Laue, T. *Sergei Witte and the Industrialization of Russia.* New York: Columbia University Press, 1963.

Voprosy partiinoi raboty (Problems of Party Work). Moscow: Gosudarstvennoe Izdatelstvo Politicheskoi Literatury, 1955.

Voznesensky, Andrei. *Selected Poems of Andrei Voznesensky,* trans. Anselm Hollo. New York: Grove Press, 1964.

———— "Oza," trans. George L. Kline, in *Tri-Quarterly,* Spring 1965.

Weber, Max. *The Theory of Social and Economic Organization,* trans. A. M. Henderson and Talcott Parsons. Glencoe: Free Press, 1947.

Weissberg, Alexander. *The Accused.* New York: Simon and Schuster, 1951.

Who's Who in the USSR, 1961–1962, ed. Heinrich E. Schulz and Stephen S. Taylor. New York: Scarecrow Press, 1962.

Wiles, Peter. "Die Macht im Vordergrund," *Soviet Survey,* no. 29 (April–June 1959).

———— and Leon Smolinski. "Economic Problems and Prospects," *Problems of Communism,* XII (November–December 1963).

WORKS CITED

Willets, Harry. "The Wages of Economic Sin," *Problems of Communism,* XI (September–October 1962).

Wolfe, Bertram D. *Communist Totalitarianism.* Boston: Beacon Press, 1956.

Yaroslavsky, Ya. *Tretya sila* (The Third Force). Moscow: Partiinoe Izdatelstvo, 1932.

Zinoviev, M. A. *Soviet Methods of Teaching History,* trans. A. Musin-Pushkin. Washington, D.C.: Russian Translation Project of the American Council of Learned Societies, 1952.

Zlobina, V. M. *Rukovodstvo kommunisticheskoi party promyshlennymi predpriatiami i proizvodstvennymi yacheikami v pervye gody NEP* (Communist Party Leadership of Industrial Establishments and Production Cells in the First Years of the NEP). Moscow: Izdatelstvo Moskovskovo Universiteta, 1962.

NOTES

All of the book and article titles cited below are given in condensed form; for full data see Works Cited. A few frequently cited and widely known sources and journals are given in abbreviation throughout:

CSP	*Current Soviet Policies* (Gruliow, ed.)
CW	Lenin, *Complete Works* (*Polnoe sobranie sochineny*)
Komm.	*Kommunist*
KPSS v Rez.	*Kommunisticheskaya partia sovetskovo soyuza v rezolyutsiakh i resheniakh syezdov, konferentsy, i plenumov TsK*
PS	*Partiinoe stroitelstvo*
PZ	*Partiinaya zhizn*

Full listing for records of party conferences and congresses are included in Works Cited under Communist Party. Citations are abbreviated in notes as:

I Konferentsia
I Syezd

1. INTRODUCTION

1. Almond and Coleman, eds., *Politics of Developing Areas,* introduction, esp. pp. 17–26.

2. Lerner, *Passing of Traditional Society,* chaps. 2 and 3, esp. pp. 51, 56–57, 60, 64, 67–68, 71, 85, 97; MIT Study Group, "The Transitional Process," pp. 618–641.

3. See Hayek, *The Counter-Revolution,* esp. pp. 121, 137; Markham, ed., *Henri Comte de Saint-Simon,* pp. 2–11, 70–71, 76–80.

4. See Weber, *The Theory,* pp. 337–339, 403; Gerth and Mills, eds., *From Max Weber,* pp. 49–50, 70–72, 82, 91, 231–233; Michels, *Political Parties,* esp. p. 383.

5. Haas, "Technocracy," p. 70.

6. See Croan, "The Politics of Marxist Sovietology"; Deutscher, *Russia in Transition;* Marcuse, *Soviet Marxism;* Rostow, "Rostow on Growth," esp. p. 414; Brzezinski, "Communist Disunity"; Ulam, "The New Face."

7. Brzezinski, "Communist Disunity," p. 17; Ulam, "The New Face," p. 407.

8. Achminow, *La Puissance dans l'ombre.*

9. Berliner, "Marxism and the Soviet Economy," pp. 9–11; Lichtheim, "Reflections on Trotsky," p. 60; Kautsky, ed., *Political Change*, p. 112; Aron, "Soviet Society," p. 7.

10. See Berliner, *Factory and Manager;* Granick, *Management;* Schwarz, "Heads of Russian Factories"; Rush, "Economic Managers"; Nicolaevsky, "The Party Men"; Conquest, *Power and Politics;* Hough, "Role of Local Party Organs."

11. See Truman, *The Governmental Process*, esp. pp. 27–39, 46, 63–64.

12. Meyer, "USSR Incorporated," p. 21.

2. BOLSHEVIK MANAGEMENT DOCTRINE BEFORE THE REVOLUTION

1. *Pravda*, July 10, 1964. In the following discussion I shall focus almost exclusively on those works of Lenin written before the revolution.

2. Lenin, quoted in Souvarine, *Stalin*, p. 309; Trotsky, *Terrorism and Communism*, pp. 132–133. Trotsky considered that "the organization of labor is in its essence the organization of the new society" — a view that makes his concession the more remarkable. For statements of other Bolshevik leaders to similar effect, see *XIII Syezd*, p. 100 (report of Zinoviev), and Osinsky, quoted in Carr, *The Bolshevik Revolution*, II, 60.

3. See, for example, Bell, *The End of Ideology*, pp. 346–354; de Schweinitz, *Industrialization*, p. 191; Nove, *Economic Rationality*, p. 53; Gershenkron, *Economic Backwardness*, pp. 276–280.

4. Sorel, *Reflections*, p. 59.

5. See Gershenkron, *Economic Backwardness*, pp. 276–277; Kautsky, *The Social Revolution*, p. 149.

6. Marx, *Capital*, III, 380. The discussion here concerns joint stock companies in particular.

7. See Marx, *Capital*, III, 428–430.

8. See Lenin, *CW*, XXXIII, 1–117, and XXXIV, 287–339.

9. See Marx, "The Civil War in France," in Feuer, ed., *Marx and Engels*, p. 367. Marx switches his reference from "organs" to "functions," thereby obscuring his meaning, which is obviously that old governmental organs are to be retained provided they perform "legitimate" — that is, "not merely repressive" — functions.

10. Lenin *CW*, XXXIV, 307. See also Fetscher, "Marx, Engels and the Future of Society," pp. 101–102.

11. See, for example, Schapiro, "The Party and the State," p. 113.

12. See Black, "Revolution, Modernization, and Communism," p. 18.

13. See, for example, Engels, *Socialism*, p. 38; Lenin, *CW*, XXXIII, 17.

14. I borrow the term "imperative coordination" from Weber but here place the stress on "imperative," as he does not.

15. Quoted in Lichtheim, *Marxism*, p. 390 (italics added). See also Dahrendorff, *Class and Class Conflict*, p. 250.

16. Engels, "On Authority," in Feuer, ed., *Marx and Engels*, pp. 483–484. See also Lenin, *CW*, XXXIII, 61–62.

17. Quoted in Nomad, *Aspects of Revolt*, pp. x–xi. See also Feuer, "Marx and the Intellectuals," pp. 102–103.

18. Quoted in Nomad, *Aspects of Revolt*, pp. 120–121.

19. *Ibid.*, pp. 99–100. See also Machajski, "On the Expropriation of the Capitalists," pp. 427–436; Bell, *The End of Ideology*, pp. 335–336.

20. See, for example, Lenin, *CW*, XXXIII, 109–110.

21. See Markham, ed., *Henri Comte de Saint-Simon*, pp. 1–11.

22. See, for example, Marx and Engels, "The German Ideology," in Feuer, ed., *Marx and Engels*, p. 254; Engels, *Anti-Duhring*, pp. 277, 405–406; Lenin, *CW*, XXXIII, 101–102, 116.

23. See, for example, Lenin, *CW*, XXXIII, 96.

24. Marx and Engels, *Selected Correspondence*, p. 493. See also Lenin, *CW*, XXXIV, 311–312.

25. See Ulam, *The Unfinished Revolution*; Nomad, *Aspects of Revolt*, p. 27, n. 15; Carr, *The Bolshevik Revolution*, I, 240, n. 3.

26. Lenin, *CW*, XXXIII, 101.

27. See Chapter 3, for evidence that Lenin was not completely successful in his efforts to avoid misleading his own followers.

28. See, for example, Lenin, *CW*, XXXIII, 101–102, and XXXIV, 307–308. Indeed, at one point Lenin makes it clear that even the "simple" functions of "accounting and control" will become truly simple only gradually and that some time will pass before they "will finally die out as *the special* function of a special stratum of the population" (XXXIII, 50).

29. *Ibid.*, XXXIII, 49.

30. *Ibid.*, XXXIII, 114; XXXIV, 311–312, 320.

31. See also *ibid.*, XXXIII, 109, for a sentence in which Lenin stresses that the socialist state apparatus will consist of *"the very same workers and officials"* as did the old bourgeois state apparatus. The italics are omitted in the authorized English translation (*Selected Works*, VII, 101).

32. One of the principal items in Machajski's critique of Marx and Engels was precisely this intention to retain the engineers and man-

agers of capitalist industry; see "On the Expropriation of the Capitalists," esp. p. 428.

33. Lenin, *CW*, XXXIII, 101.

34. See, for example, *ibid.*, XXIV, 164; XXXIV, 307–311.

35. See Marx and Engels, "Manifesto," in Feuer, ed., *Marx and Engels*, pp. 10, 14; Marx, *Capital*, III, 379–381, 427–429.

36. See Marx, *Capital*, III, 427–428, I 459–460. Marx refers in these pages to the exploitation by the capitalist owners of all workers "from the manager down to the last day laborer." See also, Volfson, *Intelligentsia*, pp. 28–29, where Marx's appendix to *The Theory of Surplus Value* is quoted; *World Marxist Review* (September 1961), pp. 66–68; and Michels, "Sulla scadenza," where the insistence of European socialists and Marxist socialists in particular that the managerial and white-collar groups in society are members of the working class is discussed in some detail and refuted with some passion.

37. Marx and Engels, *Correspondence*, p. 493; Lenin, *CW*, XXXIV, 312. See also Lenin, *CW*, XXXVIII, 116. This last reference is Lenin's report to the Eighth Party Congress, which convened in 1919. Lenin makes much of the fact that in Germany "engineers and managers" are joining the Spartakists in increasing numbers.

38. See Lenin, *CW*, XXXIV, 312, for the role of the revolution as an accelerator.

39. Quoted in Feuer, "Marx and the Intellectuals," p. 104. Later Kautsky amended this proposition to read that the members of the intelligentsia lack a common class-consciousness, thereby reverting to orthodoxy (see *The Social Revolution*, p. 46).

40. See, for example, Engels "Letters on Historical Materialism," in Feuer, ed., *Marx and Engels*, p. 405.

41. Kautsky, *The Social Revolution*, p. 46–47.

42. Lenin, *Selected Works*, III, 15; also, *CW*, XLII, 345–346; XLIV, 50–51; XXXVII, 166–169.

43. The fullest analysis of the political import of professionalism among technical and managerial personnel from a Leninist point of view can be found in Beilin, *Kadry*, chap. 7. For Lenin's own remarks on this score, see the works cited immediately above. See also Marx and Engels, *Correspondence*, p. 493; Engels, "Letter to von Bënigk," August 21, 1890, in *Voprosy istory* KPSS, no. 2 (1964), p. 4. For Marx on the payment of higher wages to skilled cadres, see Nomad, *Aspects of Revolt*, pp. 25–28.

44. Lenin, *CW*, XXXIII, 100–101. See Marx, "The Civil War in France," in Feuer, ed., *Marx and Engels*, p. 366, for the Commune of 1871 as composed of "workingmen or acknowledged representatives of the working class." In "State and Revolution," Lenin quotes this passage without particular comment, but in "Will the Bolsheviks

Retain State Power?" he makes it clear that the "acknowledged representatives of the working class" would be characterized above all by their membership in the party (*CW*, XXXIV, 313).

45. See esp. Lenin, *CW*, XXXIII, 45–51.

46. *Ibid.*, XXXIII, 49. Putting the word "managers" in quotation marks was one of the techniques Lenin utilized to rally anarchist support.

47. See Markham, ed., *Henri Comte de Saint-Simon*, introduction; Hayek, *The Counter-Revolution*. As for subsequent events, the experience of various Western European countries would be worth exploring for the role of managerial and technical cadres in socialist movements, as well as in various quasi-socialist, supranational planning and development movements associated with European integration.

48. See, for example, Chapter 3; Miloscz, *The Captive Mind*.

49. See above, note 43; Marx, *Capital*, III, 427–432. See also Marx and Engels, "Manifesto," Feuer, ed., *Marx and Engels*, pp. 17–18, for the hyperconservative role of the petty bourgeoisie, a stratum to which the managerial and technical intelligentsia could well be compared within the framework of Marxist theory. See Kautsky, *The Social Revolution*, p. 180, for the petty bourgeois leanings of the intelligentsia.

50. Marx and Engels, *Correspondence*, p. 493. See this same letter and Lenin, *CW*, XXXIV, 308, for the use of terror.

51. Rapid economic development would, of course, be a high-priority item for any socialist regime. In the *Manifesto*, Marx and Engels proclaim that the proletariat will use its power "to increase the total of productive forces as rapidly as possible" (Feuer, ed., *Marx and Engels*, p. 28). For Lenin the problem was more urgent. As he put it shortly after the revolution, life "poses the question with brutal clarity: either to be ruined or to catch up with and overtake the advanced countries economically."

52. See Lenin, *CW*, XXXIV, 310–311, for recognition of the problem of "passive sabotage." See also Lange, "On the Economic Theory of Socialism," pp. 123–124.

53. Marx and Engels, *Correspondence*, p. 493. See also Engels, "The Peasant War in Germany," in Feuer, ed., *Marx and Engels*, p. 435, for the well-known statement: "the worst thing that can befall the leader of an extreme party is to be compelled to take over a government in an epoch when the movement is not yet ripe for the domination of the class which he represents and for the realization of the measures which that domination implies . . . [He] is compelled to represent not his party or his class but the class for whose domination the movement is then ripe."

54. This awareness runs throughout "Will the Bolsheviks Retain State Power?" Lenin, *CW*, XXXIV, 287–339.

55. Lenin, *CW*, XXXIV, 307–308.

56. The figure 15,000 is an approximation based on data provided in *PZ*, no. 4 (February 1963), p. 22; Katuntsev, "Rol," p. 85; Fedyushkin, *Privlechenie*, p. 39.

57. For a retrospective acknowledgment on Lenin's part that he proceeded precisely as indicated in this paragraph, see Lenin's "Our Revolution: Apropos of the Notes of N. Sukhanov," written in 1923 (*CW*, XLV, 378–382). In this brief memorandum Lenin made no secret of the fact that his actions at the time of the Bolshevik seizure of power had been governed by the slogan *on s'engage et puis on voit*. He freely conceded his Napoleonic outlook and defiantly proclaimed that in the absence of such an outlook "revolutions could not be made at all." Above all, it had been right and proper for the Bolsheviks to launch the revolution without worrying about the "incontrovertible proposition" that Russia had "not attained the level of development of productive forces that makes socialism possible" or the basic cultural prerequistes for socialist construction. In effect, he was saying that the charges of those critics who had accused him of rank adventurism were valid from the point of view of Marxist orthodoxy. All that he claimed in his own defense was one indisputable, though theoretically irrelevant, fact: "now there can be no doubt that . . . we have been victorious."

3. THE BOURGEOIS SPECIALISTS

1. On the campaign of absenteeism and insubordination, for good examples see Fedyushkin, *Privlechenie;* Undrevich and Kareva, *Proletarskaya*, pp. 106ff; Dan, *Dva goda*, pp. 15–16; Price, *My Reminiscences*, pp. 165, 208. No precise data are available on the number of industrial specialists who joined the Whites, but the fact that Bolshevik sources which are generally hostile to the specialists are silent on this score suggests that the number was small. As for the scale of emigration among the specialists, data are once again lacking, but, given the number of specialists who remained on the scene after the Civil War, it could not have been extensive. The one contraindication on this score is a report that, in 1921, the metallurgical and coalmining industries of southwestern Russia retained only some 20–25 percent of their prewar complement of engineers (Beilin, *Kadry*, p. 34). But a substantial part of this loss can be attributed to the repatriation of foreign engineers (who made up almost 50 percent of the total number of engineers during the prewar period) and the transfer of Russian engineers to other

regions. In addition, emigration was much easier from southwestern Russia than from most other regions.

2. Judging by data on the class origins of students in the higher technical schools of prerevolutionary Russia, it is likely that at least half of the engineers on the scene in 1917 were of lower-class origin (see Hans, *History,* pp. 229–242). The sobriquet "bourgeois specialist" was more valid where members of the nontechnical intelligentsia were concerned, though even in their case it was often misleading. In any event, it was applied to all holdover cadres without discrimination.

3. See Lenin, *CW, XXXV,* 199–200.

4. See Dan, *Dva goda,* p. 23; Rezunov, *Sovetskoe gosudarstvo,* p. 93; Undrevich and Kareva, *Proletarskaya,* p. 120; Yaroslavsky, *Tretya sila,* p. 96; Lenin, *CW, XXXVI,* 137.

5. See Chapter 2. For an explicit acknowledgment on Lenin's part that "military methods" provided no spur to active cooperation, see *CW, XXXVIII,* 166–167.

6. Lenin, *CW, XXXVIII,* 168–169. As it was, there was a steady drop in the level of production throughout the Civil War period (see, for example, Baykov, *The Development,* p. 8). But the miracle is how much production was maintained, and here the role of the bourgeois specialists was critical (see, for example, Carr, *The Bolshevik Revolution,* II, 186; Liberman, *Building,* p. 61).

7. See Gladkov, *K istory;* Fedyushkin, *Privlechenie,* p. 10; Katuntsev, "Rol," p. 85; Utechin, *Russian Political Thought,* p. 185.

8. See, for example, Lenin, *CW, XLIV,* 50–51.

9. *Ibid.,* XLII, 156. To make matters more confusing, what Lenin here identified as the "first" party program (the program worked out by Bukharin, Preobrazhensky, and others) was actually the second party program from a chronological point of view, the first having been adopted in 1903.

10. It should be noted that Lenin's euphoria was not so unmitigated that he failed to note the need to "check" on the work of the engineers and agronomists in question, though this motif was definitely subordinate to the one stressed here. See *CW, XLII,* 157. Also, *CW, XLIV,* 50, for a speech to the Third Comintern Congress in which, without ceasing to stress the immense contribution of the Goelro specialists, Lenin nonetheless emphasized that "almost all of them are disposed against the Soviet regime."

11. *Ibid.,* XLV, 290–291. See Kim, *Kommunisticheskaya,* p. 215, where it is authoritatively reported not only that "in the years of the reconstruction period only insignificant successes were achieved in the preparation of new cadres," but also that there was a substantial

decline between 1922 and 1925 in the number of engineers who were graduated from Soviet institutions of higher education.

12. Dzerzhinsky, *Izbrannie*, II, 214. For more on Dzerzhinsky's favorable attitude toward the bourgeois specialists, see Volkov, "Memoirs," pp. 197–198, 218, 221, 232–233.

13. *Pravda*, January 15, 1925, p. 3. For the expression of a similar attitude by G. K. Ordzhonikidze, see his *Stati*, II, 29. Ordzhonikidze went event further than Dzerzhinsky, stating in 1927 that the term "red director" should be abolished because "there are no 'white' directors in our plants. We can directly say that every director in the factory is our director." In effect, this was a plea for the abolition of the term "bourgeois specialist" and the abandonment of all political discrimination against holdover cadres.

14. The new wage policy was inaugurated in April 1918, in a speech in which Lenin, after acknowledging that "such a measure is clearly a compromise," proclaimed the regime's intention "to resort to the old bourgeois method and agree to pay a high price for the 'services' of the biggest bourgeois specialists" (*CW*, XXXVI, 179). In December 1920, this "compromise" was carried further with the establishment of a special wage rate for virtually all specialists. By 1925, top specialists were often receiving ten times the wage of the average worker (Fedyushkin, *Privlechenie*, p. 31). Lenin had, of course, anticipated that a compromise on the "wage front" might prove necessary (*see* Chapter 2).

15. See, for example, Volfson, *Intelligentsia;* Yaroslavsky, *Tretya sila*, p. 96.

16. Quoted in, Fedyushkin, *Privlechenie*, pp. 28–29.

17. Lenin, *CW*, XXXVIII, 220–222. This response made a very favorable impact on almost all of the members of the technical intelligentsia, and prompted Dukelsky himself to join the party (see Fedyushkin *Privlechenie*, pp. 28–29; Volkov, "Memoirs," pp. 40–41).

18. For good descriptions of the system of workers' management, see Kritsman, *Geroichesky period*, pp. 89–125.

19. It was not uncommon for managers and engineers to be "locked out" altogether, and this should be kept in mind in evaluating the phenomenon of absenteeism within the ranks of the bourgeois specialists.

20. As late as March 1918, one high official of the VSNKh wrote an article for an official journal in which he asserted that it was "treason to the workers" to allow any bourgeois engineers to resume work. Cited in Carr, *The Bolshevik Revolution*, II, 182.

21. See Sozinov, *Kommunisticheskaya partia*, p. 111.

22. See, for example, Yaroslavsky, *Tretya sila*, p. 96.

23. See, for example, Krylenko, ed., *Ekonomicheskaya kontrrevolyutsia*, pp. 182–183.

24. See Lenin, *CW*, VII, 343–344. By suprapolitical developmental nationalism, I mean a commitment to expanding the economic base of the community for the sake of national power, the latter being intensely valued for its own sake. Psychologically, developmental nationalism is surely not a contradiction in terms, and it seems to me highly dubious that it is so operationally, as Richard Pipes has suggested. His argument that "nationalism runs contrary to the needs of economic development" is based on a confusion between nationalism and traditionalism — a fact that becomes apparent when he goes on (after an interval of one sentence) to buttress his argument with the assertion, "certainly, the maximal use of economic resources requires a degree of rationalization that can not brook interference from traditionalism" ("The Forces," p. 2).

25. See Mendeleev, *Zavetnye mysly* and *K poznaniyu rossy*. The fullest discussion of Mendeleev's thought in English is to be found in S. V. Utechin's *Russian Political Thought* (pp. 183–186), and it is from this discussion that the preceding summary of Mendeleev's advice to the technical intelligentsia is drawn. I reject Utechin's designation "technocratism" for the belief system here in question because in many and probably most cases, including that of Mendeleev himself, what was involved was not a commitment to rule by specialists (which would perforce entail political involvement) but a complete withdrawal from political involvement. See Mendeleev, *Zavetnye mysly*, p. 259, for a clear-cut disavowal of technocratism as we understand it.

26. Already by 1917 one could observe in Russia a trend that has since emerged in various other "advanced" underdeveloped countries: "the increase in those with an advanced technical or scientific and specialized education [has created] . . . a body of persons whose interests are narrower than their predecessors in their own countries and whose contact with the humanistic and political tradition of the hitherto prevailing higher education [has become] . . . more attenuated. They themselves [are] . . . not merely different from the conventional political intellectuals . . . but less frequently identify themselves as 'intellectuals.'" Shils, "The Intellectuals," p. 332, n. 5.

27. See Mehnert, "Changing Attitudes," pp. 498–499; Denicke, "Links," pp. 6–7. It should also be noted that the creation of the Duma and other reforms after the 1905 Revolution gave some of the political intelligentsia a societal (within-system) vocation. But these concessions by tsardom were too halfhearted and too long-delayed to overcome decades of alienation.

28. The technical intelligentsia's ability to acquire a sense of vocational achievement within the tsarist system did not mean — although it might have prefigured — generalized identification with the established social and political order. Thus the Menshevik leader Dan was convinced that "the rapid and decisive success [of the 1905 Revolution] was to a considerable degree caused by the participation of that part of the intelligentsia which performs organizing functions in a capitalist economy and in state activities and, owing to its social position, can act as a link between the movement of the masses and that of the propertied upper classes." Quoted in Elkin, "The Russian Intelligentsia," pp. 474–475.

29. Mendeleev called his political ideas "gradualism," reserving the designation "realism" (in contradistinction to both idealism and materialism) for the philosophical tenets on which they were based. See Utechin, *Russian Political Thought*, p. 183.

30. Whether what was involved in this process was usually a conscious reappraisal of Mendeleev's doctrine (or others of similar purport) or merely *de facto* adoption of a Mendeleev-like position cannot, of course, be conclusively determined. It is noteworthy, however, that the remarks of Pitrim A. Sorokin, quoted later in my text, represent an almost exact paraphrase of one of the last sentences of Mendeleev's *Zavetnye mysly* (p. 425).

31. Quoted in Bubnov and Preobrazhensky, *Za pyat let*, p. 44. See Lenin, *CW*, XXXVII, 188–197, for an appraisal of Sorokin's letter as indicative of a trend among many SRs and Mensheviks. For other examples of the way professionalism redounded to the benefit of the Bolsheviks, see Ipatieff, *Life*, pp. 255, 256, esp. p. 259; *Pravda*, November 30, 1923.

32. Bardin, *Zhizn*, p. 108.

33. Utechin, *Russian Political Thought*, p. 184.

34. See *Protsess;* Liberman, *Building*, pp. 208–209; Ipatieff, *Life*, pp. 255–256, 295; Volkov, "Memoirs," pp. 1–2, 36.

35. See Lenin, *CW*, XLV, 93, for the rapid spread of smenovekhism. Lenin was echoed a year later by Stalin, who asserted at the Twelfth Party Congress that smenovekhism had "acquired a mass of supporters among Soviet officials" (*Works*, V, 249). This smenovekh movement should not be confused with the more famous movement of the same name organized after the 1905 Revolution by Struve, Berdyaev, and other of the political and philosophical leaders of the moderate intelligentsia. The spread of post-1917 smenovekhism was partly due to Bolshevik encouragement. The smenovekhites were allowed to publish various of their journals and books in Russia, and the regime even went so far as to recommend the reading of smenovekhite publications to the specialist-dominated commanding

staff of the Red Army (see Ustryalov, *Pod znakom*, pp. 69–70). The fullest discussion of smenovekhism in English is found in Utechin's *Russian Political Thought*, pp. 253–255. Utechin stresses the presence of nationalist themes in Ustryalov's thought. However, in his writings up to at least 1925, especially his political as opposed to his historical or philosophical writings, Ustryalov's programmatic perspective is essentially liberal. At the same time, Slavophile-tinged nationalism was always an exceedingly important component in Ustryalov's thought, and, as we shall see, it became increasingly dominant with the passage of time.

36. See *Protsess*, esp. pp. 371–462, for the fullest, though somewhat constrained, exposition of the views of the ex-Menshevik specialists. Additional information can be found in Jasny, *Soviet Industrialization*, appendix A; Valentinov, "De Boukharine" and *Doktrina*; Volkov, "Memoirs," pp. 36–37.

37. I say "liberal or socialist" because some socialists among the cooperating specialists thought that dictatorial Bolshevism would give way to a liberal, quasi-bourgeois regime in the first instance and that full-fledged socialism would emerge only after the latter had run its course. See the various renderings of this theme in *Protsess*, esp. pp. 371–462; also Volkov, "Memoirs," pp. 36–37, 58–59, 155.

38. Klyuchnikov et al., *Smena vekh*, p. 163. This passage also provides a particularly graphic example of the dominance of the motif of economic determinism in smenovekhism. In Ustryalov's own writings economic determinism is equally critical, but it is rarely stated so explicitly (see, for example, *Pod znakom*, pp. 11, 18, 26–28, 45, 51–54, 68–69, 94, 96, 101–102, 119, 142–143, 166–167). See also Volkov, "Memoirs," p. 37.

39. The hope of softening Bolshevik policy by means of cooperating in its formulation and execution was by no means peculiar to liberals and socialists; it was endorsed by professionals as well. See Gurovich, "Vysshy sovet."

40. Solomon, *Sredi*, p. 41.

41. See, for example, Jasny, *Soviet Industrialization*, appendix A; Ordzhonikidze, *Stati*, II, 176–177.

42. With regard to Spencer's influence on the Russian intelligentsia, see Rogers, "The Russian Populists," p. 466; Ustryalov, *Pod znakom*, p. 253. That Ustryalov was aware of Spencer's political views and cited them with approval is particularly noteworthy.

43. See, for example, Lenin, *Selected Works*, VIII, 390–391, ed.'s note; *IX Syezd*, pp. xii, 150, 170, 172–173, 187, 212; *Rabochaya Oppozitsia*, p. 243; Carr, *The Bolshevik Revolution*, II, 85–86; Daniels, *The Conscience*, pp. 49–50.

44. *Pravda*, January 15, 1925, p. 3.

213

45. Trotsky, quoted in Daniels, *The Conscience*, p. 189; *XVI Syezd*, pp. 199–201.

46. For the figure of 50 percent or more, see Beilin, *Kadry*, p. 48; for "White professor," see Carr, *The Bolshevik Revolution*, II, 185.

47. *IX Syezd*, pp. 50–56, 115–126. Trotsky had actually anticipated Lenin's advocacy of one-man authority or, more accurately perhaps, had dared to state explicitly what Lenin had at the time only dared to imply. Thus Trotsky used the occasion of a conference of the Moscow city party organization in March 1918 to declare: "Democratization does not at all consist — as every Marxist learns in his ABC — in abolishing the meaning of skilled forces, the meaning of persons possessing special knowledge, and in replacing them everywhere and anywhere by elective boards . . . The next step must consist in the self-limitation of the collegiate principle, in a healthy and necessary act of self limitation by the working class . . . Political, collegiate, and Soviet control everywhere and anywhere; but for the executive functions we must appoint technical experts, put them in responsible positions, and impose responsibility upon them" (*Terrorism and Communism*, pp. 118–119). See Lenin *CW*, XXVII, 309–310, 357–364, for weaker statements of what was essentially a similar position. According to one source, L. B. Krasin, one of the foremost red directors and one of the few Old Bolshevik engineers, had advocated the introduction of one-man authority even earlier than Trotsky (see *XI Syezd*, p. 169).

48. See *IX Syezd*, pp. 120, 123, 150–153, 170; and Carr, *The Bolshevik Revolution*, II, 394–395, for a note on the railroad reorganization.

49. Lenin, *CW*, XL, 271. I add the word "single" in brackets in order to stress what Lenin himself made clear in the sentence following the one quoted: "One way or another unquestioning subordination to one will is unconditionally necessary."

50. See Daniels, *The Conscience*, p. 109; Kolontay, *The Workers' Opposition*, p. 7.

51. *IX Syezd*, pp. 22–25.

52. Bukharin, "The Economics of the Transition Period," excerpted in Daniels, *Documentary History*, pp. 179–180.

53. See Kolontay, *The Workers' Opposition*, esp. pp. 7, 12–13; *X Syezd*, p. 102 (speech of Kolontay).

54. For Lenin's defeats in the period immediately preceding the Ninth Congress, see Schapiro, *Origin of Communist Autocracy*, p. 230; Lenin, *Selected Works*, pp. 427–428 (ed.'s note).

55. Kritsman, *Geroichesky period*, p. 201.

56. *XII Syezd*, pp. 41, 57; Lied, *Sidelights on Economic Situation*, pp. 14, 16.

57. Kritsman, *Geroichesky period*, pp. 91, 95.

58. Lenin, *CW*, XLII, 346. This directive was aimed specifically at Communists in Gosplan, but it was obviously intended to have general application. Thus, in 1922, Lenin asserted that "there shall be no one at the head of our commercial enterprises who has no experience in this field" and warned that "the next purge will affect those Communists who imagine that they are administrators" (*CW*, XLV, 14, 16).

59. *XI Syezd*, p. 271; Schapiro, *The Communist Party*, p. 273.

60. See, however, Carr, *The Bolshevik Revolution*, II, 376, 379–380, for the view that Lenin initially opposed the establishment of Gosplan and was a good deal less than enthusiastic about extending its powers.

61. *Direktivy*, I, 552–553, 669, 680.

62. *XV Syezd*, I, 70–71.

63. Here I do not even refer to the opposition's belief that their direst predictions had long since been fully confirmed. Thus, by 1922, some members of the opposition had convinced themselves that the revolution had been suborned and the technical intelligentsia brought to power. See "The Appeal of the 'Workers' Truth' Group," excerpted in Daniels, *Documentary History*, p. 221; Daniels, *The Conscience*, p. 161.

64. Jasny, *Soviet Industrialization*, p. 436.

65. Gurovich, "Vysshy sovet," p. 327.

66. The terminology here is borrowed, of course, from Herbert Simon's conceptualization of administrative decision making in his *Administrative Behavior*.

67. Lenin, *CW*, XLV, 95.

68. Gurovich, "Vysshy sovet," pp. 327–328. See also Solomon, *Sredi*, for what is in some respects a book-length elaboration of this theme.

69. Gurovich, "Vysshy sovet," pp. 329–330. See also Deutscher, *Stalin*, p. 242.

70. Inkeles and Bauer, *The Soviet Citizen*, pp. 289–290. It is worth noting that the party leadership, including Lenin, was well aware of the "bolshevizing" effect of work involvement and constantly cited this effect in justification of official management policy. See, for example, Lenin, *CW*, XLII, 345–347; XLIV, 50–51; *XV Syezd*, I, 70–71, report of Stalin.

71. See Kritsman, *Geroichesky period*, pp. 144–146, for the results of a 1922 survey which revealed that only 13 percent of a fairly comprehensive survey of holdover managerial cadres professed loyalty to the Bolshevik regime as such — this despite the fact that there was every incentive to do so. After 1922 the conversion rate was un-

doubtedly higher, but the evidence suggests that it never assumed more than modest proportions.

72. For good discussions of organizational developments within the party during this period, see Carr, *The Bolshevik Revolution,* I, chaps. 7–9; Carr, *Socialism in One Country,* II, 196–227; Fainsod, *How Russia Is Ruled,* chaps. 5–8; Schapiro, *The Communist Party,* esp. chaps. 13, 17.

73. Stalin, *Works,* VII, 173.

74. Liberman, *Building,* p. 13.

75. Party members comprised over half of the management boards of industrial glavks in 1921 and virtually monopolized the directorships of *large* plants and factories by 1923 (Kritsman, *Geroichesky period,* pp. 90–96; Rozenfeld, *Promyshlennaya politika,* p. 310; Stalin, *Works,* V, 215–216). By 1924, 56 of 64 trust heads were party members, of whom 60 percent were Old Bolsheviks (Zlobina, *Rukovodstvo,* p. 37).

76. Whereas in 1924 only 49 percent of all plant directors were Communists, by January 1926, 78.3 percent were Communists. By January 1928, the figure was 89 percent. (Rozenfeld, *Promyshlennaya politika,* p. 310; Riutin, "Rukovodyashchie kadry," p. 27.) It should be noted that these changes cannot be explained in terms of the incorporation of bourgeois specialists into the party.

77. The phrase "institutionalization of mutual suspicion" is borrowed from Fainsod, *How Russia Is Ruled,* p. 388.

78. See *Direktivy,* II, 120–126; *Kratky ekonomichesky slovar* (1958 ed.), p. 75.

79. See, for example, Stalin, *Works,* XIII, 53–82.

80. *Ibid.,* XIII, 53–82. See also *Direktivy,* II, 172.

81. Prokofyev, *Industrial Intelligentsia,* pp. 47–48. On the rejection of offers of party membership, see Volkov, "Memoirs," p. 224; Ipatieff, *Life,* p. 362.

82. Fedyushkin, *Privlechenie,* p. 76; Ogarkov, "Borba," p. 73; *PS,* no. 10 (May 15, 1937), p. 24.

83. Liberman, *Building,* p. 179. Liberman was a former specialist who left Russia prior to the rise of Stalinism.

84. On the planning debate, see Ehrlich, *The Soviet Industrialization Debate.* The term "bacchanalian" planning is Naum Jasny's. The view the specialists adopted toward Stalin's approach was prefigured in their attitude toward Trotskyism (see Volkov, "Memoirs," p. 232).

85. Quoted in Daniels, *The Conscience,* p. 358.

86. Ustryalov, *Nashe vremya,* pp. 6–7. Ustryalov was certain that this view "reflected the mood at the time of the bulk of the serving intelligentsia," which, he asserted, "aligned with the Right Deviation in the party" on the ground that the rightist approach to industrializa-

tion "seemed the most sober and intelligent, answering the interests of the country."

87. See, for example, Molotov, "Na dva fronta"; Yaroslavsky, *Tretya sila,* esp. p. 33. On the whole subject of the Right Opposition and the bourgeois specialists, see Valentinov, "De Boukharine" and *Doktrina.* See Alexandrov, *Kto upravlyaet,* pp. 297–298, for the view that Rykov "entered into agreement with important representatives of Gosplan, the VSNKh, etc." — that is, with nonparty specialists — and in meetings of the higher party organs utilized material received from them to refute official reports presented at these meetings.

88. Lunacharsky, *Ob intelligentsy,* p. 18. For Lenin's commitment to this position, see Bonch-Bruevich, *Izbrannye,* III, 200–203. For Stalin's own formulation of the Leninist line, see his *Works,* VII, 351. This last reference is to the section in Stalin's report to the Fourteenth Party Congress where it is said of Ustryalov that "he can speculate about the degeneration of our party as much as he likes so long as he does his work [as an émigré specialist on the Manchurian railway] properly."

89. Ustryalov, *Pod znakom,* p. 49. See Stalin, *Works,* XII, 336–337, for an explicit repudiation of Ustryalov's doctrine of collaboration — this at the Sixteenth Party Congress in 1930.

90. Harper, *Civic Training,* pp. 11–12.

91. Fedyushkin, *Privlechenie,* p. 45.

92. *XVI Konferentsia,* pp. 135, 186.

93. Stalin, *Works,* XI, 225.

94. Quoted in Ustryalov, *Na novom etape,* p. 26. The same point was made less apocalyptically but in an immediate sense even more ominously in an *Izvestia* article in the same year: "In the present state of affairs apoliticism can be construed only as sheltering wreckers, only as support for the counterrevolution" (quoted in *Itogi . . . 17–21 dekabrya 1930,* p. 213).

95. For the showtrials of the specialists, see *Protsess;* Milyutin, ed., *Kondratevshchina;* Krylenko, ed., *Ekonomicheskaya kontrrevolyutsia;* Rothstein, *Wreckers.* See Trifonov, *Ocherki,* pp. 160–161, for the statement that "not more than two to three thousand" of the old engineering cadres proved to be wreckers. A well-informed émigré source, however, suggests a higher figure, reporting in 1931 that, "of the 35,000 engineers in the country, a figure which includes the latest graduates, over 7,000 have been arrested" (*Sotsialistichesky vestnik,* no. 6–7 [April 3, 1931], quoted in Abramovitch, *The Soviet Revolution,* p. 382).

96. For widespread disbelief of the charges against the specialists by Communist economic executives, see *XVI Syezd,* pp. 319, 330. On the later resumption of important posts, see *XVI Syezd,* p. 502;

Beck and Godin, *Russian Purge*, p. 8; *Za industrializatsiu*, May 23, 1931; Ordzhonikidze, *Stati*, II, 309.

97. The purge of the bourgeois specialists was also designed to terrorize oppositionists within the party. Commenting on the trial of the Gosplan specialists, the so-called trial of the Menshevik Center, Yaroslavsky remarked: "Like the other trials of the specialists, the trial of the Mensheviks was aimed at the opportunists in our own ranks — the Trotskyites and the Rights." *Pravda*, March 6, 1931.

98. Quoted in Joravsky, "Soviet Scientists," p. 567. See Baykov, *Development of the Economic System*, pp. 151–152, 216, for a multitude of complaints to this effect in the Soviet industrial press.

99. *Sbornik pyatiletki*, p. 132.

100. In 1936, 10 of the 23 heads of glavks who had higher education were pre-1917 graduates. Among the deputy heads and chief engineers of glavks, the corresponding ratio was 29 to 57. Among heads of sections of the Peoples' Commissariat of Heavy Industry, it was 6 to 13. Among heads of trusts, it was 13 to 81. Among enterprise directors, it was 21 to 230. Petrovsky, ed., *Kadry*, pp. 172–173.

101. For a contrary view, see Jasny, *Soviet Industrialization*, appendix A; Labedz, "The New Soviet Intelligentsia"; Schapiro, *The Communist Party*, p. 341. In support of my opinion, see Denicke, *Links*; Armstrong, *Politics of Totalitarianism*, p. 94; Feldmesser, "Aspects of Social Mobility," p. 210; Maynard, *The Russian Peasant*, pp. 345–346.

102. See Arakelian, *Industrial Management*, p. 89, for the figure of 7,000; Azrael, "Political Profiles," appendix C, for a full analysis of figures relating to the rate of attrition among the specialists.

103. Ustryalov, *Na novom etape*, pp. 18, 27–28. Ustryalov returned to the USSR in 1935 (see *Bolshaya*, 1956 ed., XLIV, 414).

104. See Ustryalov, *Na novom etape* and *Nashe vremya*. On the revival of nationalistic symbolism and sentiment, see Barghoorn, *Soviet Russian Nationalism*.

105. See Molotov, "Na dva fronta," pp. 10–11, for Bazarov's declaration, made while he was still employed in Gosplan. Shortly after, he was arrested and eventually brought to trial as a member of the Menshevik Center, although in fact he was an ex-Bolshevik.

106. See *Protsess*, pp. 371–456, for statements similar to Bazarov's by a number of prominent ex-Menshevik specialists. The possibility that venality played a prominent role can be ruled out.

107. *Ibid.*, p. 223. Groman was abroad at the time.

108. See, for example, Labedz, "Deutscher"; Croan, "Marxist Kreminology: Otto Bauer's Vision."

109. Quoted in Fedyushkin, *Privlechenie*, pp. 62–63.

110. Trevor-Roper, *The Last Days of Hitler*, pp. 205–206.

111. Schapiro, *The Communist Party*, p. 363.

112. See Churchill, *The Second World War*, IV, 447, for Stalin's own recognition of the insecurity of his rulership and perhaps of the Soviet regime itself during these years.

113. Arendt, *On Revolution*, p. 230.

4. THE RED DIRECTORS

1. Carr (*The Interregnum*, pp. 40–43, 355) tends to blur the distinction between the bourgeois specialists and the red directors, apparently in the mistaken belief that many bourgeois specialists became Communists in the first years after the Revolution.

2. For Communist domination of the "commanding heights" and strategic bluffs of the industrial establishment during the period 1917–1928, see Chapter 3. As for the subsequent period, it can be noted that, as late as 1936, almost 60 percent of the heads of heavy-industry glavks and a very substantial percentage of trust and large-enterprise directors, as well as most of the top cadres working directly in the Peoples' Commissariat of Heavy Industry, had held high-level management posts for over ten years. Moreover, with few exceptions, they were veteran party members who had been Communists for some time before becoming managers (*see Trud v SSSR*, p. 311; *Sostav*, pp. 16, 47; Granick, *Management*, p. 44). From *Sostav* we also learn that in 1934 almost 50 percent of the directors in the machinebuilding industry were Old Bolsheviks, and that 25 percent of all plant directors had been in the party since before 1921. Granick states that, of the men who headed heavy-industry glavks in 1934, 60 percent had worked in the particular branch of industry in question for over ten years.

3. Fischer, *Machines*, p. 61. See also Weissberg, *The Accused*, esp. pp. 55–56. Weissberg returns again and again to such statements as "all the superhuman energy of this man went completely into his work" and "he was completely taken up with his work," in his reliable and intimate portraits of the red directors.

4. For the comment of a former bourgeois specialist on the "trade off" between energy and technical competence in the case of the red directors, see *Project B*, III, no. 26, p. 9.

5. Harbison, "Entrepreneurial Organization," p. 367. Harbison goes on to say of organization builders that, "such persons . . . do not always have new ideas nor do they necessarily carry out new combinations. They may be simply good leaders and excellent administrators." See also Schumpeter, *Capitalism*, p. 132.

6. It is noteworthy in this connection that Erik Erickson (*Childhood and Society*, pp. 398–400) sees close similarities between the psychologies of the early Marxist revolutionaries in Russia and the

early Calvinists in Western Europe. See McClelland, *The Achieving Society*, Hagen, *On the Theory of Social Change*, and Pye, *Politics, Personality, and Nation Building*, part 4, for the generally accepted view that the authoritarian and the entrepreneurial personalities are essentially incompatible and even diametrically opposed.

7. Ulam, *The Unfinished Revolution*, p. 199.

8. Kritsman, *Geroichesky period*, p. 78.

9. *Ibid.*, p. 78. See Lenin, *CW*, XXXVI, 193–194, for one among many examples of official concern that top-flight organizers be assigned to managerial posts.

10. *XIII Syezd*, p. 243 (speech of Zinoviev); *Itogi partiinoi raboty*, pp. 74–77, for data on the red directors. Those of the latter who had belonged to other parties were not bourgeois specialists, but men like Pyatakov, who had been an anarchist until 1910, or Bogdanov who was a Menshevik before 1905.

11. See, for example, *VIII Syezd*, pp. 203, 289–290, 292; *IX Syezd*, pp. xii, 150, 172–173, 187; *X Syezd*, pp. 27, 57–58, 68, 255, 563, 565.

12. Gladkov, *Energia*, p. 545; Ehrenbourg, *Out of Chaos*, p. 109.

13. For examples of such charges, see *XII Syezd*, pp. 174, 222–224, 619–620; *KPSS v rez.*, I, 772.

14. See *XI Syezd*, p. 395, for the particular applicability of these charges to "comrades placed at the summit."

15. The managerial regrouping at the time of the Twelfth Congress (1923) was headed by men who were without exception not only Old Bolsheviks but venerable Old Bolsheviks. As for the rank and file for whom these men spoke, they were acknowledged to be the party's "best people." Presumably, the trust heads were representative of the entire group, and, in 1924, 60 percent of all trust heads were Old Bolsheviks. See *XII Syezd*, pp. 619–620; Zlobina, *Rukovodstovo*, p. 37.

16. *X Syezd*, pp. 563, 565, 567.

17. *XI Syezd*, pp. 548, 551. Indeed, the acknowledged slogan of the congress was "specialization" (p. 447).

18. See Carr, *The Interregnum*, p. 43.

19. *X Syezd*, pp. 566–567, 587; *XI Syezd*, pp. 532, 687.

20. *XI Syezd*, pp. 687, 398–399, 500.

21. *XII Syezd*, pp. 42, 55–56.

22. *Ibid.*, pp. 618–620, 652–656, 660–661, 57.

23. *Ibid.*, pp. 115–116, 42, 120, 142–143, 147; Carr, *The Interregnum*, p. 19, n. 3; Ustryalov, *Pod znakom*, p. 128.

24. *XII Syezd*, pp. 42, 43, 113–115.

25. *Ibid.*, pp. 132–133, 84–85.

26. *Ibid.*, pp. 42, 44, 204; Souvarine, *Stalin,* p. 327; Carr, *The Interregnum,* p. 19.

27. *XII Syezd,* p. 42.

28. *Ibid.*, pp. 66–67. For Nogin's representative character, see Zlobina, *Rukovodstvo,* pp. 40–41. According to the author, Soviet archives show that "the work of the Central Committee in 1923 in connection with a review of the leading cadres of the trusts called forth opposition from the leaders of the VSNKh — Pyatakov, Bogdanov, and others — who protested some appointments by the Central Committee's Accounting and Assignment Department, considering that these 'interfered' with the proper conduct of work by the VSNKh's cadres department."

29. *XII Syezd,* p. 334. Bogdanov was replaced by Rykov as chairman of the VSNKh almost immediately after the Twelfth Congress. Rykov, in turn, was soon replaced by Dzerzhinsky.

30. At the Eleventh Congress, Zinoviev had asserted that "we will form the leading economic organs, but having formed them, we will let them work and not interfere with them and harass them at every step." *XI Syezd,* p. 500.

31. Schapiro, *The Communist Party,* p. 321.

32. *Ibid.*, p. 321.

33. See, for example, *XII Syezd,* pp. 124, 174.

34. Alexandrov (*Kto upravlyaet,* p. 59) argues that Krasin had strong power-political ambitions, but all other sources indicate that this was not the case. See, for example, *XII Syezd,* p. 124, for Radek's assertion that he did not think Krasin's speech was "the candidacy speech of the economic executives." See also Zinoviev's report to the Eleventh Congress (*XI Syezd,* pp. 401–402), for a specific acknowledgment that the managerial regrouping in contrast, for example, to the Workers' Opposition, was "a nonpolitical grouping."

35. The abrogation at issue was, of course, purely *de facto.* The most antimanagerial resolutions of the Twelfth Congress paid lip service to the promanagerial resolutions of the preceding congress. See *XII Syezd,* p. 618.

36. Some change in management policy might have occurred in any event, since Lenin himself was concerned over the possibility that the industrial establishment would become too autonomous. In particular, it was Lenin who had proposed that the CCC and Rabkrin be merged — this in his next-to-last article, written in late January 1923 (*CW,* XLV, pp. 383–388). But Lenin had envisioned this merger as a means to control the party apparat as well as the state bureaucracy, and the last thing he wanted was that it should redound

to the benefit of Stalin and his secretarial apparatus (see, for example, Trotsky, *My Life*, p. 479; Azrael, "The Central Control Commission"; Neuwald, "The Origin"). As for the other measures at issue, there is no hint that they were initiated by Lenin or that Lenin knew of or approved them. Where the strengthening of the Central Committee's accounting and assignment department is concerned, it is almost certain that Lenin would have supported the red directors' position, and it is most unlikely that he would have favored increased party involvement in economic decision making, in view of his strong stand at the Eleventh Congress and the clear purport of his last known thoughts on economic development in general. See Schapiro, *The Communist Party*, p. 273, for Lenin's advocacy in December 1922 of Trotsky's idea of greatly strengthening the powers of Gosplan, a measure clearly incompatible with the line taken at the Twelfth Congress.

37. A. A. Heller (*The Industrial Revival*, p. 78) found on his trip to Russia in 1921 that "nearly all the younger men who are holding responsible positions in Russian industrial establishments served their apprenticeship in the Red Army." See also Ivanov and Kanev, *Na mirnoi osnove*, p. 12, where it is reported that 1,322 Communists were demobilized from the Red Army and assigned to work in the VSNKh between November 1920 and February 15, 1921.

38. Trotsky's theses on the trade unions were frequently referred to as the theses of the VSNKh or the theses of the "producers" (*proizvodstvenniki*) — that is, of the managers (see, for example, *Ekonomicheskaya zhizn*, 19 [January 29, 1921]; *X Syezd*, p. 351). Support was forthcoming, moreover, even from those red directors, a large proportion of the total, who had been union officials prior to becoming managers. The rapidity with which these men assimilated a managerial point of view in derogation of the rights of the trade unions and the workers at large was a source of wonder and despair to their former colleagues. See Carr, *The Interregnum*, p. 44, for a quote from the trade-union newspaper *Trud*, which complained in September 1922 of "a special obstinacy" in resisting workers' demands on the part of "managers who have recently come from trade-union work."

39. See *XI Syezd*, pp. 133–134. Trotsky had compounded this credit in the period immediately subsequent to the Eleventh Congress by taking a stand against the majority of the Central Committee in support of Krasin's effort to establish an effective state monopoly of foreign trade and by throwing his weight behind the VSNKh's efforts to establish a single unified economic center for the direction and administration of Soviet industry. (See Trotsky, *My Life*, p. 481; Daniels, *The Conscience*, pp. 198–202; Carr, *The*

Interregnum, p. 141.) Carr notes that Trotsky mentioned but did not support the VSNKh plan in his report to the Twelfth Congress, but even to mention it or to mention it without attacking it was a clear sign of support. Moreover, Trotsky was in favor of a "single unified economic center" as such, even if he would have preferred that Gosplan rather than the VSNKh form its core (*The Bolshevik Revolution,* II, 381).

40. See, for example, Gurovich, "Vysshy sovet," pp. 321–323; Bendix, *Nation-Building,* pp. 154–157; Krassin, *Leonid Krassin,* p. 269. Krasin was not so much a superindustrializer as an admirer of American efficiency, but it is noteworthy that even he went out of his way in his remarks to the Twelfth Congress to characterize his economic approach in terms of the Smirnov-Preobrazhensky phrase, "primitive socialist accumulation" (*XII Syezd,* p. 352).

41. See *XIII Syezd,* p. 171, for a statement by S. S. Zakharov to the Thirteenth Party Congress that in his district of Moscow province and, in fact, "almost everywhere" in the country, nearly all party cells in state and economic organs voted in favor of the opposition in the so-called discussion of late 1923 and early 1924.

42. See *XI Syezd,* pp. 808–862 (brief biographies of delegates and others who figured in the proceedings of the congress). For purposes of analysis here, a man has been defined as a red director if he was engaged in economic work at the time of the Eleventh Congress (March–April 1922) or entered such work in the period preceding the Twelfth Congress. Given the nature of the data, it would be wrong to treat the figures at issue as anything other than approximations, though reliable as such. Krasin is not here identified as a Trotskyite nor was he so identified during his lifetime. In the post-purge period, however, he was so identified (see, for example, *History of the CPSU: Short Course,* p. 262).

43. It is interesting that Smilga, a leading Trotskyite red director, had been particularly insistent that the party introduce the famous ban on factions and groupings adopted by the Tenth Congress (*X Syezd,* pp. 261, 571–573). Although some red directors had been adherents of the democratically inclined Workers' Opposition and Democratic Centralists in 1920–1922, it is probable that this adherence signified nothing more than initial resistance to the idea of investing the bourgeois specialists with status and authority — quite apart from the fact that by 1922 it was only those red directors who had broken with the groupings in question who retained their posts. (See Chapter 3; Schapiro, *The Origins;* Daniels, *The Conscience;* XI Syezd,* pp. 808–862.) Where later opposition groupings are concerned, we can wonder whether the rapid industrialization advocated by the Trotskyites and later leftists could have been accomplished

223

through other than dictatorial means. The Trotskyite idea that "a program of national centralized planning for the purpose of hastening the development of . . . production and exchange . . . was . . . unrealizable without freeing the 'main productive force in society,' the working class, from the tightening vise of secretarial bureaucratism" was scarcely vindicated by events and was unconvincing at the time it was articulated (Trotsky, *The New Course*, p. 155).

44. See, for example, Leites, *Study of Bolshevism*; Daniels, *The Conscience*.

45. *XII Syezd*, pp. 291, 306–308, 313, 316–320, 334, 583–584.

46. See Bubnov, *VKP (b)*, p. 220; Popov, *Outline*, II, 185; Trotsky, *My Life*, p. 490. It is more probable that most of the red directors knew that Trotsky was pulling his punches because, in the period immediately preceding the Twelfth Congress, Trotsky had written an article in which he stressed that the economic functions of the party should be fairly narrowly circumscribed, that "the task of the party is to direct (*pravit*) not to manage (*upravlyat*)" (Bubnov, *VKP(b)*, p. 220).

47. *XIII Syezd*, p. 87. Actually Zinoviev is elaborating on a decision of the Thirteenth Party Conference, which convened in January 1924 (*KPSS v Rez.*, I, 791). The Thirteenth Congress resolved that economic policy stress "the production of the means of production."

48. Stalin, *Works*, VII, 130–131, 306.

49. *XIV Syezd*, p. 81.

50. See *Direktivy*, I, 419, 442; *XIV Konferentsia*, pp. 14–15 (report of Molotov); *Partia v borbe za vosstanovlenie*, pp. 223–227 (Central Committee letter of February 24, 1924). This drive owed a great deal to the exertions of Felix Dzerzhinsky, who, appointed head of the VSNKh in February 1924, almost immediately emerged as a vociferous advocate of managerial rights and prerogatives. (See Davies, "Some Soviet Economic Controllers, II"; Volkov, "Memoirs"; Dzerzhinsky, *Izbrannye*, II; Trotsky, *My Life*, p. 487). Dzerzhinsky's rapid conversion to promanagerialism at once conformed to the established pattern of regrouping and set a precedent subsequently followed by his successors, Kuibyshev and Ordzhonikidze. These two men (in 1926 and 1930 respectively) also came to the chairmanship of the VSNKh from posts as chairmen of control organs (in their cases the CCC-Rabkrin rather than the Cheka) but quickly assimilated or at least became spokesmen for a managerial point of view (see Davies, "Some Soviet Economic Controllers, II and III"; text discussion below).

51. Stalin, *Works*, VIII, 146.

52. None of the red-director delegates to the Eleventh Congress

are identified as having become adherents of the Left Opposition. *XI Syezd*, pp. 808–862.

53. See Ivanov and Kanev, *Na mirnoi osnove*, p. 287; Stalin, *Works*, VII, 306.

54. See Stalin, *Works*, VIII, 126–129; Schlesinger, "A Note on the Context of Soviet Planning," pp. 28–35. Systematic work on the elaboration of a five-year plan began in March 1926 (but see Daniels, *The Conscience*, pp. 294, 323).

55. *XV Konferentsia*, pp. 276–283.

56. See, for example, *ibid.*, pp. 394–395 (speech of Zhukov); pp. 198–199 (speech of Rukhimovich); p. 229 (speech of Lobov); p. 276 (speech of Tomsky).

57. At the Fifteenth Party Congress, M. S. Mikhailov, who had violently denounced Tomsky's proposals, was promoted to the Central Committee, while A. F. Radchenko, who had strongly supported Tomsky, was removed from that body.

58. It should be noted in this connection that Stalin had always been careful to let his colleagues in the leadership (especially Zinoviev) advance the most comprehensive and unqualified claims for apparat primacy, while himself maintaining a relatively moderate tone; this made it seem that many of the powers accruing to the organization that he headed did so without any active solicitation on his part.

59. See *XI Syezd*, pp. 808–862. Of the 40 red-director delegates to this congress, only two (V. V. Schmidt and Ya. M Shatunovsky) became Right Oppositionists. It should be noted, however, that a sizable number of the men concerned had been assigned to non-managerial posts in the period since 1922, and that the sample at issue is therefore less reliable than it was in regard to managerial adherence to the earlier opposition movements. Still the sample retains some value, and no other sources suggest that it errs in its testimony that managerial adherents of the Right Opposition were few and far between (see, for example, *XVI Syezd*, p. 363, speech of Lobov). On the defection of the Trotskyite red directors to the Stalinist camp, see Daniels, *The Conscience*, pp. 371–372; *Pravda*, February 29, 1928; Deutscher, *The Prophet Outcast*, pp. 62–82; Valentinov, "Sut bolshevisma."

60. Schapiro, *The Communist Party*, pp. 361–362.

61. *Ibid.*, pp. 363–364; Schlesinger, "Note on Soviet Planning," pp. 35–44; Daniels, *The Conscience*, p. 352; Davies, "Some Soviet Economic Controllers, III." It should be stressed that I refer here exclusively to the early variants of the plan, variants in which the prescribed development tempo, while high from the start and ever increasing, was not yet utterly fantastic.

62. *XV Syezd*, II, 1059–1060. Krzhizhanovsky also spoke out against maximalist planning, as one would have anticipated, given that he was a skilled engineer (*ibid.*, II, 888–914, esp. 895). It should be stressed that neither Lomov nor Krzhizhanovsky was or subsequently became a Right Oppositionist. It is worth noting that Lomov had been one of the most fanatical "Americans" in the early years of the VSNKh (see Gurovich, "Vysshy sovet," pp. 321–323).

63. In 1929 and again in 1930, the Moscow Industrial Academy had to be thoroughly purged, while in 1932, a radical reorganization of the "faculties of special purpose" proved necessary because the latter were so badly "soiled," (*XVI Syezd*, p. 114, speech of Leonov; Petrovsky, ed., *Kadry*, pp. 107–108). See also Pistrak, *The Grand Tactician*, pp. 61–68, for some interesting speculation on the role of Khrushchev in the purge of the Moscow Industrial Academy, of which he was party secretary between May 1930 and January 1931.

64. Ordzhonikidze, *Stati*, II, 178; *Bolshevik*, no. 17 (September 15, 1930), p. 30, and no. 19–20 (October 31, 1931), p. 53. No doubt, part of the resistance these reports depict can be attributed to the bourgeois specialists who continued to occupy high posts in the industrial establishment. However, it is clear that most of the resistance originated with the red directors who dominated the industrial establishment and comprised almost the entire student body of the industrial academies and similar schools.

65. Ordzhonikidze, *Stati*, II, 443–444, 457.

66. *Direktivy*, II, 120–126.

67. See *XVI Konferentsia*, report of Yakovlev (pp. 444–492, esp. pp. 459–461) and the speech of Birman (pp. 482–501). See *Metal*, no. 2 (1929), for a representative article by Birman, who was also an advocate of lower tempos. For additional attacks on Birman, see *XVI Konferentsia*, pp. 505–510 (speech of Gurovich); pp. 527–529 (speech of Zatonsky); pp. 552–560 (speech of Rozengolts).

68. Stalin, *Works*, XI, 143; *XVI Syezd*, p. 324.

69. *PS*, no. 23–24 (December 1932), p. 47; no. 11–12 (June 1932), p. 5.

70. Ordzhonikidze, *Stati*, II, 447. On the creation of plant party organizers, see *Direktivy*, II, 372–377; *PS*, no. 15 (August 1933), p. 39; no. 7 (April 1934), pp. 9, 12; no. 8 (April 1934), p. 2. For additional organizational changes in the period in question, see Azrael, "Political Profiles," pp. 205–230.

71. On the groupings and their platforms, see Rezunov, *Sovetskoe gosudarstvo*, p. 89; *Bolshevik*, no. 21 (November 15, 1930), pp. 3–7, 29, 35–36; *Itogi . . . 17–21 dekabrya 1930*, pp. 248–249, 268–270, 272, 283; *KPSS v Rez.*, III, 198.

72. In regard to the close ties of some of the leaders of these groupings to the red directors, we can note that Syrtsov was chairman of the Council of Ministers of the RSFSR; Riutin was a member of the VSNKh presidium; Eismont and Tolmachev were both members of the Economic Council of the Russian Republic; and Smirnov (a former Right Oppositionist) was until 1931 head of the Soviet timber industry.

73. For personnel changes in 1930, see Alexandrov, *Kto upravlyaet*, pp. 345–348; Ordzhonikidze, *Stati*, II, 450, for personnel changes in 1932.

74. See Chapter 5.

75. None of the red-director members of the Central Committee was dropped at the Sixteenth Congress, while A. Ye. Badaev, I. D. Kabakov, I. I. Zhukov, and V. V. Mezhlauk were added, the latter two as candidate members. Also, whereas economic executives comprised 2.3 percent of the delegates to the Fifteenth Congress, they comprised 3.3 percent of the delegates to the Sixteenth Congress (*XVI Syezd*, p. 599). On lower-level party committees no precise data are available, but the general tenor of the party press in the period supports my statement in this regard.

76. See Davies, "Some Soviet Economic Controllers, III." Among other indications that a full-fledged intraparty struggle ranged around the adoption of the Second Five-Year Plan is the fact that this plan was approved only after a two-year delay (Baykov, *Development of the Economic System*, p. 182).

77. *XVII Syezd*, pp. 435–436.

78. It is inconceivable that Stalin was forced to accept the high tempos envisioned in Molotov's theses.

79. See, for example, *Pravda*, February 7, 1964, p. 2.

80. It is worth noting that Pyatakov (who supported Ordzhonikidze's "correctives") was elected to the Central Committee by the Seventeenth Congress. See also *Pravda*, November 17, 1964, p. 4.

81. In his report to the January 1933 Central Committee plenum, Stalin had explicitly recognized this logic — perhaps, though not necessarily, under duress (Stalin, *Works*, XIII, 187–191).

82. In the organizational realm (where incidentally the interests of Kirov and Ordzhonikidze might well have diverged), the Seventeenth Congress introduced a number of measures that tended to strengthen the party Secretariat at the expense of the industrial establishment. See Fainsod, *How Russia Is Ruled*, pp. 193–195.

83. See Barmine, *One Who Survived*, pp. 246–247. Barmine attributes the assignment of so many ex-oppositionists to managerial posts directly to Ordzhonikidze.

84. *PS*, no. 13 (July 1935), p. 28. Enukidze was known to have interceded with Stalin on behalf of many purge victims (*Letter of an Old Bolshevik*, p. 54). Although Enukidze was not officially linked with the industrial establishment and there is no "hard" evidence that his intercessions were weighted in favor of economic cadres, it is worth noting that he may have had particularly close personal links with the latter. He was himself a technician and had worked years before the revolution under Krasin, with whom and presumably with whose associates, he retained very close ties (see Liberman, "People's Commissar Krasin," p. 312).

85. See, for example, Ordzhonikidze, *Stati*, II, 771; *The Anatomy of Terror*, pp. 59–60; Weissberg, *The Accused*, p. 56. For a letter to Ordzhonikidze from S. P. Birman requesting that Ordzhonikidze intercede for the red directors, see *Bolshevik*, no. 8 (April 15, 1937), pp. 38–39 — cited by Molotov.

86. See, for example, *PS*, no. 17 (September 1936), p. 15; no. 18 (September 1936), pp. 25–26.

87. For Ordzhonikidze's exertions on Pyatakov's behalf, see Weissberg, *The Accused*, p. 56.

88. See *PS*, no. 23 (December 1936), pp. 62ff; *Anti-Soviet Trotskyite Center*. In addition to Pyatakov, the defendants at this trial included N. Ya. Lifshitz, a deputy commissar of transport, and three of his top assistants; S. A. Rataichak, I. A. Pushin, V. O. Norkin, I. D. Grashe, and Ya. N. Drobnis, leaders of the Soviet chemical industry; A. A. Shestov and M. S. Stroilov, key figures in the coal industry; and others. All of the men listed were sentenced to death.

89. That Ordzhonikidze committed suicide was confirmed by Khrushchev in 1956 (*Anatomy of Terror*, p. 60).

90. Beck and Godin, *Russian Purge*, p. 97. This was not necessarily true in all cases. For example, M. M. Kaganovich, one of the red directors who survived, was Lazar Kagonovich's brother and he had openly disagreed with Ordzhonikidze's recommendation that Molotov's theses be moderated (*XVII Syezd*, p. 473).

91. See Kravchenko, *I Chose Freedom*; Beck and Godin, *Russian Purge*; Weissberg, *The Accused*; Ciliga, *The Russian Enigma*; Barmine, *One Who Survived;* Tokaev, *Betrayal*. See Azrael, "Political Profiles," appendix B, pp. 333–336, for a partial list of purged red directors.

92. *The Land of Socialism*, p. 349.

93. *Ibid.*, p. 349.

94. For what was in effect an explicit and authoritative order from Molotov to the aspirants for membership in the new managerial elite to denounce the red directors, see *PS*, no. 10 (May 1937), pp. 32.

5. THE MANAGERIAL ELITE AFTER THE PURGE

1. *The Land of Socialism,* p. 43. The successors to the red directors were also commonly designated "proletarian specialists," but in fact only a minority, though a sizable one, was of proletarian origin. A majority, and probably a large one, *was* of lower-class origin, but at the highest levels of the postpurge industrial establishment, cadres of bourgeois origin tended to play a very prominent role. See Feldmesser, "Aspects of Social Mobility," and Azrael, "Political Profiles," for more on the class origins of the red specialists as a group.

2. Among these acts and actions were Stalin's own assumption of the premiership in 1941; the transferral of the extraordinary powers of the wartime "supercabinet," the State Defense Committee, to the Council of People's Commissars in 1946; the placing of great emphasis on the need to enhance the status of the state, indicated by the decision in 1948 to rename the Council of People's Commissars, the Council of Ministers; the listing of the state ahead of the party in all joint decrees, with Stalin signing in his capacity as head of state; the promotion of the managers Pervukhin, Saburov, Malyshev, Tevosyan, and Kabanov to the Presidium (as the Politburo was renamed in 1952); and the more or less firm insistence throughout much of the postwar period that the party concentrate its attention on ideological rather than economic questions.

3. Among Stalin's deputy premiers during the postpurge period were men such as Molotov, Kaganovich, Beria, Malenkov, Mikoyan, and Vyshinsky, none of whom was a "manager" in any meaningful sense. Party involvement in economic affairs was encouraged after Zhdanov's death in 1948, but even during this period excessive interference was vigorously condemned, and the plant directors retained more direct access to the center than their party counterparts did.

4. See Bauer, *The New Man.* On the eve of the Great Purge, the party's leading theoretical journal described the ideal red specialist as a man distinguished by "unlimited loyalty to the party and to socialism, unlimited hate for all enemies, and an ability to master the Bolshevik style of leadership which combines American know-how with Russian revolutionary vision." *Bolshevik,* no. 14 (July 15, 1937), p. 9.

5. *Izvestia,* June 29, 1963, p. 4. There is no discernible basis in fact for the hypothesis that the explanation for the two-year delay in the promulgation of the Fifth Five-Year Plan (the plan that ostensibly was to cover the period 1951–1955 but was not announced until late 1952) lies in Stalin's inability to overcome managerial opposition to high output targets. The delay may have been caused by Stalin's inability to decide between proposals for a more or less "realistic"

plan and a traditional high-tempo plan, but that is quite a different matter (see Leonhard, *The Kremlin*, pp. 40–41).

6. The shakedown of new cadres was launched under Malenkov's auspices at the Eighteenth Party Conference in 1941. In part what was involved was a relatively nonviolent continuation of the Great Purge, whereby most of the few red directors who had survived the latter were removed from their posts. To a much larger extent, what was involved was a drive for greater efficiency, whereby men whose primary merit was their proletarian origin were replaced by better trained or more competent cadres, even, if need be, by cadres of "alien" social origin. Also in some, though by no means all, cases, men who had been trained hurriedly and inadequately in the late 1920s or early 1930s were demoted in favor of men who had graduated later, when the educational milieu was less chaotic. The shakedown process was largely completed by 1942, although it continued on a diminished scale throughout the first several years of the war. See, for example, *Bolshevik*, no. 22 (November 1944), p. 3; Goure, *The Siege of Leningrad*, p. 74.

7. The two leaders who were purged were N. A. Voznesensky and A. I. Shakhurin (see *Key Officials*). Voznesensky, chairman of Gosplan from 1939, candidate member of the Politburo from 1941, and full member of the Politburo from 1947, was purged in 1949, probably at Malenkov's initiative. He has since been posthumously rehabilitated (*Pravda*, December 1, 1963, p. 6; *Izvestia*, December 1, 1963, p. 6). Shakhurin was exiled after the war on ostensibly nonpolitical charges. He was subsequently rehabilitated and re-emerged as a top member of the managerial elite (*Who's Who*, p. 674). It is also worth noting that almost all of the men who became top leaders (as defined above) after 1942, in conjunction with the creation of new ministries, survived in high office throughout Stalin's reign. The only one whose demise seems likely to have been political was G. V. Alekseenko, minister of the communications equipment industry and candidate member of the Central Committee, who disappeared early in 1953 (see, Conquest, *Power*, p. 177; according to *Key Officials*, p. 29, however, Alekseenko survived until after Stalin's death).

8. It is indicative in this regard that in 1957 in Vladimir oblast, 77.5 percent of those engaged in "leading economic work" had been so engaged for over 10 years, and 44.5 percent had been so engaged for over 15 years (*Komm.*, no. 3, February 1957, pp. 41–42). Less indicative, but still suggestive, is the fact that in 1962 a majority of the directors of the leading plants of Leningrad had apparently held their *current* posts for between 15 and 30 years, and some no doubt had held other directorships before. Among those directors whose

"biographies" are available, most began their careers as workers and then acquired education. This was a pattern characteristic of the red specialists, the cadres trained in the late 1920s and early and mid-1930s (*Ekonomicheskaya gazeta*, January 5, 1963). See also, *Izvestia*, December 26, 1963, p. 6, for an article on a director who graduated from a technical institute in 1938, at once became a plant director, and has been one ever since. The article clearly suggests that men of this "profile" comprised a large group within the managerial corps. Finally, it is worth noting that Soviet industrial novels suggests that the turnover rate among the red-specialist directors was quite low throughout the Stalin period.

9. See, for example, Leonhard, *The Kremlin*, pp. 35–49; Conquest, *Power*, chap. 8, esp. pp. 176–178, 185–187; Nicolaevsky, "The Party Men," p. 10.

10. *CSP*, I, 242. Pervukhin, Saburov, and Malyshev were made full members of the Presidium, while Tevosyan and Kabanov were made candidate members. Simultaneously, some thirty ministers, nearly all of whom were economic administrators, were elected to the Central Committee (see Armstrong, *Politics of Totalitarianism*, p. 231). See *CSP*, II, 187 ("secret speech" of Khrushchev), apropos of Stalin's plans to purge the Old Guard.

11. *CSP*, I, 242. Kosygin was demoted from full to candidate membership in the Presidium, a drop that may have been the prelude to a rapid descent but was not necessarily so. Kosygin, like Voznesensky, had begun his career in Leningrad at a time when Zhdanov was party boss in that city, and he seems clearly to have owed his rapid rise into the ranks of the top leadership to Zhdanov's sponsorship.

12. Among those who disappeared, by far the most prominent were Tsyren, deputy minister of state supply, and P. A. Zakharov, minister of geology (Conquest, *Power*, p. 177). The highpoint of the show trials came in December 1952, when a number of economic officials in the Ukraine were sentenced to be shot (Leonhard, *The Kremlin*, p. 43).

13. See Conquest, *Power*, p. 177. As noted earlier, it is not in fact certain that Alekseenko, minister of the communications industry, disappeared during Stalin's lifetime, as Conquest claims. He was elected to the Central Committee at the Nineteenth Party Congress (see above, note 7).

14. See the articles dealing with economic affairs in *Komm.*, no. 20 (October 1952), no. 21 (November 1952), no. 1 (January 1953), and no. 3 (February 1953), for the most highly politicized criticism of the managerial elite during this period.

15. See *CSP*, I, 1–20, esp. pp. 5, 14–15.

16. *Ibid.,* I, 117–120 (report of Malenkov).

17. See Leonhard, *The Kremlin,* chap. 3, for a good account of the chief measures of depressurization.

18. See McLean and Vickery, eds., *Year of Protest;* Blake and Hayward, eds., *Dissonant Voices;* Laquer and Lichtheim, eds., *The Soviet Cultural Scene,* for examples of the advocacy of full-fledged depressurization by certain groups within the scientific and cultural intelligentsia.

19. See, for example, Leonhard, *The Kremlin,* p. 13. Leonhard asserts that "the qualified economic officials have nothing to fear from a change in the political system, provided that economic planning and public ownership are retained." Largely on this basis he concludes, "leanings toward reform are particularly marked in this group."

20. The joint decree of the Central Committee, the Council of Ministers, and the Presidium of the Supreme Soviet announcing the formation of the new regime after Stalin's death began with a statement on the importance of ensuring "uninterrupted and correct leadership of the whole life of the country, which in turn demands the greatest unity of leadership and prevention of any kind of disorder and panic" (*CSP,* I, 247).

21. See Granick, *Management,* p. 45; Deutscher, *Stalin,* pp. 568–569, for some among the multitude of statements suggesting or assuming the existence of such high positive correlations.

22. See Inkeles and Bauer, *The Soviet Citizen,* parts 3, 4, 5; Dicks, "Observations on Contemporary Russian Behavior."

23. See Azrael, "The Educational System," for official criticisms of the new-class home environment. See, for some among the near infinity of attacks on the managerial elite for perpetuating a harsh and disciplinarian managerial style, *Komm.,* no. 5 (April 1956), pp. 26–27; no. 13 (September 1960), pp. 52–54; no. 15 (October 1961), esp. p. 62; no. 10 (July 1962), pp. 65–68; *PZ,* no. 22 (November 1962), pp. 51–54; no. 3 (February 1963), pp. 15–20; *Pravda,* August 27, 1963, p. 2.

24. McLean and Vickery, eds., *Year of Protest,* pp. 156–157. Paustovsky's speech, never published in the USSR, was delivered at a meeting of writers called to vilify Dudintsev's *Not by Bread Alone.*

25. See Fainsod, *How Russia Is Ruled,* chap. 17, for an excellent summary of the pattern of evolution that is involved. See Brzezinski, *Ideology,* chap. 1, for a general discussion of totalitarianism and rationality. See also, Inkeles and Bauer, *The Soviet Citizen,* part 5. Inkeles and Bauer conclude (p. 389) that Soviet managers are "largely withdrawn from politics, 'organization men' similar to their counterparts in the United States. Their main complaint in the past was

. . . over arbitrary political interference in predominantly technical decisions, the unreasonably high goals often set in the face of insufficient resources to meet them, and the treatment of failures in judgement of performance by management as if they were acts of political defiance or criminal negligence. Since Stalin's death such abuse has been tremendously reduced. Soviet managers seem, on the whole, quite satisfied with the situation."

26. Bienstock, *Management*, p. 28 and chaps. 2, 9. See also Laskovsky, "Reflections," esp. pp. 49–50, for a 1958 example of a similar argument on this point.

27. See Moore, *Soviet Politics*, p. 286, for "vested interest in confusion."

28. Panferov, *Borba*, p. 87.

29. *Pravda*, July 18, 1955, p. 2. In the Lugansk oblast in 1960 or 1961, 37 percent of the secretaries of primary party organizations in the mining industry lacked even complete secondary education, and few of the others were industrial specialists (*PZ*, no. 15, August 1962, p. 9). As late as 1956, only 25.7 percent of all raikom and gorkom secretaries had higher education (*Komm.*, no. 8, May 1962, p. 15). Even more recently, in Penza oblast, of the 54 raikom secretaries with higher education (out of a total of 74) only 2 were engineers (*PZ*, no. 1, January 1963, p. 5). Apropos of the Khrushchev campaign to recruit engineers into the apparat, the following statement from an editorial in the party's leading organizational journal is typical: "It is essential that engineers and technicians, people who know and love production, enter the party committees. The proper selection of secretaries of party committees and the strengthening of cadres in the [party committees' industrial] branch departments are necessary conditions for the improvement of the [party] leadership of industry" (*PZ*, no. 15, August 1962, p. 7).

30. It is quite probable that Hough is correct when he argues ("Role of Local Party Organs," pp. 92–94) that the typical engineer-become-apparatchik of the postpurge period is Malinov, an obkom first secretary described by Panferov in *Volga-matushka reka* (pp. 184–185). Panferov writes that, even when Malinov was a student at the renowned Bauman Technical Institute, he "had one main gift — the ability to speak and to imitate . . . Thanks to such oratorical gifts [he] was 'loaded' [with political work and 'social obligations'] . . . And science? Science remained somewhere to the side." According to Panferov, it was because he was a political activist that Malinov was allowed to graduate. Along the same lines, only from a quite different point of approach, the party's leading theoretical journal recently cited the case of a young engineer who refused to become a party worker because he loved his specialty and feared that even a short

interval in party work would mean to lag as a specialist and then went on to suggest that the case was by no means atypical (*Komm.*, no. 7, May 1960, pp. 64–65). Equally indicative, one of the engineer-heroes of a Soviet novel of the war period, a man who graduated from a technical institute in 1929, joins the party only on 1941, out of zeal for the party's leadership in the war. He explains his failure to join earlier: "It always seemed to me that entering the party was only a formality . . . In the institute and in my first years at work, I thought that, if I entered the party, social work and various [political] assignments would separate me from my studies, from profound knowledge of technology. And, in fact, I could see this happening with my comrades" (Azhaev, *Daleko*, pp. 199–200). This outlook may help to explain why only 20 percent of the specialists in the Soviet economy were Communists in 1941, despite the fact that an active recruitment campaign had been underway among specialists for the five years preceding (see *PZ*, no. 1, January 1962, p. 48).

31. Of top officials of the postpurge industrial establishment, only M. F. Nadtochy, who was a deputy minister of the building-materials industry from 1947 to 1953 and thereafter continued to occupy equivalent posts until his retirement in 1962, is known to have held a full-time party post for any substantial length of time. He served for five years as a secretary of the Sverdlovsk *obkom* (Pravda, March 30, 1963, p. 4). Kosygin also held a full-time party post (as head of the industry and transport section of the Leningrad obkom), but for less than a year (Andronnikov, *Rost*, p. 30). According to Nicolaevsky ("The Party Men," p. 8), P. F. Lomako and other members of the top echelon of the postpurge industrial establishment served as secretaries of the party cells of their institutes during their student days; but this experience antedated recruitment into the managerial elite and in the long-run was probably more effective in preventing the growth of virulent "functional role consciousness" in the form of technocratism than in breeding real identity with the apparat.

32. Thus Armstrong (*The Soviet Bureaucratic Elite*, p. 67), after noting the large number of industrial managers who served on the Ukrainian central committee in the postpurge period, goes on to observe: "For all the recognition accorded them in Party circles, industrial managers do not seem to play a major part in deciding the most important questions taken up by the Central Committee . . . The higher Party officials appear to maintain control over all matters outside the sphere of enterprise management itself."

33. *Komm.*, no. 10 (July 1962), pp. 66, 75; no. 7 (May 1960), pp. 64–65; also no. 18 (December 1962), pp. 92–93.

34. *Ibid.*, no. 7 (May 1960), p. 65. This and the preceding citations derive from the period after Stalin's death, and it should be noted that

such frankness — on all sides — was uncommon prior to 1953. But there is every reason to believe that the managerial attitudes and sentiments (and apparat resentment thereof) here at issue were equally characteristic of the preceding period. Thus managers were incessantly chastized during the Stalin period for shunning party-sponsored indoctrination programs, standing aloof from political assignments, skipping party meetings, and denigrating the role of the party. See, for example, *Bolshevik*, no. 12 (June 15, 1938), p. 78; no. 15 (August 15, 1947), pp. 3–4; no. 11 (June 15, 1948), p. 26; *Komm.*, no. 20 (November 1952), pp. 85ff; no. 21 (November 1952), pp. 71–72.

35. See Schapiro, *The Communist Party*, p. 506.

36. These were not, of course, the only lines of division. Division also proceeded in terms of personal rivalries, in terms of line-staff conflicts, in terms of differences between planners and producers, etc. With regard to the last set of differences, see Schenk and Lowenthal, "Soft Goods vs. Hard Goods, 3," esp. p. 18.

37. See, for example, the spate of complaints by directors which followed in the wake of the publication in the spring of 1955 of a strong statement by Glebovsky, director of the Urals machinebuilding plant (*Pravda*, May 20, 1955).

38. See Slusser, *Soviet Economic Policy*, esp. pp. 36–56, for a reliable firsthand account of the intense interministerial competition that arose in conjunction with German reparations after World War II and of the role of crossfunctional alliances in this competition.

39. See *ibid.*, pp. 36–56, for some of the patronage relationships that existed between industrial officials and members of the "power elite" in the postwar period. These relationships grew out of the fact that various of Stalin's top lieutenants had supervisory authority over broad sectors of the industrial front. These relationships hence had a basically departmental character. In addition, there were regional patronage relationships based on the fact that some of Stalin's top lieutenants served as viceroys for particular geographical regions and tended both to control appointments within those regions and to fill all central posts with men from "their" regions. Zhdanov, for example, led a Leningrad group, Khrushchev a Ukrainian group, etc. (See, however, Armstrong, *The Soviet Bureaucratic Elite*, pp. 67–68, for a suggestion that Malenkov led a Donbas subgroup within Khrushchev's Ukrainian bailiwick.) Finally, there were patronage relationships based on the fact that, at various times, some of Stalin's top lieutenants had special authority for "cadres policy" as such and were hence in a position to promote their favorites and build a pool of indebtedness among successful aspirants for high office. Malenkov was in a particularly favored position in this regard.

40. See, for example, Dzerzhinsky, *Izbrannye*, II, 6, 7, 11–14, 16.

41. In 1936, a separate Peoples' Commissariat of the Defense Industry was created out of the Peoples' Commissariat of Heavy Industry. In 1937, a separate Peoples' Commissariat of Machine Building was created, and thereafter separate heavy-industry ministries continued to proliferate at a rapid rate. By 1941 there were 15 commissariats dealing with heavy industry and, by 1948, over 30. Thereafter, a process of consolidation set in, but on a relatively modest scale prior to Stalin's death. See Fainsod, *How Russia Is Ruled*, pp. 391–393.

42. Also, the prepurge industrial establishment had, as the postpurge did not, its own patron, Ordzhonikidze. During Stalin's lifetime, no postpurge leader of comparable stature was identified so closely with the industrial establishment.

43. See, for example, Aron, ed., *World Technology*, p. 59.

44. Such an outcome was clearly anticipated by Philip Mosely who contended, in 1952, that "within the party real power . . . [is] handled in the main by the managerial elite" (*The Kremlin*, pp. 346–347).

45. See *CSP*, II, 247–248, 256–258, for the relevant decrees. See Conquest, *Power*, p. 234, on the background of Kosyachenko, Saburov's successor as head of Gosplan. The heavy-industry ministers who lost their posts because of the merger were Khlamov, Goremykin, Kostousov, Parshin, Maksarev, Fomin, Kazakov, Pavlenko, Yefremov, Lomako, Rayzer, and either Alekseenko or his successor as minister of the communications equipment industry (see *Key Officials;* above, note 7, for Alekseenko).

46. Leonhard (*The Kremlin*, p. 88) argues that Kosygin backed Malenkov, but this seems most unlikely in view of Kosygin's background, the fact that he was demoted in 1952 in conjunction with Malenkov's rise, and the fact that he alone among the top managers retained a seat on the Presidium after Khrushchev's consolidation of power. As we shall see, Leonhard's argument that Pervukhin and Saburov supported Khrushchev also seems implausible. Zademidko's background of close association with Khrushchev is noted by Conquest (*Power*, p. 257), who also suggests that Zasyadko may have been less than wholehearted in his support of Khrushchev and may even have defected to the Malenkov camp (pp. 257–258). Kucherenko had been a close associate of Khrushchev's in the Ukraine from 1939 to 1950 and obviously remained a particular favorite of Khrushchev's right up to his death in 1964 (see Ploss, "Some Political Aspects," p. 25, for the period 1939–1950; *Pravda*, June 29, 1963, for Khrushchev's going out of his way during a speech before the Central Committee to speak of "my old friend, that outstanding builder, Comrade Kucherenko").

47. See Ebon, *Malenkov*. Franz Borkenau (cited in *ibid.*, pp. 103–104) has suggested that the promotion of the managers was intended by Stalin as a counterweight to Malenkov's growing power, but this seems improbable in view of the career patterns of the men concerned. That Saburov, Pervukhin, and Malyshev were long-time associates of Malenkov is clear. According to Conquest (*Power,* p. 256), this was also true of Tevosyan, but others have argued that Tevosyan was a protégé of Mikoyan's or Beria's (see, for example, Armstrong, *Politics of Totalitarianism,* p. 261).

48. Malenkov's speech to the Eighteenth Party Conference in February 1941 is often cited as a promanagement speech, but, in fact, it was full of harshly critical comments on the leadership of the industrial establishment and called for *increased* party control over economic operations. To be sure, it stressed that such control should be efficient and technically competent, but this scarcely justifies a "promanagement" label (*PS,* no. 4–5, February–March 1941, pp. 9–33). Similarly, Malenkov's struggle with Zhdanov in 1946–1948 cannot legitimately be interpreted as a struggle of "technocracy" against "verbocracy." Malenkov was certainly less an ideocrat than Zhdanov, and this may have won him some sympathy from the managerial elite. But in the crucial organizational realm Malenkov stood for much greater party involvement in economic operations, and his emergence as Stalin's top lieutenant after Zhdanov's death in 1948 was followed by an intensification of party control (see, for example, Fainsod, *How Russia Is Ruled,* p. 191).

49. In his speech to the August 1953 session of the Supreme Soviet, Malenkov laid particular stress on the need for use of "biological" rather than "barn" yields in Soviet statistical computation (*Pravda,* August 9, 1953). See also the decrees, issued immediately after Stalin's death, ending prosecutions for "offenses committed in an official capacity" and economic crimes, and amnestying all those who had earlier been convicted on these grounds (Berliner, *Factory,* p. 312). See also the announcement, on April 4, 1953, of the reversal of the Doctors' Plot, which emphasized the role of the Soviet government while ignoring the role of the party in "guarding the rights of the citizens in our country" (*Pravda,* April 4, 1953).

50. See, for example, Armstrong, *Politics of Totalitarianism,* p. 308. Leonhard (*The Kremlin,* p. 88), Pethybridge (*A Key,* p. 36), and Rigby ("How Strong is the Leader?" p. 4, n. 8) also assert that Pervukhin, Saburov, and most of the heavy-industry ministers actively opposed the new look and therefore supported Khrushchev rather than Malenkov during the first phase of the succession struggle. They fail, however, either to buttress their assertions with persuasive evidence or to explain their reasons for dismissing the arguments in sup-

port of an opposite conclusion of the sort adduced here. Regarding Saburov's support for the new look in particular and Malenkov in general, see Garthoff, "The Role of the Military," where attention is drawn to Saburov's "Anniversary of the Revolution" speech on November 6, 1954 — a speech that failed to call "for even the maintenance, let alone increase, of military strength" (p. 8). On the virgin lands, see Pethybridge, A Key, pp. 54–55; Conquest, Power, pp. 249ff. It is worth noting in this connection that, after Khrushchev's consolidation of power, it was intimated that the virgin-lands program encountered vigorous opposition from the managerial elite (see Pethybridge, A Key, p. 51; Conquest, Power, p. 237). On the international dimensions of the new look, it has been variously assumed that, being "reasonable" and consumption-oriented, the managers were for détente with the West or that, being deeply involved in "defense" production, they were against détente (see Dinerstein, War, for an approach tending toward the former view; Pethybridge, A Key, p. 36, for an approach tending toward the latter view). In fact, no information is available on the foreign-policy attitudes of the managerial elite as a group, and one estimate seems as good as another. What does seem probable is that foreign-policy calculations weighed less heavily than domestic calculations in determining the managers' political stance. As for the most prominent top managers, Dinerstein cites persuasive evidence that both Saburov and Pervukhin backed détente, a fact which suggests that they did not oppose the economic line of the new look (see Dinerstein, War, pp. 101, 119).

51. Pravda, April 26, 1953 (italics added); Pravda, May 20, 1953. With regard to "repromotions," Saburov was reappointed head of Gosplan on June 29, 1953; Pervukhin, Malyshev, Saburov, Tevosyan, and Kosygin were renamed deputy chairmen of the Council of Ministers on December 7, 1953; Kostousov, Kazakov, Rayzer, Parshin, and Pavlenko were reappointed heads of independent ministries on April 19, 1954, as Lomako had been before them on February 8. See Key Officials.

52. See, for example, Pethybridge, A Key, pp. 45–46; Conquest, Power, pp. 41–42. Schapiro (The Communist Party, p. 552) considers this interpretation conjectural but quite plausible.

53. Had Malenkov viewed the state apparatus as the most potent power base within the system, he would almost certainly have opposed the drastic antimanagerial organizational and personnel changes that were introduced immediately after Stalin's death, and it is difficult to believe that the managers could have been dealt so severe a blow had Malenkov been opposed. Hence, the severe setback suffered by the managers is potent testimony against the hypothesis that Malenkov viewed the state bureaucracy as the main fulcrum of power

in the Soviet system and planned from the start to make it the chief base in his campaign for the succession. This is certainly the case if it is true, as much speculation has it, that the reconstitution of the regime was first and foremost the work of Malenkov and Beria (see Pethybridge, *A Key*, p. 43; Boffa, *Inside the Khrushchev Era*, p. 27).

54. The July 1928 Central Committee plenum ordered the immediate dispatch to institutions of higher technical education of "not less than 1,000 Communists who have passed through the serious school of party, soviet, or trade union work" and decreed that an additional 1,000 of this sort be similarly dispatched in each of the next several years (*KPSS v Rez.*, II, 524). The November 1929 Central Committee plenum ordered that the annual party draft quota be raised to 2,000 in 1930–31 and to 3,000 in 1931–32 and that the trade unions and Komsomol introduce even more extensive draft programs (*KPSS v Rez.*, II, 639). In fact, the "thousandite" plan was overfulfilled, the party alone sending 5,000 men to technical institutes in 1931–32 (Ogarkov, "Borba," p. 158). In consequence of the thousandite program, institutions of higher technical education filled a very high percentage of their enrollment quotas with party members. As early as 1929, 42 percent of those admitted to all universities were Communists, and, by 1930, 71 percent of those admitted to heavy-industry institutes held party cards (*XVI Syezd*, p. 78, report of Kaganovich; Ogarkov, "Borba," p. 143).

55. The "party maximum" was in force until 1929 or 1931. See Moore, *Politics*, pp. 185 and 445, n. 99; Mosely "Some Vignettes of Soviet Life," pp. 61–62.

56. Except where the Old Bolshevik thousandites are concerned, Schwarz ("Heads of Russian Factories," p. 321) probably goes somewhat too far in describing the graduates of the late 1920s and early 1930s as men who "did not, as a rule, regard themselves simply as technicians but considered their present technical work a continuation of their previous activity influenced chiefly by social and political motives." Such a description underrates the change in the level of active ideological commitment which did occur in conjunction with the "renewal of cadres," though the point is well taken insofar as any description of the members of the postpurge managerial elite as technocrats is concerned.

57. Kravchenko, *I Chose Freedom*, p. 61.

58. See, Haimson, "The Solitary Hero," p. 546, and "Three Generations," p. 241; Schwarz, "Heads of Russian Factories," pp. 334–335; Dicks, "Observations on Russian Behavior," p. 141; Bauer, "The Psychology of the Soviet Middle Elite," p. 639. Bauer notes that among former members of the Soviet middle elite one often finds no real definition of self, no internalized code that validates action, and

he concludes that these cadres, "having no essential self-conception . . . are dependent entirely on cues from their environment. . . . Needing constant reaffirmation of their own adequacy and worth, they strive constantly for . . . tokens of success." These tokens are, of course, disposed of by the regime.

59. See, for example, *Soveshchanie khozyaistvennikov*, pp. 134–135; *PS*, no. 19–20 (November 1935), p. 19; Kuzminov, "Soviet Productive-Technical Intelligentsia," p. 103; *PS*, no. 3 (February 1935), p. 3; *KPSS v Rez.*, III, 322–323; *Bolshevik*, no. 8 (April 15, 1938), p. 59. The last source points out that while the new Soviet intelligentsia which had been trained in the past several years represented a substantial improvement over the old, bourgeois intelligentsia, it nonetheless was often characterized by such familiar traits as "individualism, lack of discipline, disorganization . . . careerism, self-certainty, separation from life . . . skepticism, theoreticism, a sense of 'chosenness,' moodiness, egotism, etc."

60. *Bolshevik*, no. 8 (April 15, 1937), p. 36.

61. See, for example, *ibid.*, no. 12 (June 1952), p. 2.

62. See above, note 30, for dedicated professionals shunning party membership. Although the regime did call, in 1941, for the promotion of non-Communists to high-level managerial posts, in fact virtually all line officers above the rank of plant section head were party members. See *KPSS v Rez.*, III, 434.

63. Even in 1963, only half of the directors of *large* plants in Moscow and Leningrad were graduate engineers, while in Sverdlovsk oblast, a major industrial center, only one third of the plant directors had either higher or specialized secondary education. See *Ekonomicheskaya gazeta*, January 5, 1963, p. 11; *PZ*, no. 16 (August 1963), p. 15. For similar figures from elsewhere in the USSR, see *Komm.*, no. 5 (March 1961), pp. 16–17; *Pravda*, July 7, 1962, p. 3; *Kazakhstanskaya pravda*, March 19, 1963, p. 3; *Pravda vostoka*, June 7, 1963, pp. 2–4, and June 8, 1963, pp. 2–3; *Komm.*, no. 4 (March 1964), p. 100. To be sure, in heavy-industry enterprises, the great preponderance of directors were engineers, but the low percentage of engineers among the total corps of directors is nonetheless indicative.

64. Inkeles and Bauer, *The Soviet Citizen*, p. 290.

65. See Leonhard, *The Kremlin*, pp. 90–97, and Conquest, *Power*, pp. 248–256, for Malenkov's resignation. The decline in Malenkov's power was symbolized by the fact that, after August 17, 1954, the party was given priority over the state in all joint decrees. Earlier the opposite order of precedence had been consistently observed (Leonhard, *The Kremlin*, p. 90). That the members of the managerial elite rallied to Malenkov's side in increasing numbers and with increasing vigor seems likely because it became more and more obvious that

Khrushchev was not only opposed to the redemption of the promanagerial promise of the Nineteenth Party Congress, but was also inclined to the sort of organizational experiments that ran directly counter to managerial interests (see below, note 69).

66. Malenkov's protégé, Shatalin, remained on the party Secretariat throughout the first phase of the succession struggle, and it is certain that other committed Malenkovites also retained influential posts in the apparat. It is indicative of Malenkov's on-going support within the apparat as well as of this support's fairly rapid decline that in the Russian republic alone, eleven obkom secretaries were removed from their posts in 1955. See Conquest, *Power,* p. 73.

67. See below, note 75, for some graphic illustrations of Khrushchev's direct involvement in personal attacks on key ministers. Among the ministers belabored by name in the press were Akopov, Orlov, Sheremetev, Beshchev, Stepanov, Kazakov, and Rayzer. See *Komm.,* no. 7 (May 1955), pp. 7, 8, 11; no. 9 (June 1955), p. 45; no. 10 (July 1955), pp. 6, 7. One top minister to lose his post was Zasyadko, minister of the coal industry, who may have been in particular disfavor with Khrushchev for having defected to the Malenkov camp during the first phase of the succession struggle (see above, note 46). This is far from certain, however, since Zasyadko was merely demoted and eventually re-emerged as a top-echelon manager. Another top manager to lose his post was A. S. Pavlenko, minister of power stations, who was replaced by Malenkov. Pavlenko remained as deputy minister, however, and subsequently regained his post. No such qualifications are necessary in the cases of Kazakov, Akopov, Yevseenko, and Sokolov, who lost their ministerial posts in the spring and summer of 1955 (*Key Officials*). In addition, in May 1955, Gosplan was split, thus greatly undercutting Saburov's power. It should also be noted that, in the immediate aftermath of Malenkov's resignation, the Presidium of the Council of Ministers (first deputy chairmen and deputy chairmen) was enlarged. This expansion led to the promotion of a number of top economic officials, including Saburov and Pervukhin, but the net result was probably to make the Presidium a more unwieldy and ineffectual body, thus reducing its power relative to that of the party Secretariat. This result was probably intended, although Khrushchev may at the same time have been seeking through such promotions to lull the suspicions of the managerial elite. That the promotions represented rewards for last-minute defections from Malenkov's camp seems most unlikely in view of the general antimanagerial climate prevailing at the time. Had the top managers been in a position to demand rewards, they would almost certainly have been in a position to prevent Khrushchev's launching a mass campaign to discredit the entire leadership of the industrial establishment.

68. This initial campaign culminated in the July 1955 Central Committee plenum, which announced in its resolution that "the Plenum . . . considers the chief cause of the inadequate introduction of new technology into the national economy to be weak leadership from the side of the ministers and departmental leaders . . . self-certainty and complacency on the part of many leading workers in industry, their loss of a sense of responsibility for the affairs entrusted to them." *KPSS v Rez.*, IV, 92–93.

69. That Khrushchev's real intentions were suspected is strongly suggested by the fact that G. Glebovsky, director of the Urals machine-building plant and an outspoken leader in the drive of plant directors to free themselves from "petty tutelage," went out of his way in an interview in the spring of 1955 to state that the drive he was leading did not imply support for the notion of abolishing the ministries, without which, he said, "it would be simply impossible to lead industry" ("Ocherki nashikh dnei," p. 13 — see above, note 37, for Glebovsky's leadership of the campaign of the rank and file managers against petty tutelage). So far as is known, the possibility of abolition had not been mentioned by Khrushchev, but it was certainly prominent in his thoughts, and Glebovsky and probably others as well were able to penetrate the first secretary's thoughts by reflecting on his behavior.

70. *CSP*, II, 52, 140–141. Bulganin confined his suggestion to "some union-republic ministries," but he then went on to attack "certain officials of all-union ministries . . . who want to run everything from the center," thus indicating that his suggestion might have a much broader application. The fact that his remarks evoked a "stir in the hall" suggests that the full import of what he was saying did not escape his audience. It is also noteworthy that, despite its obvious impact, Bulganin's suggestion was studiously ignored by all of the speakers, most of them industrial executives, who spoke in the ensuing debate. The chief modification in Khrushchev's original plan was the temporary retention of a number of industrial ministries, most of which were associated with the defense establishment. The ministries retained were those for aviation, defense, medium machinebuilding (atomic energy), shipbuilding, radio technology, electric stations, the chemical industry, and transport. At that, it was stressed that these ministries "must be freed from the direct administration of the corresponding enterprises" (*Pravda,* May 8, 1957). An additional modification was the establishment of more regional economic councils (over 100 were established in all) than had orginally been envisioned. In this case, however, no compromise on Khrushchev's part appears to have been involved. See Leonhard, *The Kremlin,* pp. 237–241, and Armstrong, *Politics of Totalitarianism,* chap. 23, for com-

mentaries on the various modifications and for the articulation and adoption of the reorganization plan.

71. See, for examples of closer appraisals, Swearer, "Khrushchev's Revolution in Industrial Management"; Mosely, "Khrushchev's New Economic Gambit"; Nove, "The Soviet Industrial Reorganization"; Avtorkhanov, "Soviet Decentralization"; Laskovsky, "Reflections"; Hoeffding, "The Soviet Industrial Reorganization of 1957."

72. See Paloczi-Horvath, *Khrushchev*, pp. 172–173, for an unusual argument that the managerial elite supported Khrushchev's plan.

73. See *New York Herald Tribune*, February 21, 1957, for Khrushchev's acknowledgment (indeed, boast) that his plan had encountered extensive managerial opposition — this in an interview with Joseph Alsop. Alsop in discussing the reorganization plan wrote: "As Khrushchev himself pointed out to me, the plan was . . . a direct attack on the vested interests of 'tens of thousands' of the most highly placed officials, technicians, and administrators in the Soviet Union . . . As Khrushchev said with sardonic cheerfulness, 'These gentlemen are now to be sent out into the provinces to do more productive work.'"

74. See *Pravda*, May 10, 1957. One light-industry minister, V. P. Zotov, minister of the foodstuffs industry, spoke in favor of the reorganization. He was rewarded with a promotion to the deputy chairmanship of Gosplan, the chief central economic organ after the reorganization. It is noteworthy also that the newspaper of Malyshev's State Committee for New Technology was the only one of Moscow's major organs to refrain from responding editorially to the reorganization decree (Conquest, *Power*, p. 299). In the same vein, almost every minister who participated in the public "discussion" which preceded the Supreme Soviet session spoke out in favor of the retention of his particular ministry (Leonhard, *The Kremlin*, p. 238). One Soviet source reports that, at the meetings of the February 1957 Central Committee plenum which were devoted to discussion of the industrial reorganization, "almost all ministers" spoke in favor of Khrushchev's theses. The great stress laid on this point raises suspicions that ministerial dissent was substantial, as does the fact that the ministers who were allegedly favorably disposed are not identified as those associated with heavy industry, although the author of the article is at some pains to identify plant directors who backed Khrushchev as heavy-industry managers (Kolbenikov, *Sovershenstvovanie*, p. 62).

75. See, for example, *Komm.*, no. 3 (February 1957), pp. 47–50; no. 4 (March 1957), editorial; no. 6 (April 1957), p. 24. Khrushchev's initial attack on the leadership of the industrial establishment following Malenkov's resignation as premier had also been characterized

by an effort to exploit hierarchical tension within the industrial establishment. Thus one of the main forums from which the attack had been conducted was the Conference of Leading Workers of Industry, which was convened in the Kremlin in May 1955. Khrushchev tried to make it appear that the official line reflected the sentiments of the delegates to this conference, most of whom were plant officials, and at the level of appearances he was successful. As one account put it, many delegates "sharply criticized — [one] . . . would even say attacked — the ministries and Gosplan, charging their workers with bureaucratism." But there is more than ordinary reason to be skeptical of appearances in this case. It is evident from this same account that some of the more severe denunciations of the ministries and their leaders by lower-level executives were manifestations of what one anonymous member of the conference presidium openly labeled "criticism under pressure." Khrushchev, in particular, browbeat the speakers. Thus, during the speech of one plant executive named Laskov, Khrushchev interrupted after every mention of difficulties to ask "who is guilty?" and thereby "helped Laskov move from citations to analysis . . . [though] . . . it was necessary to name the minister himself." Laskov was not alone in receiving such "help," and this raises serious doubts about the extent to which the official line and rank-and-file managerial sentiments coincided even prior to the announcement of the reorganization plan. See "Ocherki nashikh dnei," esp. pp. 7, 10, 16.

76. See *Pravda*, May 4, 1957, for a protest on these counts by academician Kapitza.

77. See *KPSS v Rez.*, IV, 107–108, for the July decree, which was enacted into law in August 1955 (*Pravda*, August 9, 1955). It is true that, at the Twentieth Congress, Pervukhin criticized some central economic organs for having failed to implement this law, but it is striking that it was precisely Pervukhin who criticized this failure, while Bulganin, the law's ostensible sponsor, had almost nothing and Khrushchev nothing at all to say on the subject of directors' rights (*CSP*, II, 153–154, speech of Pervukhin; p. 133, speech of Bulganin). Apropos of the attitudes of the top managers, it is worth noting that in 1954 (before Malenkov's resignation) almost one half of the glavks, administrations, departments, and sections in heavy-industry ministries were liquidated (*Komm.*, no. 1, January 1956, p. 70).

78. See *CSP*, II. 39–40 (report of Khrushchev), 124–140 (report of Bulganin on the Sixth Five-Year Plan). See text below for more on the five-year plan. That the reorganization plan was designed to strengthen party control was explicitly stated in the authorizing resolution of the February 1957 Central Committee plenum. This resolution stressed that it was "a great defect" of the ministerial system that it

"restricted the possibilities of the local party organs . . . in the leadership of economy" (*KPSS v Rez.*, IV, 258). That many local plant executives were not persuaded by Khrushchev's efforts to gloss over this aspect of the reorganization is apparent from reports in the Soviet press. Thus, "in some plants many workers have failed to understand the significance of one-man management; unreflecting questions have been raised: how will the reorganization affect one-man management, will the latter be preserved, what forms will it take, will it be replaced by something else?" Or, more directly: "Some enterprise workers express fear that with the transfer of the center of gravity of the operative leadership of industry and construction to the local level, to the economic regions, petty tutelage over the enterprises will increase" (*Komm.*, no. 4, March 1957, pp. 10, 15).

79. See, for example, Fainsod, *How Russia Is Ruled*, p. 395; Laskovsky, "Reflections," pp. 49–50. I doubt the validity even of Leonhard's suggestion (*The Kremlin*, p. 241) that the *initial* response of the local managers to the reorganization plan was favorable.

80. See notes 37 and 69, for Glebovsky's stance prior to 1957; *Pravda*, April 4, 1957, for his opposition to the reorganization, an opposition based primarily on rejection of the notion of establishing the boundaries of the sovnarkhozes in accord with existing (oblast) territorial-administrative boundaries. Glebovsky, we might note, was a 1934 graduate of the Urals Metallurgical Institute ("Ocherki nashikh dnei," p. 14).

81. Since local-level managers, unlike their colleagues and superiors at the center, did not face either the loss of the entire institutional basis of their status and influence or the prospect of exile to the provinces, it is likely that their opposition to Khrushchev was less intense than that of the ministerial cadres.

82. Pethybridge (*A Key*, p. 175) unaccountably describes the entire 1953–1957 period as one in which "Khrushchev was only fighting a defensive battle from the apparatus against the encroachments of other interest groups." Such a description is of dubious validity where the first phase of the succession struggle is concerned; with regard to the second phase, it seems wholly untenable.

83. See Leonhard, *The Kremlin*, pp. 233–235; Conquest, *Power*, pp. 294–295, for the December 1956 plenum. Armstrong (*Politics of Totalitarianism*, pp. 309–310) dissents from the view that the December plenum was a defeat for Khrushchev, but his argument is not persuasive. Apart from the anti-Khrushchev organizational policy involved and the sharp downward revision of a plan that had been adopted to the accompaniment of assurance from Khrushchev that "we have every opportunity not merely to fulfill but to overfulfill [it]," it is worth noting that the December resolution was entirely free of

Khrushchevean invective against the managerial elite. Whereas the resolution of the July 1955 plenum had blamed defects in industry almost exclusively on "weak leadership from the side of ministers . . . self-certainty and complacency on the part of many leading workers in industry, their loss of a sense of responsibility for the affairs entrusted to them," the December plenum put the chief blame on "serious defects in planning the national economy" and stressed the presence of "a multitude of qualified workers, a qualified apparatus for managing production . . . cadres [that] are able to solve the most difficult production-economic and scientific-technical problems" *KPSS v Rez.*, IV, 39–40, 107–108). See also Schenk and Lowenthal, "Soft Goods vs. Hard Goods, 2," p. 18. Schenk here reports that in January 1957 Saburov told an East German delegation that the December 1956 Central Committee plenum sounded the victory of economic realism and then went on to say that "now the planners must prove their strength of character." However, though it seems clear that December 1956 did represent a serious setback for Khrushchev, the managers were not alone in administering it. It is misleading to assert, as does Peter Wiles ("Die Macht," p. 76), that "in December 1956 it [the economic bureaucracy] even threw Khrushchev and his henchman, weakened by Poland and Hungary, from the seats of economic power, replacing the presidium as manager of the economy by an Inner Cabinet of technocrats, dependent more on the State than on the Party for their power."

84. Rush, *Political Succession,* p. 93. When all is said and done, Pethybridge (*A Key,* p. 17) is closer to the mark when he contends that the role of the managerial elite in the succession struggle was that of a "minor group." At the same time, Pethybridge probably dismisses the managers too lightly.

85. See, for example, Rush, "The Khrushchev Succession Problem," p. 39; Wiles and Smolinski, "Economic Problems," p. 29. Rush argues that the economic bureaucracy's "own internal divisions transformed a *prospective victory* over the party machine into an overwhelming defeat at its hands (December 1956–June 1957)." Wiles and Smolinski refer to December 1956 as "a veritable 'technocratic counterrevolution.'"

86. I say "not necessarily narrow" because it is far from certain that the antiparty group would have shown any great respect for the interests of the managerial elite had Khrushchev been ousted in 1957.

87. *CSP*, IV, 198.

88. See Conquest, *Power*, chap. 14.

89. See, for example, Lowenthal, "The Revolution Withers Away," pp. 11–12; Fainsod, "Khrushchevism in Retrospect," p. 4.

90. See Armstrong, *Politics of Totalitarianism*, pp. 312–313.

91. Of the 37 industrial ministers in the "cabinet" that Bulganin headed in August 1955 (a date chosen primarily for convenience of calculation), at least 23 retained leading posts as late as 1962.

92. *Pravda*, August 21, 1961, p. 3. See also *Pravda*, December 8, 1962, p. 2, and November 19, 1963, editorial; *Komm.*, no. 18 (December 1962), p. 5, and no. 16 (November 1963), p. 5; *PZ*, no. 11 (June 1963), pp. 21–24; *Pravda*, August 24, 1964, p. 2.

93. *CSP*, III, 70. See *ibid.*, IV, 56, for a similar statement by Khrushchev at the Twenty-Second Party Congress.

94. See above, for the high percentage of technically untrained managers and the narrowly specialized and highly political education received by those who were trained.

95. Precareer experiences are relevant insofar as their upbringing and education fostered authoritarianism and insofar as the latter is in fact, as McClelland, Hagen, and others claim, associated with lack of economic enterprise.

96. See Merton, "Bureaucratic Structure and Personality," pp. 379–380.

97. *CSP*, II, 186. At the Twenty-Second Party Congress, Khrushchev put the case: "In the past, in the period of the cult of the individual such bad features of party, state, and economic leadership as highhanded rule by fiat, the hushing up of shortcomings, working with a cautious and fearful glance over the shoulder and fear of anything new were widespread. In this situation, many sycophants, hosannasingers, and falsifiers appeared" (*ibid.*, IV, 70).

98. See Willets, "The Wages of Economic Sin," for a good analysis of the new economic-crime laws.

99. Formal abolition of these sanctions came only in 1956, but in fact the laws had not been applied for some time before. Yet it is noteworthy that, in his speech to the November 1962 Central Committee plenum, Khrushchev expressed grave concern about the high rate of labor turnover and suggested that legal changes — more coercion — might be necessary to reduce it (*Pravda*, November 13, 1962). Another factor that called for the development of a new, persuasive managerial style was the emergent "automation revolution" in industrial technology.

100. A good statement regarding the proper Stalinist managerial style was delivered by M. M. Kaganovich in 1934: "The director is the sole sovereign . . . in the plant. Everyone in the plant must be subordinated to him. If the director doesn't feel this, if he wants to play the liberal and be a 'little brother,' to busy himself with persuasion, then he is not a director and should not be directing a plant. Every-

thing should be subordinated to the director. The earth should tremble when the director walks around the plant" (*Soveshchanie khozyaistvennikov*, pp. 212–213).

101. Frol Kozlov, in *Komm.*, no. 8 (May 1962), p. 15.

102. *CSP*, II, 39.

103. See *Komm.*, no. 5 (March 1955), editorial, esp. pp. 6–8, for a particularly full catalogue of the bourgeois instincts that the new class tends to indulge and cultivate. See *PZ*, no. 21 (November 1958), editorial, pp. 4–5, and no. 19 (October 1960), pp. 56–61; *Pravda*, January 22, 1962, p. 2, and March 23, 1962, p. 6; *Izvestia*, June 14, 1962, p. 1; *Komm.*, no. 13 (September 1962), pp. 65–66, for some articles directed specifically against the process of bourgeoisification among the members of the managerial elite; Babich, "Measures," for a recent Western survey. An interesting fictional account of the bourgeoisification of a high economic official is presented in V. Tevekelyan's novel, *Za moskovskuyu reku*.

104. See Feldsmesser, "The 'Classless Society,' " for a good discussion of many of these measures.

105. See *CSP*, IV, 20–32; Fainsod, "The Twenty-Second Party Congress," p. ix.

106. See, for example, Fainsod, "Khrushchevism in Retrospect"; Azrael, "An End to Coercion?" and "The Party and Society."

107. See, for example, *CSP*, III, 70; *Plenum TsK, 24–29 iyunya 1959*, pp. 481–482.

108. See *Izvestia*, November 28, 1962, p. 1, for a statement claiming that the source of various nonentrepreneurial practices (simulation, report padding, etc.) which the regime was anxious to root out was to be found precisely in economic organs above the enterprise level; *Komm.*, no. 17 (November 1962), p. 12, for an editorial suggestion that a renewal of cadres was necessary in Gosplan, the principal haven of former ministers and top ministerial officials; *PZ*, no. 19 (October 1963), p. 41, for a demand that the cadres in the state committee for the chemical and oil industries be renewed.

109. See Chapter 4.

110. For a more thorough analysis of the plenum, see Azrael, "Politics and Management." For recentralizing measures prior to November 1962, see Nove, "The Industrial Planning System."

111. Where the conduct of economic affairs at the enterprise level was concerned, the decisions of the November 1962 Central Committee plenum provided for a strengthening of party control and were thus continuous with the principles of the 1957 economic reorganization. See Azrael, "Politics and Management," pp. 93–97.

112. See esp. Linden, "Khrushchev and the Party Battle"; Ploss,

"Some Political Aspects," "Recent Alignments," and "A New Phase."

113. At the November 1962 plenum, only two members of the Presidium besides Khrushchev spoke in favor of the party-state reorganization.

114. See the articles cited in note 112; also Lowenthal, "The Revolution Withers Away," pp. 13–14.

115. See *Pravda*, November 17, 1964.

116. Kosygin, as we have seen (note 11) was on good terms with Zhdanov. Kosygin's close affiliation with Khrushchev is also noteworthy in this regard.

117. See Ploss, "Soviet Politics since the Fall of Khrushchev," pp. 26–30. More recently one manager, D. F. Ustinov, former head of the USSR Supreme Council of the National Economy, a body formed in March 1963 probably against Khrushchev's will, and a man whose relations with Khrushchev had obviously been strained, has been made a candidate member of the Presidium. *Plenum TsK . . . 24–26 marta 1965*, p. 234; also Nove, "The Uses," p. 179.

118. See the resolutions of the September 1965 Central Committee plenum (*Pravda*, October 1, 1965). Also, the reunification of the party apparat has been accompanied by strong criticism of excessive involvement by the party committees in the conduct of economic affairs. See, for example, *PZ*, no. 24 (December 1964), pp. 6–7; *Pravda*, December 23, 1964; *PZ*, no. 2 (January 1965), p. 4; *Pravda*, February 26, 1965, p. 1.

119. See Lowenthal, "The Revolution Withers Away"; Brzezinski, "The Soviet Political System: Transformation or Degeneration."

120. See *Pravda*, January 21 and 22, 1961; November 20, 1962.

121. Indeed, Khrushchev's schedule almost certainly foresaw a complete "renewal of cadres" within the industrial establishment by 1964–65.

122. It is worth noting in this connection that Brezhnev stressed at the September 1965 Central Committee plenum that the newly re-established economic ministries should be staffed with young people. *Pravda*, September 30, 1965, p. 2.

6. THE EMERGING MANAGERIAL ELITE

1. *Izvestia*, October 22, 1964, p. 4.

2. See *Plenum TsK, 24–29 iyunya 1959*, p. 482, for the insistence by Khrushchev that new managers be drawn from the ranks of men under forty. It should perhaps be noted in this connection that the number of men in their early fifties and late forties in the USSR is relatively small, since it was this age group that bore the brunt of wartime casualties. According to the best available estimates, 44 percent

of the men born between 1912 and 1921 were lost in the war (Newth, "The Soviet Population").

3. See, for example, *PZ* no. 24 (December 1962), pp. 41ff; *Izvestia,* May 19, 1963, p. 2, and August 23, 1964, p. 4.

4. See Chapter 5.

5. See Sherman, "Soviet Youth," p. 226; Voznesensky, *Selected Poems,* p. 10 (introd. note).

6. See also Callaghan, "Studying the Students."

7. *Komsomolskaya pravda,* July 17, 1953.

8. Tendryakov, *Chrezvychainy sud,* pp. 48ff.

9. During the course of a conversation with the author. For an attack on technocratism by Andrei Voznesensky, see "Oza," pp. 97–117.

10. See Dudintsev, *Not by Bread Alone* and *New Year's Tale*; Granin "Idu na grozu," and the review of the latter in *Pravda,* January 3, 1964; also Granin, *Iskateli.*

11. Dudintsev, *Not by Bread Alone,* p. 512.

12. *CSP,* III, 199.

13. *Komm.,* no. 14 (September 1959), p. 56. See also Ilichev's remarks, *ibid.,* no. 16 (November 1962), pp. 16–19. See *Komsomolskaya pravda,* February 12, 1964, for a number of technocratic statements by young Soviet engineers and scientists.

14. By 1958, some 60 to 70 percent of the students in Moscow's institutions of higher education were children of "officials" and "members of the intelligentsia." A decade earlier, when the members of the Filyukov generation were attending institutes and universities, the percentage of "new-class" children may have been even higher since tuition fees, established in 1941, had been abolished in the interim. See Khrushchev, "Educating," pp. 66ff.

15. See Inkeles and Bauer, *The Soviet Citizen,* pp. 216–218; Inkeles, "Social Change and Social Character."

16. See Azrael, "The Educational System," for a general discussion of the role of the educational system in political socialization.

17. See Counts, *I Want,* p. 54; Zinoviev, *Soviet Methods,* p. 90; Sukhomlinsky, *Vospitanie,* pp. 25–26. This last source was published in the post-Stalin period but is in most respects a reliable guide to pedagogical practice under Stalin.

18. See Zinoviev, *Soviet Methods,* p. 83.

19. See Counts, *I Want,* p. 39; Zinoviev, *Soviet Methods,* p. 91; Kalinin, *On Communist Education,* pp. 108–109.

20. Zinoviev, *Soviet Methods,* pp. 3, 84.

21. *Ibid.,* pp. 63, 79, 85–90.

22. See Hyman, *Political Socialization,* p. 19, for the important

role of party loyalty as opposed (at least partially) to programmatic loyalty in preparing the ground for the acceptance of social change.

23. Kalinin, *On Communist Education*, p. 93; Counts, *I Want*, pp. 95–96, 108.

24. Counts, *I Want*, pp. 37, 128; Cantril, *Soviet Leaders*, p. 45.

25. *CSP*, I, 2.

26. See, for example, Khrushchev, "Educating," pp. 66–67; *Pravda*, January 10, 1962, p. 4; *Izvestia*, November 24, 1961, p. 6; Bereday, *The Politics*, pp. 79–88.

27. See Callaghan, "Studying the Students"; Burg, "Observations on Students."

28. *Komsomolskaya pravda*, July 22, 1961.

29. *Ibid.*, April 16, 1958.

30. See Inkeles and Bauer, *The Soviet Citizen*, part 3.

31. This conviction derives primarily from a year (1958–59) spent in the Soviet Union. I presented some of the information in this section in the article by "Callaghan" cited in the preceding notes.

32. See, for example, *Sovetskaya Rossia*, October 26, 1962, p. 2; *Pravda*, April 9, 1962, p. 2, and October 12, 1962, p. 3; *Izvestia*, January 15, 1953, p. 3, and January 15, 1963, p. 3.

33. *Pravda*, June 2, 1961, p. 1.

34. See, for example, *PZ*, no. 15 (August 1964), pp. 36–40; no. 24 (December 1964), pp. 6–7.

35. See above, Chapter 5, for the use of such short-term assignments in the party apparat among the red specialists.

36. See, for examples, *PZ*, no. 11 (June 1959), p. 15, and no. 3 (February 1962), p. 4; *Komm.*, no. 14 (September 1960), p. 66, for the growing preponderance of engineers and industrial specialists within the party apparat. The recruitment of such cadres was vastly intensified in conjunction with the November 1962 reorganization of the apparat.

37. See, for example, *PZ*, no. 4 (February 1961), p. 30; no. 24 (December 1962), pp. 41–45, for the problem of excessive pragmatism. The term "verbocrat" is borrowed from Paloczi-Horvath, who uses it as the antonym of "technocrat." For young engineer-party secretaries giving particularly niggling orders to production leaders, see *PZ*, no. 13 (July 1965), p. 18; *Pravda*, May 30, 1965, p. 2.

38. Ovalov, "Partiinoe poruchenie," p. 26. On the problem of loss of expertise, see Chapter 5; *Komm.*, no. 7 (May 1960), pp. 64–65.

39. See, for example, Lowenthal, "The Revolution Withers Away."

40. See Mosca, *The Ruling Class*, p. 60; Michels, *Political Parties*, p. 98. See also Moore, *Political Power*, p. 157. Moore refers to a "law of drift."

251

7. CONCLUSION

1. See Deutscher, *Russia in Transition*, p. 17.

2. One falls almost naturally into a Marxist vocabulary in discussing the underlying theory in question, but to call the theory neo-Marxism, as is frequently done, is something of a misnomer since, as I have said in the Introduction and again in Chapter 2, economic determinism has deep roots in liberal theory as well.

3. For one particularly stimulating attempt to advance the state of developmental theory, see Binder, *Iran*, chap. 1.

4. See Brzezinski, *Ideology and Power*, pp. 97–140.

5. See Kassof, "The Administered Society"; Rigby, "Traditional, Market, and Organizational Societies"; Groth, "The 'Isms' in Totalitarianism"; Lowenthal, "Totalitarianism Reconsidered"; Tucker, "Towards a Comparative Politics"; Friedrich, ed., *Totalitarianism*.

6. See esp. Friedrich and Brzezinski, *Totalitarian Dictatorship;* also Arendt, *The Origins;* Wolfe, *Communist Totalitarianism.* I use the word "model" in its loosest sense. In most cases what is actually involved are mere trait lists, with only the most generalized suggestions as to the interrelations among the various traits and between these traits and the broader political configuration.

7. Tucker's argument (in "Towards a Comparative Politics") that totalitarianism is merely a distinct species within a broader genus does not really constitute a fundamental critique of this view, as long as the emphasis is on the word "distinct."

8. See Moore, *Political Power and Social Theory*, esp. pp. 32–33.

INDEX

Accounting and assignment department, 72, 74, 82, 221n28, 221n36. *See also* Cadres department
Adzhubei, Alexei, 147
All-Russian Association of Engineers, 55
Almond, Gabriel, 1
Alsky, A. O., 80
"Americanism," 79, 90, 94
Anarcho-syndicalism, 34; in patristic management doctrine, 18–20; in party, 41–46, 47, 223n43. *See also* Workers' management; Opposition groups
Apparat (party): role in industrial management, 51–52, 71–75, 78–79, 83–85, 92–93, 104, 117–118, 125, 133, 134–135, 144–146, 165, 167–169; as political power base, 78, 88, 102, 106, 131–132, 142, 144–146, 148; managerial assignments in, 80, 84, 95, 118–119, 127–128, 166. *See also* Accounting and assignment department; Cadres department; Central Committee (party); Communist Party; Secretariat of the Central Committee (party)
Arendt, Hannah, 64
Aron, Raymond, 4

Badaev, A. Ye., 227n75
Bakunin, M., 16, 17
Bardin, I. P., 37
Bauer, Otto, 3
Bauer, Raymond A., 50, 130
Bauman Technical Institute, 124
Bazarov, V. A., 54, 61
Bebel, August, 25

Beria, L. P., 108
Berliner, Joseph, 4
Beshchev, B. P., 134
Birman, S. P., 91–92
Bogdanov, P. A., 75, 167, 221n28, 221n29
Brzezinski, Zbigniew, 3
Bukharin, N., 31, 45, 54, 65
Bulganin, N. A., 132, 136

Cadres department, 124. *See also* Accounting and assignment department
Central Asian sovnarkhoz, 145
Central Committee (party), 70–86, 93, 96, 97, 134, 138, 145–146; managerial representation on, 80, 84, 95
 Plenums: September 1925, 47; July 1928, 239n54; November 1929, 239n54; January 1933, 90–91; February–March 1937, 129; July 1955, 134, 242n68, 246n83; December 1956, 136, 137, 245–246n83; February 1957, 244–245n78; June 1957, 136, 137, 138, 143; November 1962, 138, 145, 248n111; October 1964, 147; September 1965, 249n122. *See also* Accounting and assignment department; Apparat (party); Cadres department; Communist Party; Economic Bureau (party); Orgburo; Politburo; Presidium (party); Secretariat of the Central Committee (party)
Central Control Commission, 42, 72, 74, 82, 221–222n36
Central Executive Committee, 99

253

Troika, 78. *See also* Kamenev; Stalin; Zinoviev
Trotsky, L. D., 78, 85, 86; on industrial organization, 12; on bourgeois specialists, 42; and red directors, 78–86, 222–223n39, 224n46
Trotskyites, *see* Trotsky, L. D.
Tupoloyov, A. N., 173

Ufimtsev, N. I., 80
Ulam, Adam, 3, 66
Ustinov, D. F., 249n117
Ustryalov, N. V., 38, 54, 55, 59, 60–61, 217n88
Utechin, S. V., 37

Veblen, Thorstein, 173
Virgin-lands program, 125
Voroshilov, K. E., 108, 136
Voznesensky, A., 154
Voznesensky, N. A., 109
VSNKh, 32, 48, 54, 74, 75, 89, 90, 167; bourgeois specialists in, 42–43, 46, 52, 58

Wage policy, 53, 210n14; in patristic theory, 22; and bourgeois specialists, 32–33; under Stalin, 112. *See also* Egalitarianism; New class
Weber, Max, 2
Workers' and Peasants' Inspection, 52, 72, 74, 82, 221–222n36
Workers' management, 33, 34–35, 42, 44. *See also* Anarcho-syndicalism; one-man authority; One-man management
Workers' Opposition, *see* Opposition groups
Wrecker trails, 58. *See also* Great Purge; Purge; Terror

Yedinolichie, see One-man authority
Yedinonachalie, see One-man management
Yevtushenko, Ye., 154, 156

Zademidko, A. N., 124
Zasyadko, A. F., 124
Zhdanov, A. A., 109, 235n39
Zhukov, I. I., 227n75
Zinoviev, G. E., 67, 71, 73, 74, 78, 83, 85, 86, 221n30

Russian Research Center Studies

* Out of print.
† Publications of the Harvard Project on the Soviet Social System.
‡ Published jointly with the Center for International Affairs, Harvard University.